Six Colts, Two Weeks

A Special Colt Starting Clinic with Harry Whitney

Volume One, Week One

SPINNING SEVENS
PRESS

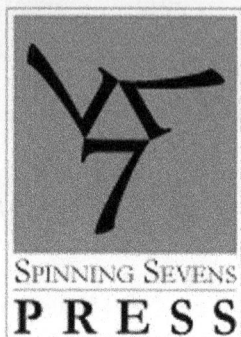

Other Books by Tom Moates:

Discovering Natural Horsemanship
Round-Up: A Gathering of Equine Writings

The Honest Horsemanship Series:
A Horse's Thought
Between the Reins
Further Along the Trail
Going Somewhere
Passing It On

Six Colts, Two Weeks

A Special Colt Starting Clinic with Harry Whitney

Volume One, Week One

Tom Moates

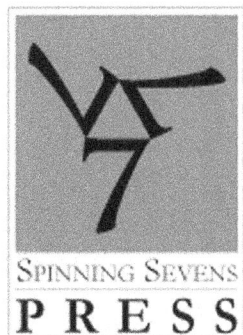

ISBN 978-0-9845850-9-0
Cover photo by Tom Moates
Cover designed by Emily Kitching.

Contents

Foreword

I really enjoy photography. I hope each photo I take is an appropriate representation of what was at that moment in time. But taken at the right moment or from the right angle, a photo can easily become an optical illusion. Without the context of more of the surroundings or the moments before and after what was captured, our minds can jump to untrue conclusions or become truly confused. A photo is only a moment captured that later takes us back to replay or relive the whole scene. The words and photos in this book are only captured moments of something greater, and hopefully they are appropriate representations of what really happened.

It is also my hope what really happened was appropriate for each horse at that moment in time and that I mislead no one in what the horses were thinking and feeling during the actual event. And, I assure you, Tom has done his very best to capture a true picture of what took place, no illusions.

During the clinic we presented several approaches to starting these youngsters, then made adjustments in the approach for each individual horse, so don't try to hang onto what was captured in a bundle of words at any one moment, but grab the philosophy behind why that was happening and was (hopefully) appropriate at that time.

Thank you, Tom, for attempting to capture with your camera and pen an appropriate representation of each of these moments in time, no illusions, just what was.

Harry Whitney
Novemnber 2015

Acknowledgements

A huge appreciation goes to Harry Whitney for sticking with his horsemanship clinics over the decades and teaching us horse obsessed folks who seek a deeper relationship with our horses all he can. I am profoundly grateful he provided me the opportunity to be a part of his once-in-a-lifetime colt starting clinic—week one of which is recounted in this volume. I'd also like to thank him for taking the time he put into reading through the chapters of this book as I completed them. It is very important to me that I get his teaching down correctly and in the proper context, and there is no better check and balance than to have Harry's own eyes on the manuscript. Thank you, Harry!

Many thanks to Chris Legg for his help in the initial phases of getting this book laid out. Spinning Sevens Press would be hurting without his generosity with his time. More of Chris's work can be seen at www.bluefinagency.com.

I'm delighted to have the incomparable Emily Kitching on board helping with the final layout and design of this book and for her wonderful talents designing the cover. Emily owns and edits *Eclectic Horseman* magazine and was one of the first editors to publish my horse based writing. I owe much to Emily's help and friendship along my path as an equestrian journalist and author. Visit www. Eclectic-Horseman.com to find out more about the magazine and other services like web design and hosting offered through Eclectic-Horseman Communications.

A talented photographer and another veteran of many Harry Whitney clinics, Nancy Lawson, allowed me to use many of her fabulous photos from the clinic in this book. Her camera angles, eye, and equipment provide a much broader visual record to the reader than mine alone could have done, and I am extremely grateful for her willingness to provide them. Her name appears with each of her photos; photos without a credit are mine.

Photographs taken by my long time friends Danielle Gruber and Ginna Ciszek also are included in this book. Thanks to both of them for their contributions.

Dr. David Williams has ridden with me through the process of writing this book over the past year and a half, editing each chapter as words tumbled along. His eagle eye and helpful comments and suggestions have done much to smooth the wrinkles in the manuscript, and I am greatly indebted to him for his many hours and enthusiasm.

I am tremendously grateful to my wife, Carol. Carol endured a 24 inch snowfall back at home in the mountains of Virginia while the events I recount in this book unfolded in sunny Arizona. There are many moving parts when it comes to keeping a writer writing and a horseman working with horses, and I am forever appreciative of her willingness to continue walking along this journey with me.

Finally, a big thanks to everybody who came out to the desert and made this colt starting clinic happen (you all know who you are)!

Introduction

"So, why are we here?" Harry Whitney asked, leaning back in his chair.

The tall, lean horsemanship clinician was not referring to the grander plight of human kind. The reference was to a group of about 30 of us eager students gathered in his bunk house who had just finished supper. It was Sunday, February 9, 2014, the evening before the first full day of clinic was to begin.

Harry Whitney, Ty Haas, and Tom Moates bringing in the saddle horses, Easy, Sandy, and Big Easy, for a day's work during the colt starting clinic. (Photo: Nancy Lawson)

I was sitting among the largest mob ever to attend a clinic at Harry's Salome, Arizona, facility. It was a capacity crowd, accommodated by (in addition to the permanent bunkhouse) a fleet of RVs, a temporary wooden framed building converted to a mini bunkhouse, porta-johns, living quarters horse trailers, and a full-time assistant cook helping the regular full-time cook.

Normally in the kitchen/dining area of the bunkhouse, a single run of tables arranged end-to-end accommodated the clinic goers with Harry sitting at one end. That typical table space had been doubled for this event. Harry now sat at the apex of a right angle made by two long sets of tables. His position at the valley of the V allowed for him to easily address folks from along either line of tables who had questions or comments.

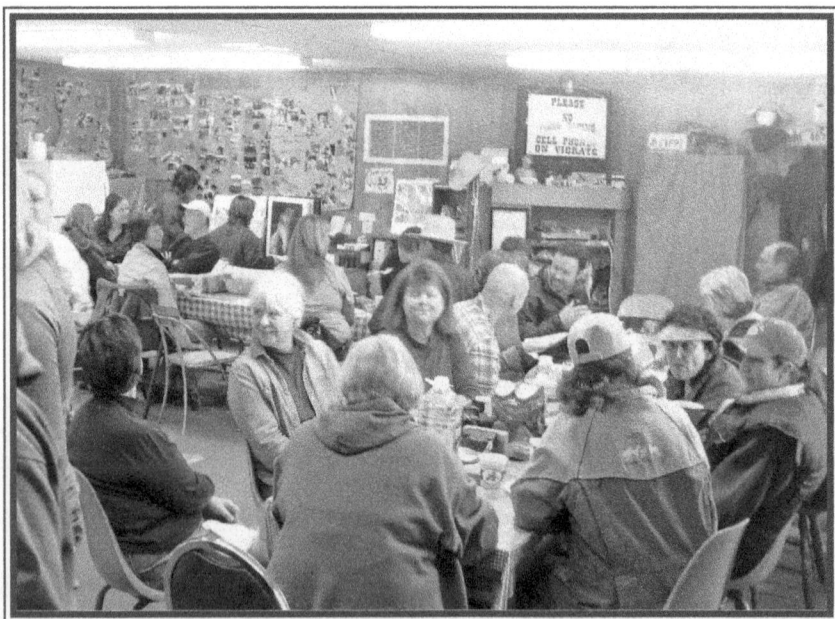

The crowded bunkhouse on day one.

"No," he continued, "I'm not asking, 'Why are we here?'" He paused, then gripped his forehead with a tan hand, "I'm asking, 'Why did I do this!'"

The room busted into laughter. Nearly everybody present had extensive experience with Harry, his clinics, and his good natured "complaints," so we knew that this clinic was now officially in-session. A huge dose of humor is interwoven into Harry Whitney's horsemanship. Frequent fits of laughter are as much a part of his clinics as are meal time discussions and round pen sessions.

This was, however, the start of no ordinary clinic. This was the beginning of what would be an extraordinary, singular opportunity to learn from a renowned horseman in a way that may never happen again. Harry continued:

"At this point in my life, I believe very strongly that you guys are witnessing two colt startings—the first and the last. I don't want to go through this again!"

We hooted and cackled a second time, but there was little doubt we all knew he really wasn't kidding. From the moment Harry told me about the plans for this clinic, I was certain that it would be the only chance to witness him dedicate two weeks to the specific task of starting colts, let alone so large a group of young horses as the six head he had lined up. That was one reason I had pushed so hard to get there, even in the dead of winter (February 10-21, 2014) which was not the best time to leave the farm in Virginia. In fact, when I left home the forecast looked reasonable, but as bad luck would have it, I was only three days in Arizona when back on the farm snow began falling that ended up dumping 24 inches before it stopped a couple of days later. It was particularly bad timing, and my poor wife, Carol, held down the fort admirably. But that's another story....

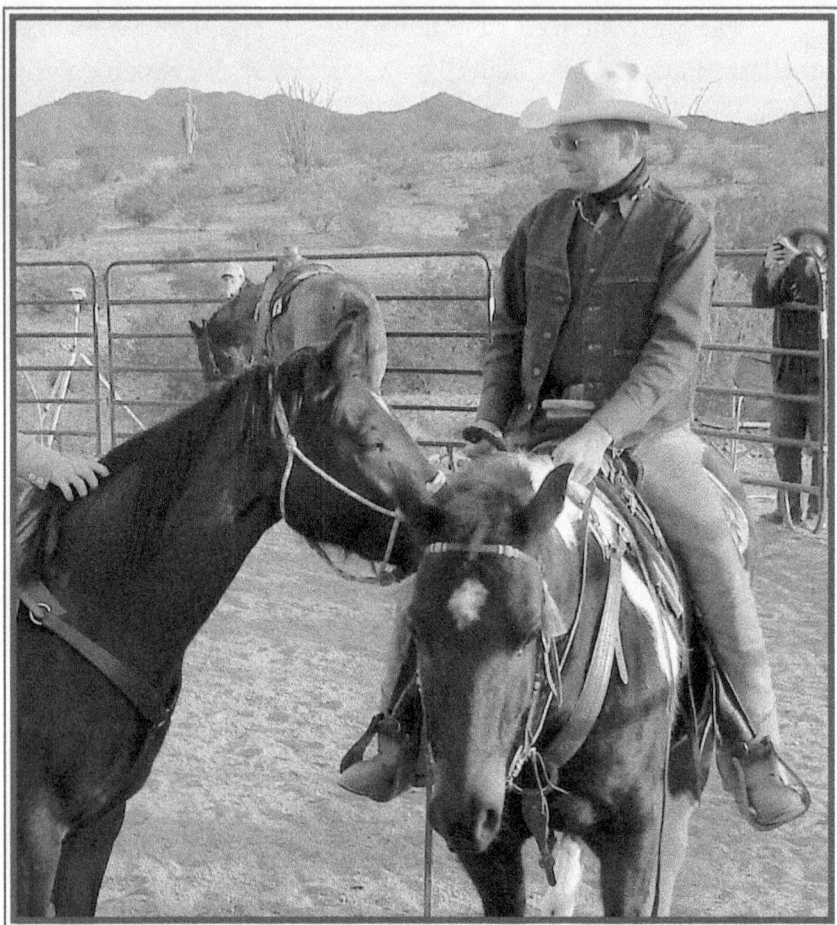

Harry Whitney

Harry occasionally works with young and untrained horses at his regular clinics. I had been lucky enough to see only a few instances of this in nearly a decade of attending and hosting Harry's clinics. It is rare enough that when I had the great fortune to see Harry work with a three-month-old, basically untouched Quarter Horse filly named Olive owned by Melissa Hanson (who happened to be one of the folks at the colt starting clinic) at a clinic at FitzFarm in Minnesota in 2010, I devoted a whole chapter to the experience in my book, *Further Along the Trail.*

Typical Harry clinics are filled with saddle horses possessing a wide range of pre-existing people-problems that he helps folks try to fix. I often had wondered how Harry would approach a group of colts to help keep them from getting messed up by people in the first place. Sure, all horses are born with certain traits, and their own experiences dictate some behaviors, but most of the big challenges we horse owners face are the ones we cause due to how we handle horses from their very first experiences with us. Thus one of Harry's regular sayings: So They're Started, So They Go! That maxim was the official title of the clinic and, given what we witnessed as evidence of its truth, it was on the lips of most everybody throughout the two weeks we were there.

I flew to Arizona from Virginia in early 2014 to learn all I could about working youngsters from my mentor, but I also was prepared to document as much of this unique opportunity as I could. In fact, my gut had been telling me something exceptional was afoot, and I already had plans for writing this book before ever booking my plane ticket. I had published four books, and a fifth was released soon after this clinic, which altogether comprise a memoir series

The view of Oklahoma from out my window as I flew from Virginia to Arizona to the colt starting clinic.

about my ongoing horsemanship journey that hinges on Harry's patient guidance with this student. Yet, I was aware that this would be a different kind of horse book from those of that series. This book would document a specific, unusual event while at the same time presenting as much information as possible of how Harry shared the task of applying his distinctive horsemanship to starting young horses.

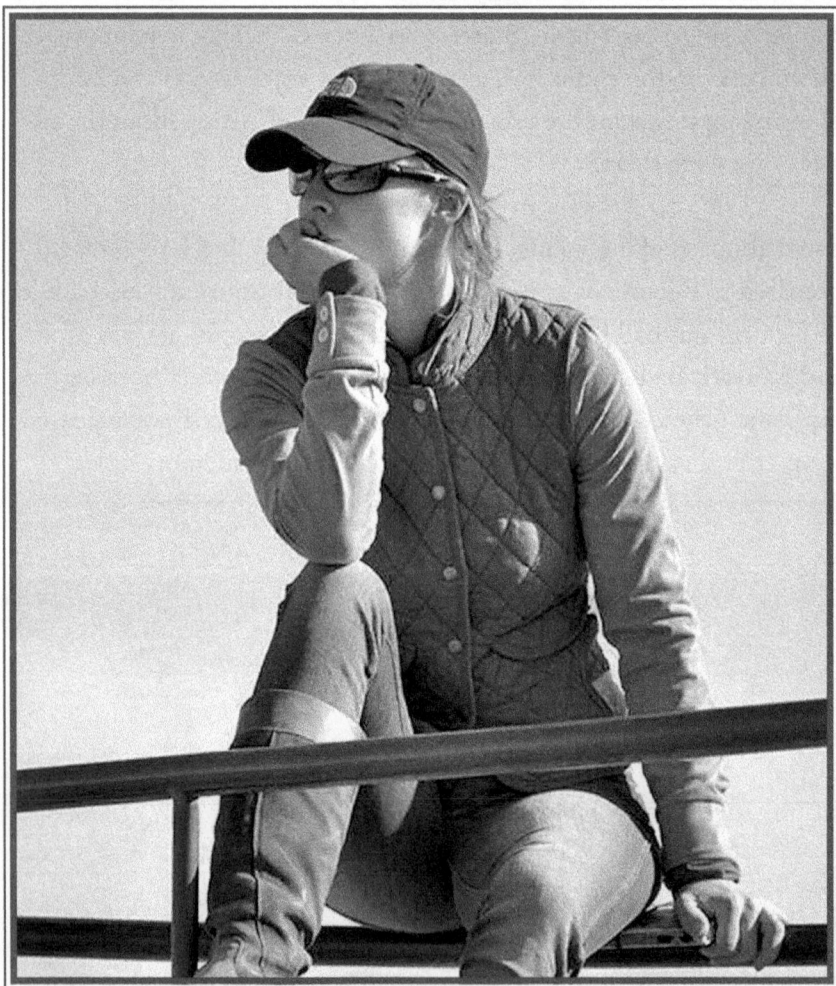

Anna Bonnage watches Harry intently as he works a young mare in the round pen. (Photo: Nancy Lawson)

"To give you a little background," Harry proceeded, leaning back in his chair, "there was a ranch a ways from here that was dispersing their horses. Some of you know Philly that I go with in Wickenburg—her sister, Resa, bought a bunch of horses from the ranch, and Philly went in on a couple of them. We're talking about 14 head of horses. They've been farmed out and so forth, some of them, but the young ones—there was a crop which are now coming on—I feel like I should help them. Last year there were a couple that were three-year-olds so we kinda gave Anna the project of starting those."

The Anna that Harry refers to is Anna Bonnage, a long time student of his from England who has made the trip to work with Harry in Arizona every year for over a decade. Anna was sitting across the table from me beside Ty Haas, another serious student of Harry's. Ty lives in Kansas. The way Harry structured this Colt Starting Clinic was that he would work the colts with the assistance of Anna and Ty, and then there would be 20 auditors. I would be there to help out (and generally make a nuisance of myself). Plus there would be the cooks and a couple of other helpers, so all-in-all about 30 head of people would be in attendance and be fed three meals a day during the course of the two five-day clinics. These would run Monday through Friday with the weekend in between off from clinic.

"Prior to that," Harry continued, "Ellen's oldest daughter (Harry is referring to Ellen Bartlett from Bishop, California, who was in attendance with us along with her son, Wes—her daughter's name is Barbara) was here and she played with a couple of them because when they got them, they weren't even halter broke. They hadn't been touched. So Barbara played with a couple of them. And then Wes came and helped for a few weeks playing with a couple of them and getting them better about their feet. He did a really nice job with them and really moved those youngsters along. Then last year, Anna started two under saddle.

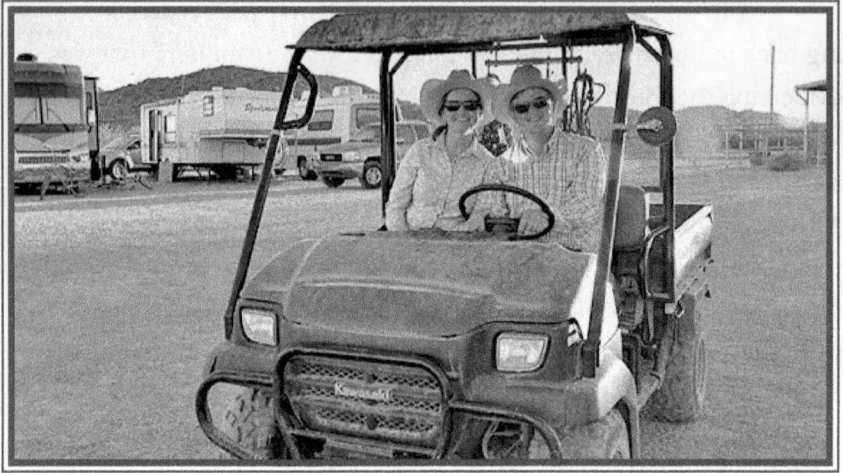

Ellen Bartlett and Wes Bartlett enjoying an afternoon of auditing.
(Photo: Nancy Lawson)

"And, we were out here at the round pen and Anna was having so much fun that she says, 'Can we start all five of those others next year?'

"And I went, 'Ohhhhh...' because last year I've got a whole clinic full of horses here, well about 6:45—and we're going to eat breakfast at 7:30—here's comes Anna with one of them on a halter....

"'Harry? Will you watch what I do?'"

Harry made a face and grabbed his forehead again with his hand which caused Anna to roll her eyes, sending us all into more fits of mirth.

"So, I was trying to coach on her, get in here and eat breakfast, look out the door, scold her for what she was doing right or wrong—and then we're done at the end of the day, my eyes are bleary, and here she comes with the other one. 'Harreeey...?'

"So when she mentioned starting the others, I was like, 'Noooo, not again!'

"I said, 'Anna, I'd have to take two weeks off. I don't have time to start that many.' And so forth.

"And she said, 'Well it's just a shame there's not a whole bunch of people sitting here watching this because they shouldn't be missing this!'

"So thus began the talk of how we could do this and not really take two weeks off from clinic time, still make the mortgage payment on time, get the colts started, and keep Anna happy—that's pretty important in itself!

"So Anna looks at me and she says, 'Well, is there anybody else you'd want to have help us?'

"And we both looked at each other and at the same instant said, 'Ty!' So we called Ty.

"He hemhawwed and finally called back and says, 'I'm on board.' He was pretty committed to coming. And at the same time we told Lynn (Lynn Weschler is the full-time cook during Harry's home clinics—she comes from Bishop, California) what we were thinking, and she says, 'I'm on board!' And about two days ago she told us that she was regretting saying that. So that's how this all came about. I presented it to Philly and her sister and they were all for doing it."

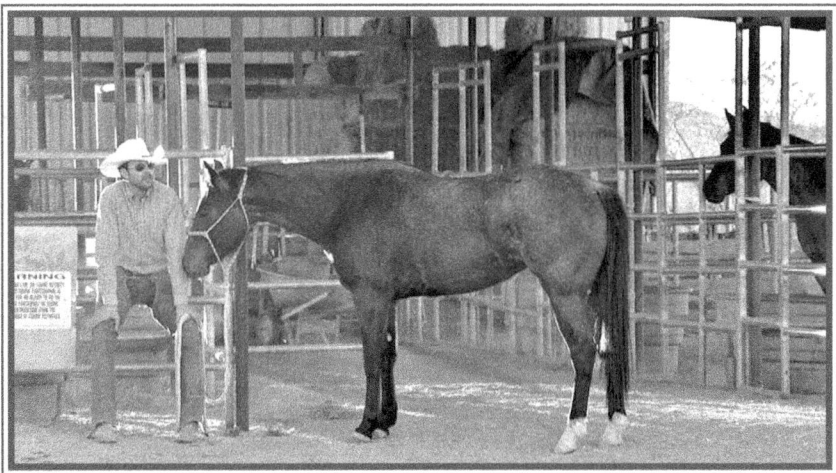

Ty Haas and Tinker relax awaiting a session to begin. (Photo: Nancy Lawson)

"I'm going to change now to a little different part of the story," Harry said, shifting in his seat. "I'm going to blame Franny for a little stuff. (Harry was talking about Franny Burridge, who was present and sitting opposite him at the end of one of those long lines of tables.)

"Those of you that don't know, Franny's from Maine. She hosts clinics in Maine. She's had a tremendous list of individuals do clinics at her place. I really respect Franny's view on things because she's seen a lot, and she thinks a lot.

"A number of years ago we were in Tennessee (Harry is referring to Mendin' Fences Farm in Rogersville, Tennessee, where he teaches a run of four to five clinics every May/June) and I was helping a lady start a young horse. It certainly wasn't a colt starting clinic, but people bring young horses that aren't started to my clinics and I help them. I never guarantee they're going to ride the horse, but I

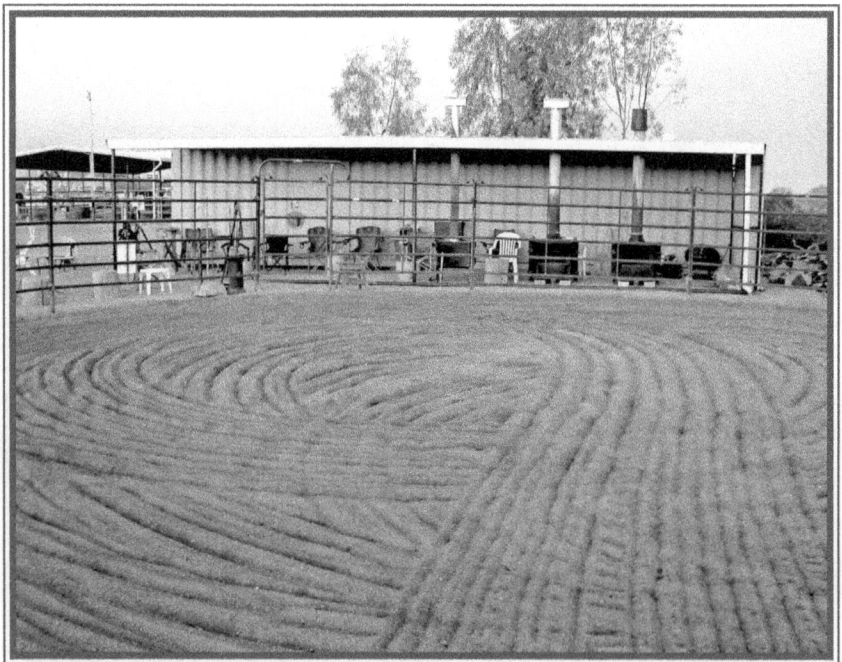

Harry's well groomed round pen ready for a day of clinic.

help them. I was coaching this lady with her horse and Franny said something that impacted me, and I'm going to paraphrase, she said, 'If this was Bryan Neubert's boys starting this horse, they'd be loping over that mountain over there, but most of us don't have the space to go over that mountain, and even if we did, our heart is too weak to do it. What Harry has given you people is how you can do it in your own back yard.'

"That really impacted me. I didn't think of it that way as such before Franny said it that strongly. And, I was glad to hear that because I would like to think that I could give people something that they could put to use when they got home.

"I know at some of these clinics they get a lot of colts started in a very short time, but I often wonder what people have to put to work when they get home. Can they duplicate it? Do they have the ability or the bravery to follow up with some of that? And so, my objective in doing this—I don't care if we ride any of these horses; I don't care when we ride them if we ride them—I want to take time with each one and look at a lot of things. I hope to vary it greatly.

"If everything goes the way I'd like for it to, I'm going to have three different saddle horses I'll be using. I hope to do a little demonstrating with them in amongst playing with the young ones. Within that, I hope to tie together what takes place in working a youngster, how that ties later with what you're going to do later down the road with a horse. I don't know if anybody is doing that to a high extent.

"I would hope that I would work a couple of these young-sters off from a saddle horse, but I'd hope also that we would end up riding one or two without ever having worked it off another horse. I would hope to work off the fence, do a bunch of fence work with some of them, and one or two, don't do any fence work before we ride them. I don't want to do any kind of a cookie cutter program—do them all the same in any way, shape, or form."

Heading to the "mare motel" with the youngsters to begin the day's work.
(Photo: Nancy Lawson)

Harry went on to say that some of the training choices made during the clinic would be based on what he thought might work well for a particular horse at a given moment, and others might just be random. The random aspect would be important to this clinic, he explained, because the average person who goes out and buys a colt may not have certain facilities, gear, or handiness. It was important to Harry that the clinic cover a variety of approaches that can be a fit for the typical horse person with the common colt.

"The average horse owner with the average young horse," Harry said, "the horse is probably leadable, probably touchable, probably trimmable—those kind of things, and that's what we have [here at the clinic]. A couple years ago they had not been touched, but they are now in your pocket, almost a nuisance at times. I see a lot of that in working horses, so I think it's pretty fitting what we have here for what people would have at home."

Harry went on to encourage us auditors to give input at any time during the clinic. Harry loves fielding questions from an interested audience and encourages questions at all of his clinics. If, for example, at home you have a saddle horse and would like to see him work on a certain thing with a colt from the saddle in the clinic, speak up and he'd see about demonstrating it. Harry was eager to include all kinds of variables in the approaches Anna, Ty, and he would use and welcomed us all to help guide what kinds of scenarios might be helpful.

This theme carried through the entire clinic. It is very important to emphasize Harry's desire to do this, I think, because it shows his deep seated convictions that success is not dependent upon what you work with—rope halter, web halter, no halter, round pen, square pen, no pen, etc.—but rather, success depends upon the priorities you keep in front of you, the goals you seek, when working with a young horse, along with developing your feel and timing. These bring a horse along in a good and lasting way.

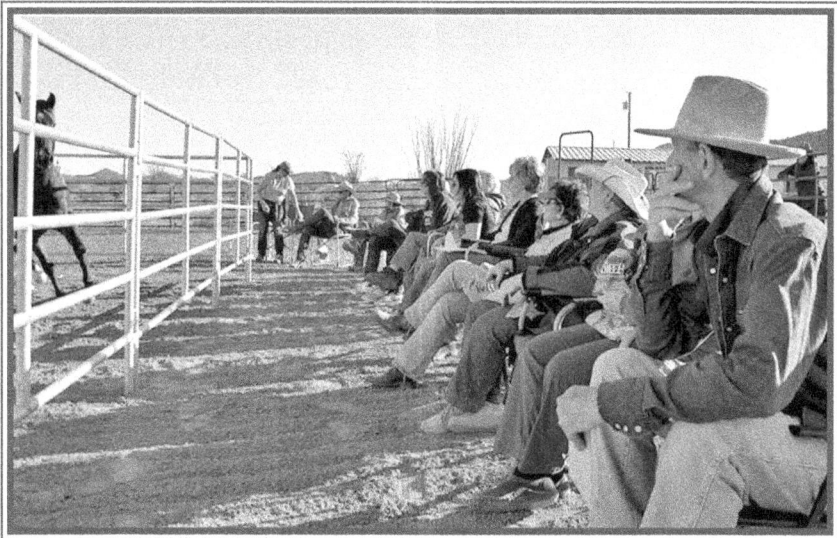

The auditors lined up along a temporary square pen set up inside the arena watch a session. (Photo: Nancy Lawson)

Harry says hello to Sky as the clinic gets going. (Photo: Nancy Lawson)

He was very keen to demonstrate that there is no "cookie cutter" program (as he dubbed it above) that spits out finished colts. Rather, an individual's awareness of approach to the individual horse's needs is paramount to achieving a good start to a horse's relationship with the human.

"I'm not trying to have an agenda, a plan, of any kind," Harry reiterated. "Anna's been bugging me since we got here, 'So what's the plan?' Well...there's not a plan. (Laughter erupted again at that remark.) I hope that nobody in this group is timid about asking questions, but if you are, look close by—I'm sure there's someone that'll ask for you."

A Note to the Reader

Each session each day for the two weeks of this special Colt Starting Clinic had plenty of moments I could go into great detail about, not to mention other insights from all that happened and was discussed at other times during the clinic. But, to keep this book from rivaling the page count of *War and Peace*, it is necessary to hit on some things and jump over others.

I have found it very difficult at times to decide what to cover in depth in these pages and what to gloss over. Ultimately, I decided to be guided by my notes taken during the clinic, which were a collection of the points that really stood out for me in the first place, and to follow my gut as to what were moments that work best to provide insights and give a true flavor on the page of what the clinic was like.

Some chapters provide a series of "snapshots" from the clinic—vignettes from different sessions—and some chapters are devoted entirely to a single situation that unfolded with one horse. Other chapters focus entirely on the after meal discussions. All of the events, however, are kept in chronological order start-to-finish across the course of the clinic to give an idea of how things with the young horses evolved day-by-day.

The Horses

The stars of the clinic definitely were the horses. All the colts at the Colt Starting Clinic had the same sire. Aside from one sorrel gelding, all the rest were mares and looked very similar. Discerning who was who was quite a challenge at times during the clinic. To help keep track of them in this book, I'll provide a list of equine characters here to provide easy reference for the reader.

In the colt crop were four roans, one grulla, and the above mentioned sorrel. All were registered American Quarter Horses that came off the YOLO ranch.

The Colts

Sky—This mare was four years old, making her the oldest of the bunch by a full year. She was one of the larger horses, a roan, and is the one Anna had started the previous year.

Bailey—She was a big roan mare, a three year old.

Smoke—This three year old mare was grulla and was of medium build.

Chic—One of the two smallest mares who were roans and looked very much alike. Both were three year olds. Chic had no white on her feet.

Tinker—The other of the smallest roan mares. Tinker had white on her hind feet which helped distinguish her from Chic.

Houston—The one gelding in the bunch. Houston was a two year old and easily stood out because of his sorrel color and slightly stockier build. He came to the clinic from Texas where he had been living, and that's how he came by his name.

The Saddle Horses

Sandy—A long time horse of Harry's. This sorrel Quarter Horse has the brand Four-Bar-J on a hind quarter because he was previously owned by Tom Johnson, a long time friend of Harry's who had that brand. Sandy traveled with Harry on his circuit around America each year for many years until Harry quit hauling horses in 2008.

Easy—A Paint Horse owned by Harry (or technically owned by Harry's son, Zack). Sandy and Easy have been together for all of the recent and medium past including Harry's many trips around the country teaching clinics.

Big Easy—A large gray Quarter Horse owned by Harry's girlfriend, Philly. Big Easy has spent many seasons at Harry's Arizona facility off-and-on over the years occasionally being used as a saddle horse.

Chapter One

Annual Floyd, Virginia Clinic
Six Months Later

"So they're started, so they go."
Harry Whitney

I stood there holding the end of the lead rope in dumbfounded amazement looking at the mare's underbelly as her hooves flew like a shadowboxer's fists in front of my face. Then her front end hit the ground and she penned her ears with a determined look in her eyes—she was ready to take me out, if necessary.

Between a sense of wonderment at her extremely aggressive actions (which I had not encountered in all of our time together since the day she was born on our place three years prior) and a delay that presents itself in my reactions at times, I was a little slow on the uptake of the seriousness of my dilemma. Immediate action no doubt would have been the better policy when facing a horse dedicated to assuring herself of my demise in the moment.

Tom works with Mirage in August 2014 at the Floyd, Virginia clinic. (Photo: Danielle Gruber)

It wasn't a personal attack, though. It never is with horses. She wasn't going out of her way to hunt me down and kill me because she didn't like me; it was, rather, a conversation. We simply had differing opinions about what should happen next in that round pen. Had I walked away right then, she would have let it go and gone about her business. That, however, in my mind was not building towards a relationship that's going to work between us if she's going to be ridden and become a solid equine citizen in the world of humans. No, such a stubborn hold on her own thoughts when I asked something of her was a recipe for disaster if she was to become "usable."

And here lies the very crux of the matter—to quote two of Harry Whitney's sayings that address the very foundation of effective horsemanship: "The best thing we can do for our horses is to help them develop the ability to let go of a thought," and, "So they're started, so they go."

Luckily, during the situation with that mare, Harry sat right on the other side of the round pen panels, (along with my wife Carol and a dozen other clinic attendees at our Bible/Horsemanship clinic in Floyd, Virginia, that summer of 2014). Harry, who possesses no delay in himself with regards to horse work, blurted out helpful things through the PA system in a timely way like, "Watch out!" "Don't get that close!" "Flag! Flag her off you!" and "*Tom!*"

I nearly got kicked, bitten, struck, mowed over, and generally pummeled, but none of that actually happened, thanks in part to Harry's quick coaching, and I was determined to get things going better with this mare with Harry's sage guidance.

The shenanigans had been triggered by my making a simple request that the mare take her thoughts to one side, look out that way with interest, and then step that direction. She pushed back mentally, and instead of letting go and having a look, she decided to push back physically, too.

We found ourselves at "The Spot," as I call it. The Spot is

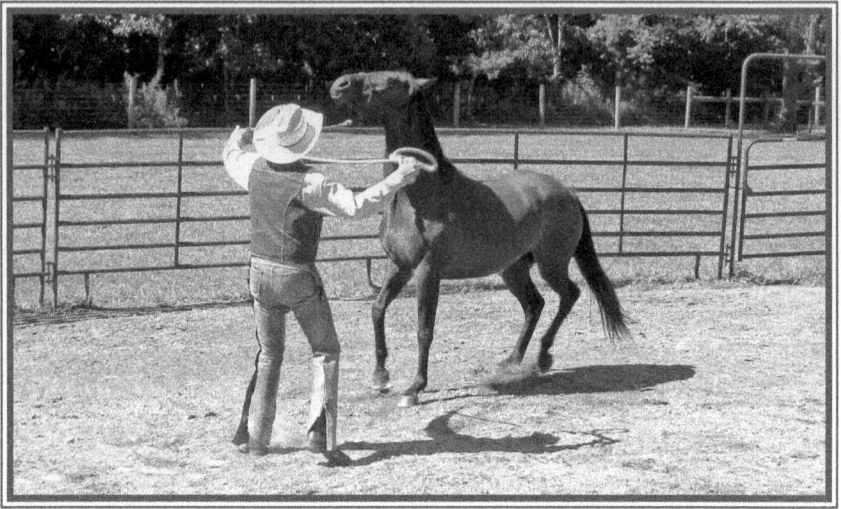

Harry and Mirage having a conversation. (Photo: Danielle Gruber)

where push comes to shove—where the person's thought comes up against a horse's differing thought. And, when the horse is unwilling to let go of her thought at The Spot, a situation can present as it had with this mare who was not the least bit timid about asserting her thoughts over the top of mine, and overtop of my body as well. I stuck in there with the flagging and got bigger with her, and then she got bigger. It escalated to the point Harry couldn't take it anymore.

"I'm coming in there!" he said.

And he did. I handed him the lead rope and the flag, but I stayed in the round pen to observe up close what would happen next. What I witnessed was Harry get really big, really soon, with the requests he made of the mare. She got bigger, and he got bigger. She got even biggerer, and Harry went to uber-extremely-biggerer.

She pawed, reared, and struck at him, thought about turning to kick him, and went through the whole spectrum of her best, loudest vocabulary, but Harry stayed ahead of all of it. Finally, after an extraordinary display of everything that you never want to see thrown at your favorite clinician by the horse you're trying to start even before the saddle gets put on her, she finally let go of one strong thought she was holding onto and went along with Harry's suggestion. At that point, things began to improve, at least a little.

I learned plenty over the course of that clinic with her, perhaps as much as I've ever learned working a horse in any clinic, because of the difficulties this mare presented. I later told Harry, "I realize I now must pay extremely close attention to this mare when I work with her to be sure that I am absolutely ahead of any little possible wayward thought of hers—which makes me realize I don't support other horses in the same way. And I should!"

And, while I learned a huge amount about how to recognize and deal with a horse with an extreme tendency to hold onto her own thoughts who is not afraid in the least about taking on a human armed with a flag, or anything else for that matter, a more important question came to me from this experience: why was that three-year-old mare so brutally stuck on her thoughts in the first place?

Clearly, she had the tendency towards being strong minded,

Harry has Mirage feeling better about letting go of her strong thoughts. (Photo: Danielle Gruber)

a trait she likely was born with. But the ultimate lesson here rests in Harry's statement, "So they're started, so they go."

This mare wasn't "started" per se. She was at that clinic to move towards being started under saddle. But her relationship with humans began the day she was born. She'd been halter broke and had learned trailer loading quite easily. And, believe it or not, when I was not brushing up against The Spot where push comes to shove between the human's desires and hers, she was an angel. She actually was quite curious, easy to lead, very groomable, etc. But, I learned at that clinic that when one asked something of her when she had another idea, it's Katy-bar-the-door and she's ready to eradicate anyone pushing into her mental space.

Clearly I had not pushed the envelope nearly enough with this mare to test the waters and ferret out The Spot in her. I had known for a long time about this kind of thing, though. I had worked with foals before. One early experience always sticks in my mind.

I had been working with a foal when I first was learning horsemanship. I'd done a ton of "pressure and release" training and had this little colt leading very nicely. Of course, we'd only worked in the pasture with his mother there close by. After many months of steady improvement I had the notion one day to lead the colt to a far corner of the pasture.

Off we went, but the other horses including his mother didn't come along. It went great for quite a distance, and then the colt realized we were at the other end of the world from the herd. This was the first time we had approached The Spot where the horse's thought was so strong he couldn't easily let it go and follow my lead. I held the rope and he reared and pulled back, panicked. It was so bad he was about to go over backwards so I let go of the rope, and off he went back to where his overpowering thought was, with the herd.

I've since discovered that this scenario is pretty common when people work with foals. It is always caused by the same thing: the horse gets a thought that he isn't able to let go of. What happens at The Spot is the indication of how well our horsemanship has prepared a horse for maintaining with-you-ness with us in all circumstances. Even though in ideal circumstances the foal leads like a champ and we humans get very confident that he has "learned to lead," all his learning may amount to nothing when we first find ourselves with him in adverse conditions.

How much more helpful would it be to work on getting a colt to readily let go of a thought when asked to, especially a strong one, than have a merely mechanical understanding of how to lead? In other words, if I'd been working from the time of the mare's birth on getting her to let go of her thoughts and come along with mine in ever more difficult circumstances, then even if she couldn't perform what I asked with perfection, at least she'd be available mentally to work on things rather than be trying to push me out of her space.

Thus I get to the central point of this book—how can we

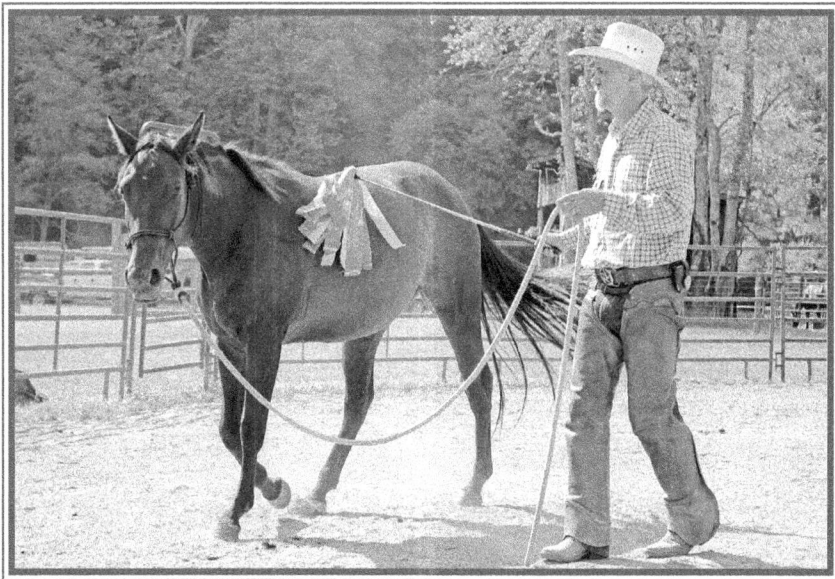

Mirage hits a nice spot and is able to follow the feel Tom presents. (Photo: Danielle Gruber)

develop horses that are willing partners? We do so by preparing them the best we can to let go of their thoughts and go along with our suggestions. So, how do we do that? That is the very thing Harry Whitney sought to demonstrate in many varied ways during his one and only Colt Starting Clinic in February of 2014. I think of it as having been a clinic on how to avoid having trouble ever get built into a horse in the first place. After all, if "so they're started, so they go," then a good start means there's never a need to fix things or cope with problems because they don't exist in the first place.

Let's rewind six months from my round pen dilemma in Floyd to the Colt Starting Clinic at Harry's place in Salome, Arizona. I'll walk through the experiences of that clinic in the pages that follow and try to shed light on what took place during those two amazing weeks.

Chapter Two

Day One, Early Morning
Monday, 10 February 2014

"A clinic is a universe unto itself."
Tom Moates

The cozy stillness of the bunkhouse remained undisturbed at 4:30 a.m. except for the faint sound of my scribbling in a new clinic journal and the muffled hum of three refrigerators. I sat at one of the tables where the big group on-hand would gather to share meals and explore the depths of horsemanship over the next two weeks.

My early start was partly due to insomnia. I tend to be somewhat of an insomniac when I'm at clinics (the layers of possibilities I witness between horses and humans at Harry's clinics hardly allow my horse-obsessed mind time to rest!) and partly because with the two hour time difference between Virginia and Arizona, my inner clock made it feel like a more reasonable 6:30 a.m.

Harry's bunkhouse is situated about 60 feet across a flat area with a stone dust surface from the round pen and the arena. One end of it houses four furnished bedrooms and two full bathrooms. I sat at the other end in a large room that houses both the kitchen and the dining/discussion area, scribbling a note saying all the attendees had arrived safely the previous evening before I'd gone to bed. That really was no small feat considering the harsh weather that February can unload across the country and that folks were coming in from places like England, the Yukon, Maine, Georgia, Rhode Island, Kansas, Idaho, Tennessee, Hawaii, Montana, Minnesota, California, and other points in between. My own flights from Virginia had been on time, for which I was very grateful.

At quarter to five, a door with a bigger than life sized poster of Hoppalong Cassidy taped to it opened and Lynn Wechsler, the cook, entered the light of the kitchen area. She tied on her fancy new apron that sported fabric with classy, colorful vintage pinup cowgirls. We chatted a minute while she buzzed around, but soon she was in the throes of fixing a massive breakfast for the largest crew ever to attend a clinic at Harry's place. The first full day of the special Colt Starting Clinic was actively underway.

***

(From my clinic journal:)

I'm going to start a fire in the middle woodstove about 6:30. We're going to have a Christian devotional led by Ty, out by the round pen at 7:00 a.m.

There were a zillion little things we still were doing all day yesterday.

I'm ready to see the colts moved down here. Harry said he's going to prep Sandy, Easy, and Big Easy to use as saddle horses, so we'll spend some time first thing today with the older horses.

***

Harry has engineered a most ingenious arrangement: a large metal shipping container, the kind that are as large as a tractor trailer's trailer, is situated for use as a tack room adjacent to the main round pen. The rings attached to the sides of the metal container used to tie it down during shipping are ideal for tying up horses while they're being saddled. It is positioned perfectly as a windbreak for spectators watching the action in the round pen, and a shed roof has been added to the long side of the container which faces the round pen.

Two Franklin woodstoves—more like metal fireplaces than what I think of as typical woodstoves—and a more conventional looking woodstove face the container with their stove pipes going up through the shed roof. The result is an excellent space for pulling up a chair and auditing in weather extremes, whether one seeks the shade on a hot day or protection from the wind and rain, and those stoves provide a surprising amount of heat to the semi-open area on cold days.

Darkness still loomed outside in the chilly early morning air when I exited the bunkhouse, although a faint light began to show in the clear desert sky to the east and a zillion stars still glittered overhead. With my trusty headlamp stuck above the rim of my cowboy hat, I ventured to my task of starting a fire in one of the woodstoves by the round pen where we'd meet for the morning devotional.

Before long, firelight was flickering on the wall of the container, and I was warming my gloved hands. Sitting by a fire in

Fires roar in the two Franklin stoves by the round pen, ready to warm the crowd that will gather around them soon.

the Arizona desert with the dawn about to break on the first day of a very special colt starting clinic is one of life's better experiences. I drank it in as I welcomed the warmth from the flames, knowing full well how it goes with what I think of as "clinic time."

Clinic time is a shift from the experience of time in the real world to that of a clinic. During a week or two or three of Harry's clinics, an entirely different set of rhythms come into play from those of the regular world. Without appointments, television, commutes, family obligations, or other worldly activities that normally define people's days, life melts into a wonderful time-space continuum where horses, and people who want to get better with horses, spend from sun up to sun down—and longer—focused on learning from Harry.

A clinic is a universe unto itself, and experiencing it is difficult to explain. I find it to be otherworldly in the best way. And, sitting there by the flickering fire that first morning with most of the place still sleeping and dark, I knew I had the whole thing still ahead of me. The joy of knowing it wasn't yet spent and the anticipation of it just about to begin made me want that moment to hang there for longer than I knew it would.

I saw another head lamp move across the area between me and the bunkhouse toward the arena. It was Anna on the way to what would be her morning vigil, sprinkling the round pen and arena to help keep the dust down during the day. I went over and helped her maneuver the lengthy hoses and turn on several sprinklers.

As dawn began to break in earnest, we hauled the sprinklers and hoses back in, and Harry showed up in his Kawasaki Mule, a four wheel drive mini-truck. I helped him open up some fence panels and pull a large triangular metal drag into the arena and hook it to the Mule. Then off he went, a plume of wet sand rooster-tailing out behind him.

People started to emerge from their various temporary abodes. Gates clanged and tubs thunked as horses were tended to. People began to mill about. I stoked the stove again and added wood. Just before 7:00, quite a crowd gathered their chairs around the woodstoves between the container and the round pen with Harry and Ty present. The timing couldn't have been better. We prayed and Ty read a passage of scripture and spoke. As we began to share thoughts, the sun broke straight out to the east and flooded the area where we sat with its warm, golden glow. What timing!

After a closing prayer, the breakfast bell rang, and off we went to get this clinic underway....

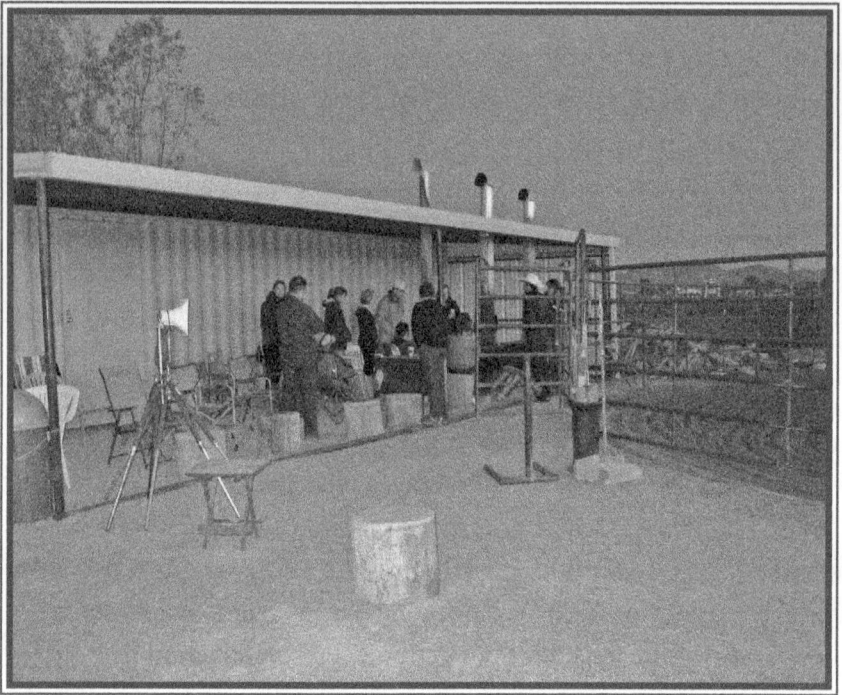

The early morning crowd begins to gather around the wood stoves under the shed roof that extends from the shipping container tack room at the edge of the round pen.

Chapter Three

Morning, Day One
Monday, 10 February 2014

"It's not the thoughts a horse is willing to let go of that get us in trouble; it's the ones they aren't willing to let go of that cause problems."

Harry Whitney

Smoke was the first of the six young horses to be worked during the clinic. But since Harry had not ridden his saddle horses, Sandy and Easy, for some time, we got the added benefit of watching him work his own older horses first before beginning with the colts.

Sandy was released into the round pen, and Harry worked him with the flag at liberty for a bit. Then Harry saddled and rode him before tying him to a hitching rail by the bunkhouse to be on stand-by. Easy went through a similar warm-up and then got the task of packing Harry around while he worked Smoke.

The first note in my journal about the young grulla mare was the answer to a general question I'd wondered about working horses: can they be brought to a new place—like these colts from wherever they'd been to Harry's for the clinic—and be expected to "be here now with the person working them?" That is, can they be expected right from the get-go to let go of other thoughts and center mentally with us and settle down.

Harry said, "Yes," they can be with-us even in an unfamiliar place. As he began working with Smoke from the saddle atop Easy,

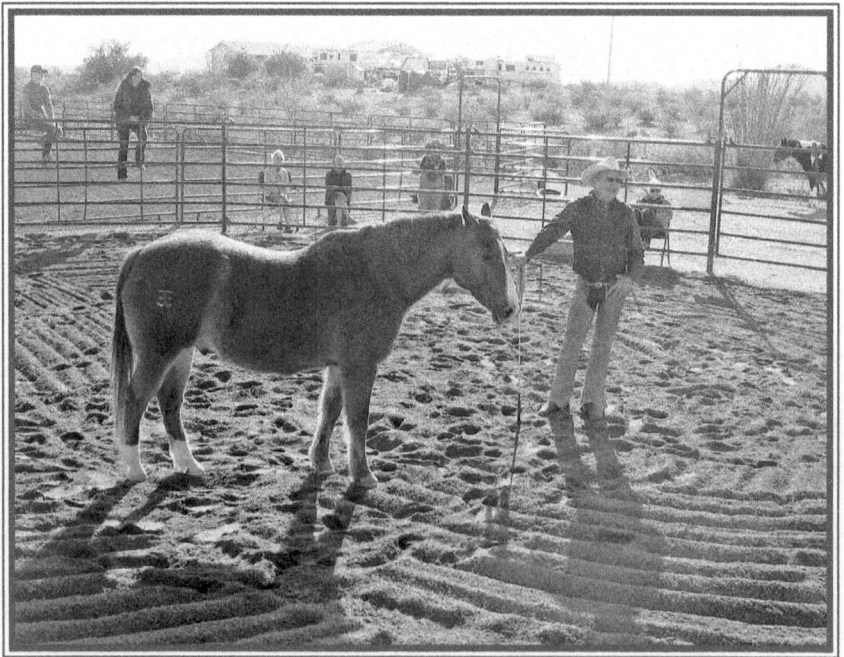

Harry and Sandy get things going in the round pen on the first morning of the colt starting clinic.

the mare was wanting to draw in and push on him a bit. Harry not only did enough there with the flag to get her more mentally centered, he also created enough of a disturbance to convince her that crowding him was not the right idea.

As is the way with Harry's horsemanship, the clinician wasn't insistent about what he asked of the young horse, never forcing Smoke absolutely to do what he asked with military sharpness. Rather, he was encouragingly persistent about it. He presented a little "imbalance" into the situation—a bit of flagging, feel on the lead rope, positioning with Easy, etc.—and she soon got the idea. She quickly picked up on the imbalances presented her and began searching for the answers to whatever Harry was asking.

"She'll start hunting that spot," Harry said. "She knows what feels good and what doesn't."

I was curious as to whether Harry would ask the young horse to line out across a spectrum of requests at once, or if he would focus more on shaping up a single thing with the horse in a given circumstance at a time. With Smoke, from the beginning, he had many complexities shaping up. In fact, only 15 minutes into that first session, Harry had Easy and Smoke bending and walking in a head-to-tail circle with Smoke being ponied on a lead line.

"She should fill out the other side of the circle," Harry commented, indicating with an arch of his hand how the two horses had fallen in synch with one another following the circle he was directing.

The next thing Harry entered into is something we regular students of his refer to as "the whole rigmarole." The whole rigmarole offers a huge opportunity to shape up a horse in many aspects while working on a task. The fact that Harry decided to introduce Smoke to this little deal while working her from off of Easy in their very first session in itself spoke volumes about what kind of complexities a young horse can be introduced to almost immediately if handled right.

Let me put my very early observations and thoughts of the clinic's beginnings this way. In my mind, as we began the clinic I wondered how much one can do with a young/unstarted horse at the earliest stages of working with him or her. This first session answered that question.

Harry did start by offering some options to Smoke and felt the feedback where she didn't seem to understand. He shaped that up a little, by having her follow the feel of the lead rope while being ponied from Easy. But very soon, Harry was asking quite a bit more. If Smoke got a little lost, the clinician just kept offering, and she'd find her way to what he was asking. But the progress seemed very rapid in my eyes.

The fact that Harry went to the whole rigmarole at all in that first session meant that Smoke was coming through with his requests and thus able to let go of other thoughts to pick up on what was being presented. It also meant without question that a young,

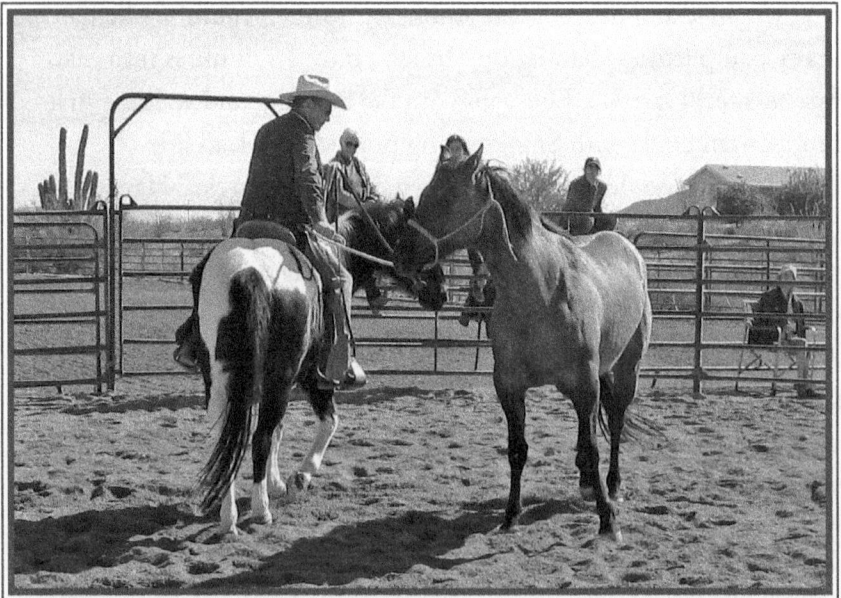

Harry and Easy work with Smoke on the whole rigmarole.

inexperienced horse is fully capable of grasping and following a full spectrum of presentations from the person and can understand them in a positive way.

Harry had Easy going in that circle, and he presented with the lead rope for Smoke's head to follow Easy's tail and get into the constant turn and make up the other side of the circle—a head-to-tail affair. Once that was nice and balanced, Harry then brought the lead rope forward towards Easy's head and offered for Smoke to come along beside them walking in the same direction.

"Pretty soon that front end is going to go because that thought went," Harry explained. "Her thought will go by me, and the front end will go here."

Harry indicated with his hand holding the rope that her head would come past him in the saddle and come to about Easy's shoulder as she came along parallel to him. And that's exactly what happened.

Next, Harry switched around and did the whole rigmarole going in the opposite direction. He mentioned that it is good to work on turns.

"We're getting some turnage going on here," he said, setting it up again with the horses turning head-to-tail. "I'd like for her thought to tip past me a little stronger there and then she'll go on past me."

If it is beginning to seem like Harry is constantly talking about a horse's thoughts, you are correct. I knew from studying with Harry for many years that getting the horse's mind on board with what the person wants to accomplish is the key to success. If you have the horse's mind, you have the horse—feet, shoulder, head, back...all those things are ruled by a horse's thinking. So often, we humans get stuck wanting the horse's body to do something and we want a simple mechanical solution to that. With Smoke, from the very first moments of this Colt Starting Clinic, it was clear that for Harry, these young horses weren't being treated any differently than older horses, really.

Harry's focus was always first concerned with the horse's mind—getting her attention and then presenting a search whereby the young horse began letting go of other thoughts until she came to the sweet spot (the one Harry wanted her to find). Also built into his progression with Smoke, as with all the other horses he worked, was his insistence that she become increasingly relaxed in the process.

It may seem that "insistence" and "relaxed" are not terms that work together. Perhaps "insistence" gives the impression of a hard, tightening, obedient, whip-cracking kind of approach. It is hard to explain on the page, but if Smoke wanted to start into a task with Harry in a tight, worried way, he'd shut her down and say, "No, not like that." Then he'd regroup and ask her to go again, but only with more relaxation, and she would find that relaxation. To witness a horse soften up in the midst of working on new things when handled right is wonderful.

Understanding and relaxation, if built in from the very beginning of a young horse's experience with people, are where willingness originates. We were to see hundreds of examples of this put into practice in myriad ways with the six colts over the two weeks that followed, many of which I hope to convey in these pages.

The complexities of the rigmarole were not too much for the young horse to take in right at the very beginning. I think they may be too much for some people to present to an inexperienced horse; not all of us have Harry's touch or experience. But Harry shows a great example what the horse is capable of.

Watching Harry and Smoke made me think that the horse is born with the capabilities to meet us humans anywhere along the spectrum of our abilities. In other words, they have the capacity to very quickly carry their end of the bargain in the relationship if we can provide ours and be soft, collected, relaxed, capable critters. The key is to have their minds present and focus on defusing tensions and blocking stressful choices on their end.

After getting the rigmarole going in each direction pretty

well, Harry stopped Easy and began asking Smoke with feel on the lead rope to walk in a circle all the way around them.

"Hey! Don't *pull* on me!" Harry said, and stressed it is important to be aware and not let a horse begin pulling, or pushing, on us.

I could see that the pulling at first was quite observable. But soon Harry was addressing it before the horse really pulled on the line. It was Smoke's thought of pulling that caused the physical pulling. Harry was addressing that initial thought and dealing with it, and soon she was walking a fine circle around him and Easy with a nice float in the lead rope.

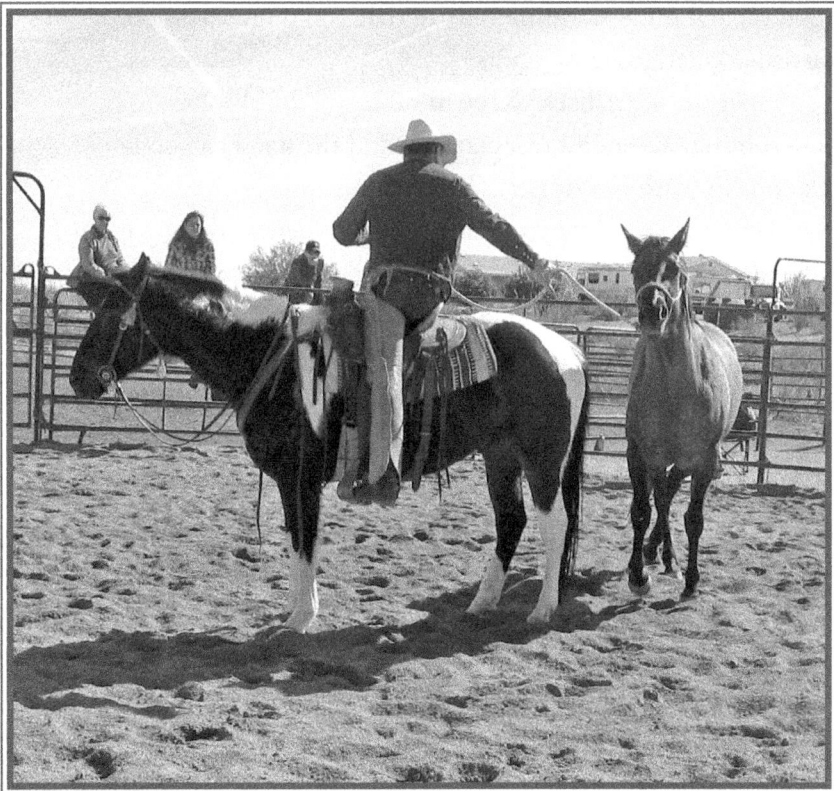

Harry offering a feel on the lead rope for Smoke to circle around him and Easy.

Harry dismounted, handed Easy off to someone outside of the pen and worked Smoke loose in the round pen for a few minutes before wrapping up her session. We broke for lunch, and afterwards we sat around the lunch table to discuss the morning. I asked a question that was on my mind anyway, but after watching the extensive amount of work Harry had done with Smoke it jumped to the forefront of my curiosity.

"With regard to the length of time working a young horse in a session, can a person overdo it?" I asked.

"Clarity," Harry answered. "If you have clarity, it is amazing what you can get done and have them be okay."

Clarity is mental. So Harry's answer said to me, "If you build mental understanding into all that you do in a session, it's not particularly fatiguing to a horse."

Again, we're back to the mind being the absolute underpinning to good horsemanship and the key to a good relationship with our horses. That first session clearly showed that there is no set time you must stick to when working colts as I had heard discussed over the years. I had heard things like, "You can only work these youngsters for 20 minutes or they start to get overwhelmed." I saw now that such advice really means, "If your approach lacks clarity, you only will be able to work a young horse a short time before he or she burns out."

Harry's session with Smoke lasted about an hour, and she was so much more relaxed and let down after the work than before, it was truly a testament to Harry's statement, and his approach.

Chapter Four

***

Day One,
Afternoon, Bailey at the Stall
Monday, 10 February 2014

"If in every experience we share with a colt we establish the kind of communication, consistency, relaxation, and willingness Harry did with Bailey when simply going to fetch her from the stall, just consider how all the big things might go when it is time to approach them."

Tom Moates

After lunch and the discussion that followed, we headed outside and across a large, open parking area from the bunk house, round pen, and arena to a set of pipe stalls situated under a large roof. Each morning, we fetched the colts from a pasture at one corner of the property and put them into the stalls so they would be close by for the day's work.

Bailey was the second horse to go on the first day. She was one of the larger horses in the group. Harry decided to start her session at the very beginning most point—entering the stall, haltering the horse, and exiting the stall.

I had witnessed Harry help people at his regular clinics many times with the seemingly simple task of getting their horses from the

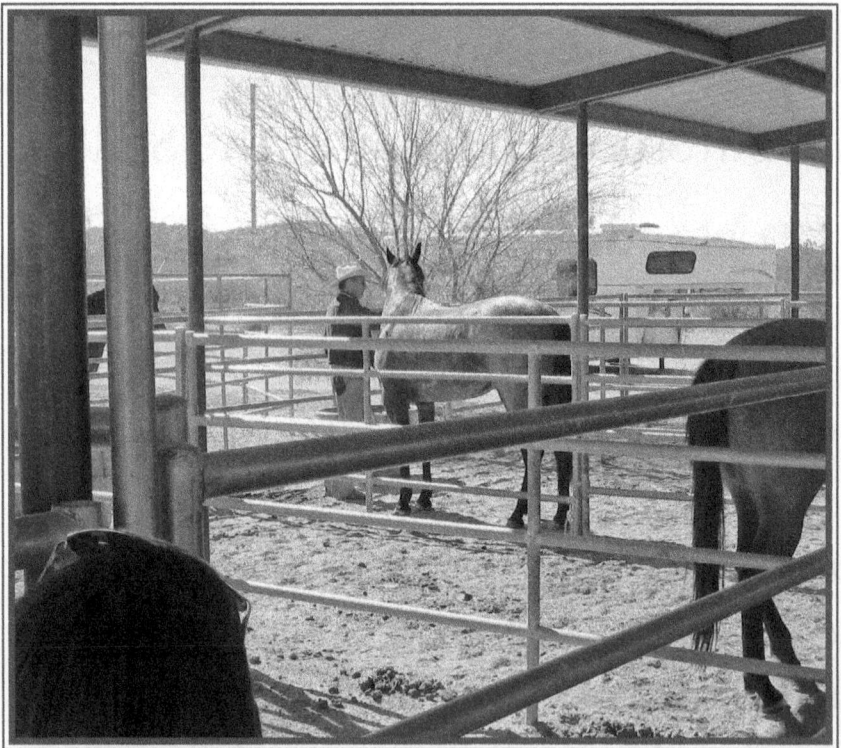

Harry puts the halter on Bailey in the stall at the beginning of her first session.

stalls. Sometimes, a whole session ended up unfolding at the stall and never getting to the round pen or the arena due to the work that got done there on those "simple things." I greatly appreciate that this happens at Harry's clinics because it points to the fact that the trouble our horses experience can be present in all the things we do with them, big or small.

If somebody comes to a clinic with a horse that isn't thinking forward and has been having trouble with the walk-to-trot transition for example, there's a very good chance Harry can address this holding back of their thought in the stall, on the walk to the arena, or pretty much anywhere. So often, people don't see such troubles in the microcosmic moments until they are pointed out to them. Finding the trouble with horses in the smaller presentations always has fascinated and challenged me, and has prompted me to improve my awareness to look for such things in my own horses. Thus, I was eager to see what Harry would find in this young horse in the stall environment, since she would have far fewer established people problems than the older horses at clinics I'd seen before.

What unfolded at the stall took very little time, less than 10 minutes, but I found it to be a great lesson. Harry entered the stall with a halter and met Bailey who was towards the back, opposite the gate. He had no problem approaching her. He offered the halter and she was fine about sliding her nose into it, and he tied it in place.

Next, they took a couple steps together, and Harry centered her up mentally by asking her to back a step, stop, and then look him up. They moved around a little bit more and Bailey was looking pretty good. But when they headed to exit through the gate, the mare crowded him and went to rush through it.

Harry was ahead of the situation and quickly got pretty big with the lead rope asking for a back up. Bailey's head flew up and she staggered a couple of steps back as this sudden intervention on Harry's part interrupted her strong forward thought. The scene repeated with Harry needing less and less bigness to break the crowding/rushing thoughts in her mind. The result was three fold: she got her mind centered in the stall following Harry's feel rather than her mind jumping out of the stall before her body was there, she got more light and responsive to Harry's request on the lead rope, and she got more soft and relaxed throughout her body.

Once she realized Harry was going to block any rush on him or the open gate with a request to reverse, she started thinking about this situation. That also set up a search in the young horse to try other ways to get this deal to work out.

Within a couple of minutes, Harry was on the other side of the open gate in the aisle facing her, lead rope in hand and offering

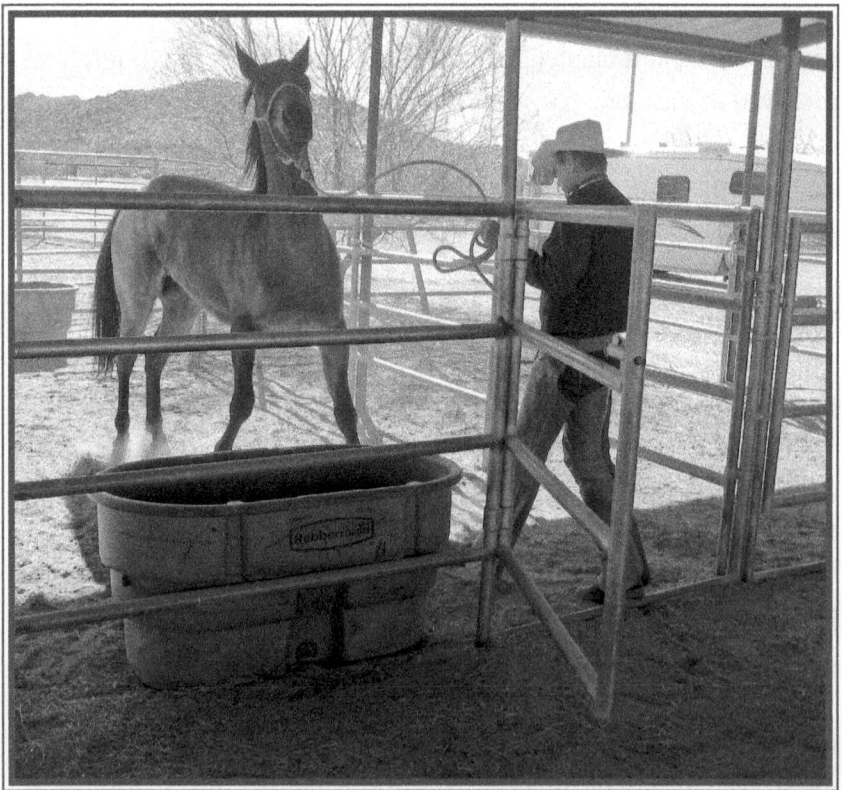

Harry "got pretty big with the lead rope" asking Bailey to back up rather than rush through the gate.

a feel to come forward—but only if relaxed, calm, and ready to stop, back, or step forward at any given moment. She had the ticket. At first, Harry set it up so she could step up to the open gate, but not step through it, and he'd stop her there and pet her on the forehead. Then, he would ask her to take a step through the gate and stop, back up, come forward again...basically just be mentally available at every moment regardless of where she was in relation to the gate.

What a wonderful thing to instill in a colt. I thought how, if all horses from their very first experiences with people had a human who was mindful in this way and was careful to tend to keeping the horse with him or her at the most basic tasks, there may never be other issues further along the line. How many big problems would be solved by preventing them in the first place?

Said differently, how many big problems are the result of a horse getting a strong thought of her own (like running through the gate or through the bit) rather than being with us and following the thought we present? Well, pretty much all of them. And, how many people just completely overlook how they approach a horse in the stall? People don't seem to consider that something as mundane as putting a halter on the horse and walking out the stall door has meaning to the horse, but it surely does.

I've heard Harry talk many times about how a person thinks what happens in the round pen is important and that he or she must take great care with how to work the horse when in that space. Then, the second that person walks out of the round corral gate, he or she ignores the horse and undoes everything just worked on. The person can seem to punch off the clock the second that person is out of the round pen, but the horse never, ever punches out, ever. Every one of our interactions with horses has the same level of meaning and influence, and if we're not nurturing with-you-ness, we're allowing the opposite, not-with-you-ness, to build into the relationship.

This few minutes with Bailey sticks with me as profoundly important. Here, in the second session of the clinic, it was obvious that for whatever reason, the young horse was pushy. Certainly, horses are pushy with each other and constantly jostle around to see who can move the other around. But, as this example showed, people must be careful to not only consider moving a horse's body when it is time to, but to consider the mental aspects of moving the horse.

With Bailey at the stall, Harry was very careful to not only back the mare's feet away from the gate when she went to rush through and crowd him, but to back her until she had a change of thought. It is possible to back a horse who still hasn't changed the mental aspect of pushing, in which case you haven't affected a true change. You've momentarily moved the horse, but mentally she can be pushing every bit as hard as before if you don't get a mental shift, and that will again become a physical push at her first opportunity.

Harry was very particular to be certain he made his presence useful and effective by getting big enough so that she let go of her pushy-ness and relaxed and became quite willing to follow his feel

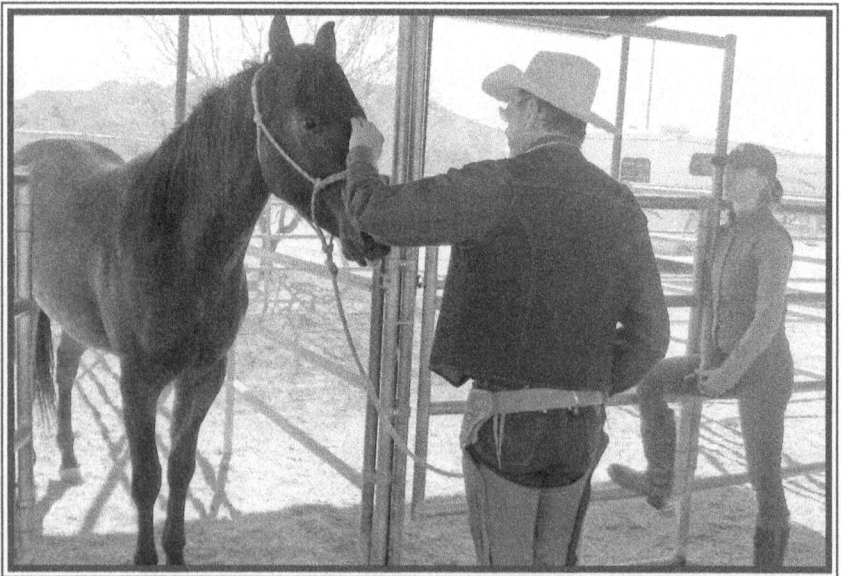

Harry gets Bailey to relax and not rush the gate at the stall as Anna Bonnage watches intently.

to mindfully step with him. Honestly, before long that became the situation with her wherever she was. The gate became irrelevant. In the stall, in the gate, in the aisle way between the stalls, in the parking lot area, or in the pasture...it no longer mattered where she was located once Harry had her mind centered with him and she was following the feel of whatever he presented.

This stall session with Bailey, which happened before her main session, although short and dealing with a seemingly routine task, seems to me to perfectly represent the idea Harry is fond of saying, "so they're started, so they go." If in every experience we share with a colt we establish the kind of communication, consistency, relaxation, and willingness Harry did with Bailey when simply going to fetch her from the stall, just consider how all the big things might go when it is time to approach them.

Chapter Five

Day One, Afternoon Continued,
Chic and Tinker

*"One of the best rewards a
horse can have is <u>nothing</u>."*
Harry Whitney

After Bailey, Harry worked Chic. The most striking point
to me about that session came at the beginning. Chic was turned
loose in the round pen. Harry untied Sandy from the hitching rail,
tightened up his cinch, and mounted. When Sandy and Harry
approached the gate from outside of the round pen, Chic rushed

towards them and crowded the unopened gate. Rather than pushing Chic aside and entering the round pen to begin work on something inside, Harry took that opportunity to help Chic center mentally and let go of the tension she was carrying before he and Sandy ever entered the gate.

Harry got a flag and, positioned on Sandy just outside of the gate, worked on Chic's pushiness right there. When the mare rushed up to the gate, Harry made a ruckus with the flag until she began to let go of that pushy thought and to move back further into the pen, at which point he quit flagging.

Sandy just stood there relaxed like the trooper that he is. Chic, on the other hand, at first did some exaggerated head wringing and jumping around when she moved away from the gate. Her little fits clearly were an opinion about not wanting to let go of her strong thought to crowd them at the gate rather than about any fear of the flag.

A view of Harry's place before Bailey's session on day one. The shipping container tack room with the shed roof is on the left by the round pen. The gate to the arena is on the right behind Easy, Big Easy, and Sandy who are tied to the hitching rail, and the bunkhouse is just out of the photo to the right.

The scene repeated with Chic coming in strong and Harry matching her assertiveness by getting just big enough with the flag to get her to let go of the thought of pushing on them, but not big enough to send her rushing away into flee mode. It was interesting to observe that, in a way, Chic really was the one in control of the flag. That is, if she pushed into the gate, the flag activated. If she let go of that thought, relaxed some, and backed away, then the flag went still and silent. If she pushed into the gate, she essentially pushed into her own pressure, i.e. the flag getting busy in response to her actions. The situation really got her thinking and got her able to step away from the gate and eventually to stand calmly.

That business took about ten minutes to sort out. Finally, Harry was able to reach over, unlatch the gate, and ride into the pen on Sandy without Chic coming over to crowd them. It registered with me that Harry took advantage of a semi-problematic situation that presented itself in the course of preparing for the session to help the mare get to a better frame of mind before ever getting to what many people would consider the "starting" of the session.

It was a great example of, "it is not an A, B, C program (like every colt must go to the round pen and have X, Y, Z groundwork done just so before going to the next step), but rather, what is critical is how you approach things with horses, whatever you do with them." The horse is always "on," so stopping to work on some issue that presents itself wherever it presents itself, can be the most effective place to sort it out.

This theme would permeate the next two weeks as we watched Harry with Anna and Ty bring the six young horses along in their relationships to humans in a huge variation of circumstances. I thought about how Chic, Sandy, and Harry happened to be at a round pen in this situation. But what Harry worked on there could have been accomplished at any gate in any fence, or even done over a section of solid fence for that matter, and need not have been related to a round pen at all. In other words, what counted with Chic was

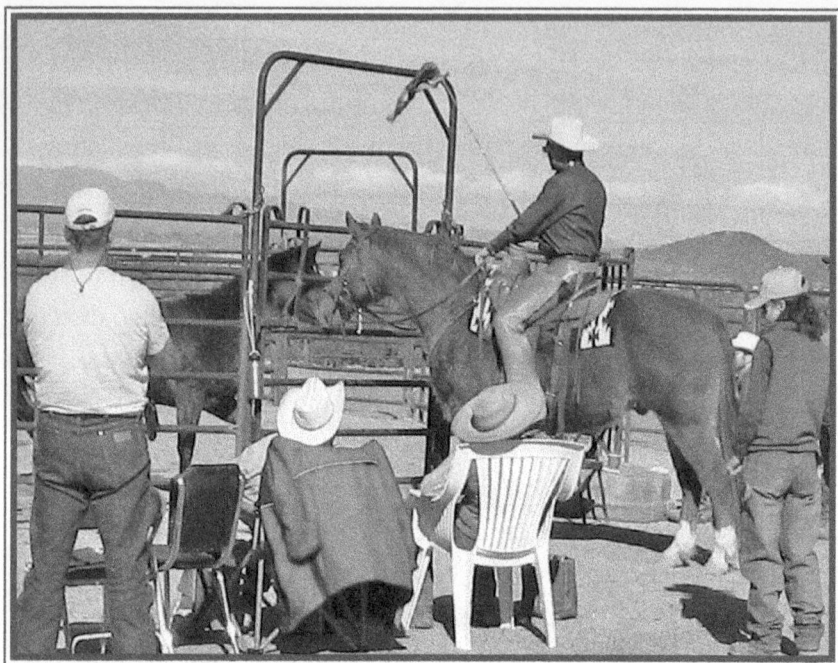

Chic crowding the gate as Harry flags her from atop Sandy as auditors watch the action unfold.

not gear or place specific; what counted was seeing the pushiness in her and addressing it right where it manifested.

Likewise, it was a lesson to us observers that we might keep an eye out for any opportunity at any time to help a horse we are working with, even if it presents itself while on the way to do what we have in mind. The situation earlier in the day when Harry went to fetch Bailey and she took to pushing on him before ever exiting the stall was quite similar. Harry dealt with that situation in the stall right there in real-time rather than ignoring it and going a hundred yards to the round pen before "starting" to work with the mare.

In other words, Harry's actions with Chic at the round pen gate showed an important lesson. If you get on autopilot to go into the round pen because that's what you have set out to do (so by golly that's what you're going to do), and just push the horse that's crowding you out of the way to get started working on something else you have in mind, then you might miss a wonderful chance to work on your horse in the midst of where she needs it, right when she needs it, regardless of whether you are where you set out to be or not.

***

The next horse was Tinker. A group of us clinic goers hauled in some panels on the back of Harry's pickup and set up a sizable square pen inside the arena. Back in England, Anna does not have regular access to round pens but often has access to small "yards" where she can work colts. The square pen was to give yet another example of a how a person can work a colt in a different environment and still get the desired results.

The best way to describe what unfolded with Tinker in the square pen is to say that eventually she "made the square pen round." It wasn't, however, without the mare getting stuck in the corners at first when her focus was thinking outside of the pen.

Harry entered the corral with Tinker loose, and he worked her at liberty with a halter and lead rope in his hands.

"I flagged those others," Harry said, "so, I'm not going to flag her."

Essentially, what he did looked no different than it would have if he had worked her in the round pen, and he said it really was no different. The mare made her own circle in the pen to move freely around Harry, simply cutting off the corners of the square. But Tinker wasn't without her challenges.

"This is why you hear a lot of people talk naughty about the Hancock/ Driftwood type lines," Harry said while working on getting the little mare to let go of her focus that was outside of the pen and to connect with him. "Because, a lot of them are pretty strong minded like this, and it often comes out in—then things don't work out— they end up bucking and stuff. And so, they have some ill thoughts about them. But, they're a horse first. Doesn't matter who their daddy or their granddaddy or their greatgranddaddy was. You take care of what the horse needs to feel better about what's taking place—get some clarity and understanding. See, her mind is gone...gone!"

Harry would slap a chap with the end of the lead rope to attempt to break Tinker's outward interest and see if she would take an interest in him. When she was particularly far gone (mentally), Harry would toss the halter at her bum to get her to consider what was happening around her in the pen. As this work with Tinker progressed, he began increasingly to gain her focus, and she began to make shorter trips around the pen before stopping to check in with Harry, and she quit getting stuck in the corners she was favoring at first.

"If there was a chance of her thinking about following

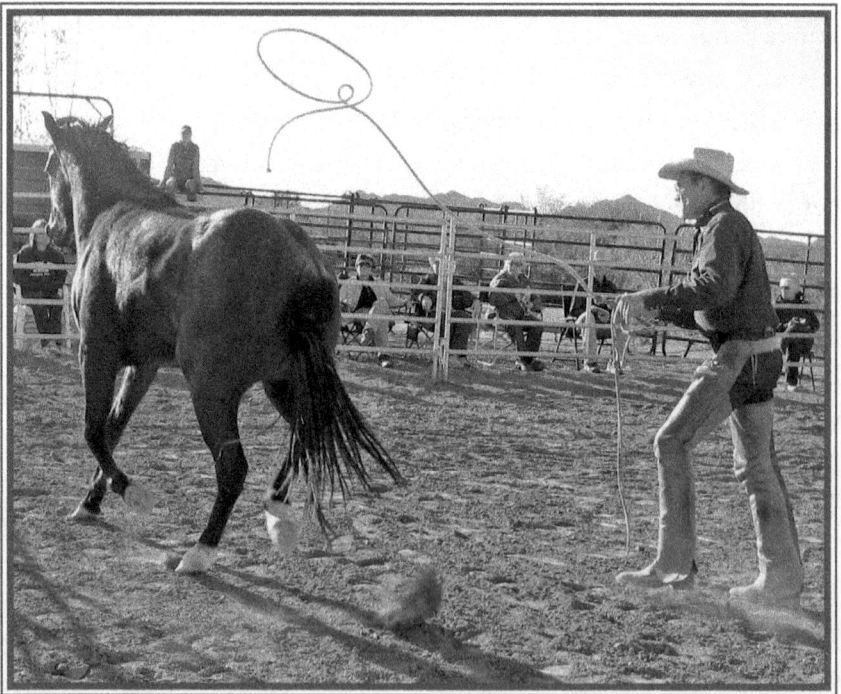

Harry tosses the rope at Tinker's bum in the square pen that we set up inside the arena.

The young mares turned out after their first day of clinic.

me," Harry continued, "it would be if I come off over here [in the direction of the stalls] where she keeps thinking about her buddies. So, you can use that to your advantage. But, to just step off over here [Harry indicated the side of the pen in the opposite direction of where the other horses were kept], and just see if she'll even look [at me]. That's why I didn't ask her to come off over this way—[but tried to see] if I could just get her to look over here, even."

Harry worked awhile on gaining Tinker's focus. The clinician continued at times to slap the rope against his chaps to break her mind loose or toss the lead rope at her butt to snap her mind back into the pen and towards him.

"Again, I want to remind you guys," Harry reiterated to us sitting there, "that when I toss that rope, it's not about her going. It's about her not getting stuck in the corner maybe, but it's more a reminder that I'm here, that there's something important here—not out there."

Before long, she was able to let go of those outside thought magnets and was more content to connect with Harry. Once she was standing quietly beside the clinician, Harry haltered her and did a little ground work on line.

"If she's relaxed and has clarity," he shared with the sea of auditors sitting on the other side of the panels taking everything in, "then I'll build anything you want in there one day."

***

(From my clinic journal:)

Personal note: I've been to a lot of clinics, but one thing that struck me about today was how much these colts either pushed against or pulled away from Harry (and/or his saddle horse)...establishing space [was a big focus].

Chapter Six

Day Two, After Breakfast
Discussion
11 February 2014

"But, we don't have them take us somewhere.
We just make them go."

Harry Whitney

     Discussions always are a huge part of Harry Whitney's clinics, and the special Colt Starting Clinic was no exception. In fact, the discussions were particularly energetic and insightful all through both weeks of the clinic. I'm sure that resulted from the large crowd of folks on-hand. Nearly all of the people present were long-time students of Harry's and thus quite comfortable with putting questions out there in front of the group.

Clinic goers are encouraged to ask questions anywhere and anytime at a Harry clinic, but official discussion times always ensue after a meal in the bunkhouse when Harry holds court to field questions and ponder reflections on what has been observed so far in a clinic. The second day of the clinic provided the first after-breakfast opportunity to discuss the previous day's progress with the colts. Sometimes, a group's sleep on the previous day's events can provide very fertile ground for vibrant ponderings.

To get things going, Harry asked Ty to summarize what happened the day before because a guest of Harry's had arrived late and missed the first day.

"Here's what we did yesterday," Ty said. "Harry worked two

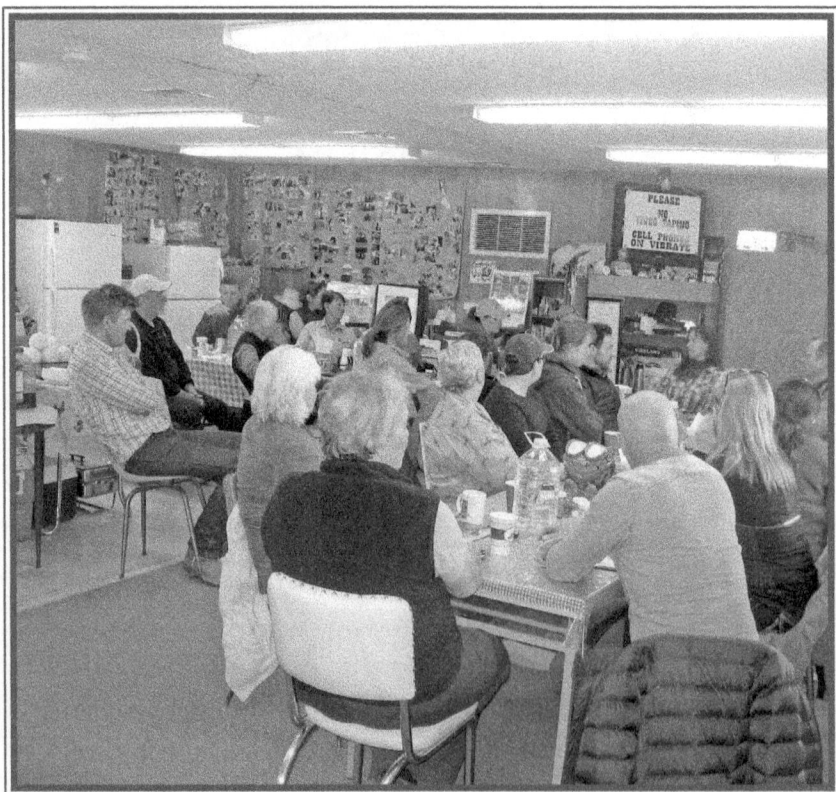

A packed bunkhouse after-meal discussion.

saddle horses, [there was an extended pause as Ty masterfully held the group's attention before continuing...] and then Anna and I worked our tails off all day!"

The bunkhouse shook with the roar of side-splitting laughter. The inside joke was that Anna and Ty hadn't gotten to do much of anything with the colts on the first day, and that the newcomers might be persuaded by Ty to believe otherwise. Such good natured ribbing and general silliness always adds great fun to Harry's clinics.

"And, if he does that to us again today..." Ty continued....

"You might go home," Harry completed the sentence, punctuated with a hearty cackle.

When we had caught our collective breath, Harry proceeded to give the quick recap.

"I played with Sandy and Easy, who had not been ridden since April, and played with each one of them for a few minutes—too many minutes. And then, two of the fillies we worked from horseback [Smoke and Chic] and on the ground a little bit. The other two [Tinker and Bailey] we just strictly worked on the ground... trying to keep it varied so we're not doing identical things to everybody.

"They brought a gelding out yesterday [Houston] and we didn't work him. He's been doing a lot of hauling, so he got to rest yesterday and we'll work him today. Our plan is—and that could change—is to just work him on the line, not even turn him loose in a pen, and maybe do everything on the line up to riding him just to show people you can get it done without having a pen if you really want to.

"We didn't work Sky [a mare who is a year older than the others] yesterday. She's the one that Anna started last year. So we have the gelding and Sky to play with."

***

Houston begins his first session on day two.

Some talk about working colts in small versus large spaces got started. Frannie Burridge from Maine got things really rolling with her input:

"It occurred to me that back east we do things totally opposite from what they do out west. Mainly because of the availability of land. But, they never kill the go in a horse because they never keep it confined. They wouldn't start a colt in a confined area. They might get it saddled in there."

"Right, right," Harry agreed. "Soon as it's rideable enough to go, they're going."

"And that way," Frannie continued, "they never kill the go. They never kill the straightness, because it's in those confined areas you take the straightness out of them. And then, you try to put it back in.

"I remember, you said, 'First you go where the horse wants to go, and then you ask if he'll go with you a little ways, and then you let him go where he wants to go...eventually, you're going somewhere together.'"

Harry sat up in his chair which was at the bottom of the V of the two long lines of tables. Frannie sat facing him at the opposite end of one of them.

"The thing I think about there is," Harry said, "if you get his mind lined out thinking forward, then you keep the straightness. It's when we're *making* them go [that they get crooked]. It's like that guy I was talking about, that I saw in that demo, and that little horse was so counter-bent going around that pen just looking for a way out—and he's pulling on the rein trying to keep it from falling into the middle too far. But, it never turned to that rein. And so, he's building in a crookedness there that was phenomenal 'cause he wasn't working getting that colt to think about going, whether it went around the pen or across the middle. What matters is as long as he was taking himself and the rider somewhere, then he'll line out and go straight. But, when you're trying to make him go and there's nowhere to go in his mind, things get crooked in a hurry.

"And, I think everybody in this room has heard me use the little analogy of one of those little trains that's cut out of pieces of wood and is hooked together with strings. If a little kid gets ahold of that string and takes off, that train just pulls right straight. It doesn't matter if that kid's going in a straight line or around a curve, everything is lined up straight. I think of that little kid just like a horse's thoughts. It's just drawing him right out there straight wherever it's going. But, most of us are riding our horse just like that little train that you walked up and pushed on the caboose. It's not planning on going anywhere; there's nothing drawing it out there straight. You push on the caboose and things get crooked.

"Now, if you want a stronger example of what a lot of people do, they're hanging onto the reins, so take the string on that engine, go around behind it and push on the caboose and you've got a complete train wreck! And that's what Frannie's talking about in a small pen, is people create a complete train wreck and now you work for years to try to get him straight. Because, he doesn't know anything about getting straight because his mind isn't going out there and drawing him right out there straight.

"It's probably a little more difficult or limited in a round pen, but in an arena—and you could have an arena half the size of this one even if that's the biggest space you had—get that horse to take you somewhere. But, we're interested in going round and round. Why? We think we're big wheels; we just want to go in circles. Line out and get him to take you to the corner. If you're younger and spryer than me, jump off. Go kick the panels in the corner. Get on him; get him to take you to another corner. Kick the panels. Pretty soon he'll line out and take you, and it doesn't take a very big space.

"You can get some of that done in an area the size of this room if you want to do it. But, we don't have them take us somewhere. We just make them go."

Chapter Seven

Day Two,
Morning, Bailey and Big Easy
11 February 2014

*"Yesterday she wasn't feeling of me much,
but today she's starting to."*
Harry Whitney

    Day two started off with Harry working Big Easy in the round pen to prepare him to be his saddle horse for the day. What unfolded took me back to my first trip to Arizona when I met Harry and attended two weeks of clinics the first season he opened his new facility in 2006.

The whole encounter is described in detail in the final chapter of my book, *Passing It On*, so I won't recount it all again here. Suffice it to say, I had quite the déjà vu experience. I was sitting on the rail of the panels of the same round pen in the same spot as eight years previous, watching Harry work the same horse, and the same thing happened. After a little work in the round pen, Big Easy relaxed and began moving around pretty nicely when Harry took his lariat and roped the gelding across his rump. The loop hung nicely in the seat of the saddle and draped around across the back of his legs, which sent him forward with great concern.

I remember distinctly in 2006 thinking how I would have been lulled into thinking Big Easy was doing great, and that I would

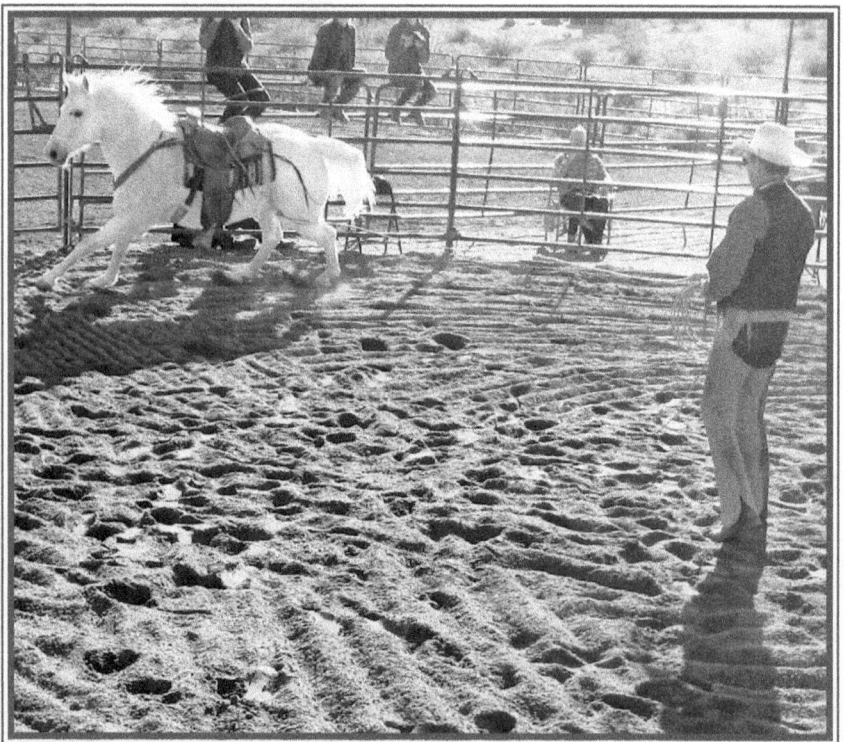

My déjà vu experience—Big Easy being very uneasy about Harry roping him around the posterior.

have missed this great worry lingering in him about the rope touching his hind end. This situation bringing me full circle eight years later made a powerful impression on me and caused me to reflect on my personal horsemanship journey...but, on to Bailey who was the first colt of the day.

At this point, Harry was riding Big Easy and had built a loop with his lariat and had been swinging it all around. He made several throws onto the ground near the gelding. He also allowed the loop to land against Big Easy's legs and back end while he rode him around. Soon, the horse's angst about the rope relaxed and things looked pretty settled with him.

Anna fetched Bailey and put her in the round pen with Harry still in there on Big Easy. At first, Harry was inclined to work the mare from the saddle horse. But adjusting to something in the situation with her (I'm not sure exactly what), he dismounted and handed off Big Easy to someone outside of the pen. Again, I was struck by how Harry constantly morphs his approach to what unfolds before him with the horses he works with rather than forcing horses into some pre-ordained program.

Bailey was at liberty in the round pen. Harry offered for her to connect and come to him, but at first she turned away from him. Harry asked her to move around.

"Today she has not nearly the need to protect herself," he said, after playing with her a little bit.

Harry roped her rump and legs; she kicked, but he just kept letting her work at getting accustomed to the rope and finding the feel he was presenting in different ways.

Several times when it seemed like Bailey was leaving him mentally and physically, rather than presenting something bigger to instigate a look from her, Harry just waited, let her work at it, and the mare eventually made it back to him.

"So often we miss those spots because we believe the horse is leaving," he mentioned at one point when he let the mare walk

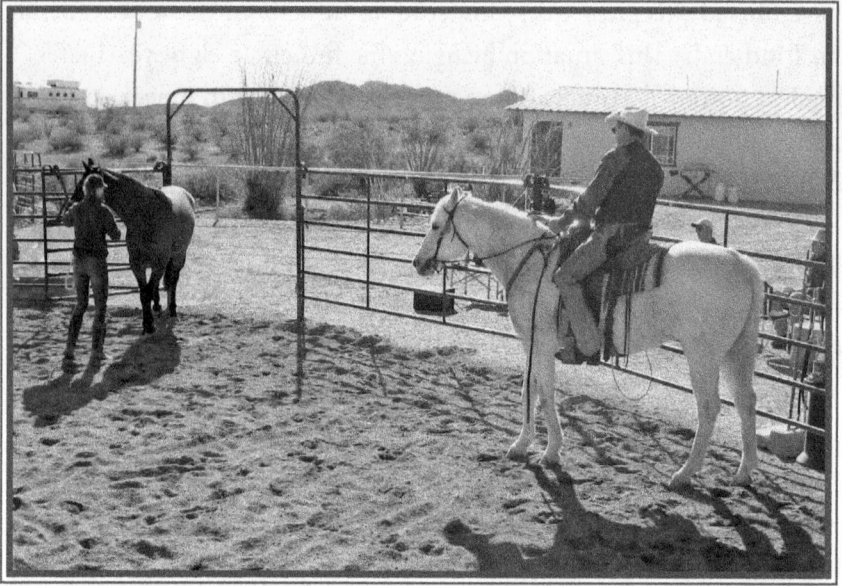

Anna turns Bailey loose in the round pen as Harry sizes things up on Big Easy.

straight away from him several steps. Because he waited and did not intervene to pressure her, she turned back to face him on her own before she reached the panels.

At times, the rope caused her to flee quite rapidly, but Harry just kept up his same, even, confident presentation.

"You just don't panic," he offered us as advice. "If those [somewhat wayward] things happen, just let it work out. Yesterday she wasn't feeling of me, but today she's starting to."

Soon, she was turning to face him with regularity. It was a quiet moment with her when the clinician easily slipped the loop of his lariat over her head. The young mare was docile about it, and Harry backed away and began to work with her on line with the lariat loop at the top of her neck close to the base of her head.

Essentially, he treated the situation as if he had a halter and lead rope on the horse. With her standing and facing him, Harry would offer a feel on the rope for the mare to take an interest and look strongly in a direction. She would search for a moment as to what he was asking, but soon she found it. He would release and stroke her on the nose. He built on that, and soon she was readily stepping along with his requests, and he had her circling him both directions quite nicely. After about 20 minutes of groundwork, Harry remounted Big Easy with the lariat in-hand and still around Bailey's neck.

Harry asked in a gentle way for Bailey to move around Big Easy and him. The added dimension of his being above her rather than on foot and with another horse in close proximity caused Harry to again let the mare search at discovering what the feel he presented on the line meant. Soon, however, she was moving around them with more ease. He would have her walk a half circle in front of Big Easy, then turn and walk back the other way past his head. Eventually, he had Bailey able to come right in beside the gelding, with her head close to the saddle, which Harry petted, and her butt out beyond Big Easy's nose.

Harry asks Bailey to circle around him and Big Easy.

Harry worked her about 10 minutes from the saddle horse, and with a nice spot achieved, he wrapped up with her and called for Ty and Houston to come into the arena.

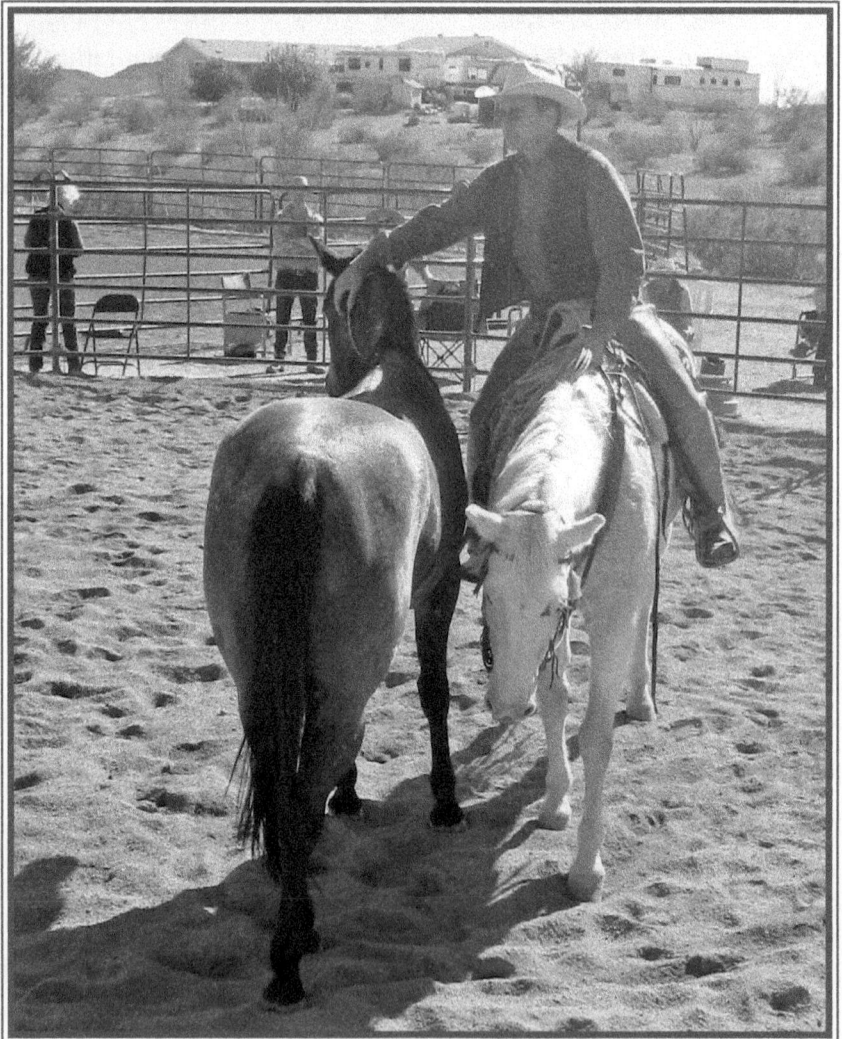

Harry, Big Easy, and Bailey all ending the session on a good note.

Chapter Eight

Ty and Houston, First Session
11 February 2014

"A lot of people say, 'Well look at him. He's so relaxed. He's doing great.' And yet, there are spots here that there's more tension than you realize a lot of times."

Harry Whitney

Next, Ty entered Harry's spacious arena with Houston for the dun gelding's first session of the clinic. Harry's familiar giant saguaro cactus reached its arms up towards heaven, towering as the tallest feature in the background in a wash near the far end of the arena. The plan was to work the youngster only in open spaces throughout both weeks of the clinic to show how things can be approached for folks who do not have a round pen or small corral at home.

We have a round pen at home. But Carol's young horse, Mirage, is pastured on another farm close by that doesn't have any small fenced-in spaces, so I realized I'd often be in this very predicament when working her upon my return to Virginia. Watching Houston's progress during the clinic proved to be very helpful to me with the project of starting Mirage.

Ty walked into the arena a ways with Houston who was on a lead rope and halter. They stopped, and Ty began to get acquainted with the gelding on-line. Just approaching Houston from the front, the gelding showed to be a little apprehensive of Ty and shied away.

To address this, Ty repeatedly walked head-on towards the colt with his arms and a chaotic bundle of the lead rope waving around above his head. This is a move I picked up from Harry years ago that I call the "windmill." The arm-flapping Ty approached the gelding's head assertively, and the gelding shied away with concern. Ty just kept presenting his flapping arms and the rope in close proximity to the horse's head until Houston began to relax and let down a little realizing he wasn't in trouble and the strange person meant him no harm, at which point the strange person would stop with the flapping and pet on Houston. This scenario repeated multiple times until Houston was able to take Ty's flappy approach in stride.

Harry made the comment that Houston is "gentle, easy to load, but knows nothing of a little direction."

We broke for lunch after only a short, half-session, planning to return after lunch to finish up with Houston. The post-lunch discussion is covered in the next chapter, but I want to share some of the second half of Houston's session on day two here.

With lunch and discussion wrapped up, we returned to the arena and Ty went back to working with Houston, addressing situations where the gelding became tense and working to bring relaxation to him in those areas. Before long, Ty was walking closely along side Houston and was placing an arm over his back where the saddle would go. He hopped up and down in that area and got Houston settled about his being in that spot, and also directing about his movements from there as well. It worked out so well he took the notion to hop up and lie across the gelding's back in the "sack of potatoes" position.

Houston stood there like a trooper with Ty lying across him. This got repeated a few more times and looked so good I could tell Ty was thinking about going ahead and throwing a leg over his equine companion. Then, as Houston was walking along with Ty lying

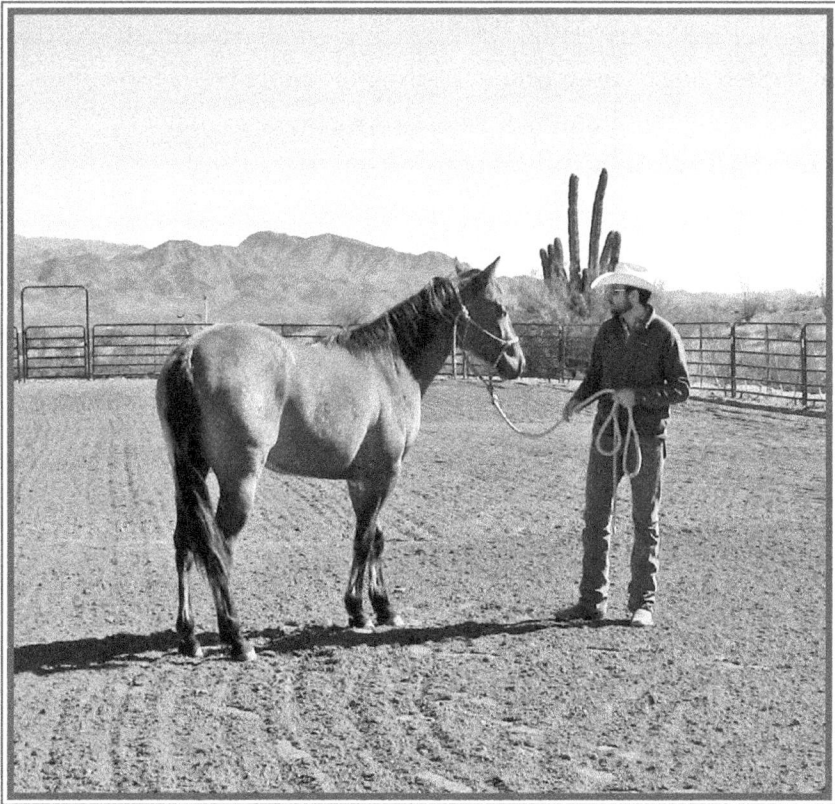

Ty and Houston beginning their first session together with Harry's huge saguaro cactus in the background.

across his back, Ty brought a leg over and sat up on the young horse. It went perfectly. He repeated this several times before calling it a day with Houston.

Observing how Ty and Houston got along not only provided some idea of what it looks like to work with a colt in an open environment, but it showed that some horses will present opportunities to play with something you might not have thought you'd get to in a session.

In other words, I bet not a person there expected that Houston would have someone sitting on his back for at least a few days at the earliest. It just was not the focus of this colt starting clinic to see how fast a colt can be saddled and ridden. Quite the opposite was true, and Harry made it clear at the beginning that some of these youngsters might not get ridden during the entire two weeks. What was of paramount importance was that whatever got done with the colts, it would be their understanding, relaxation, and positive progression that counted.

But, that said—and this first session with Houston proved the point—if the opportunity presented itself to get something unexpectedly advanced done with a colt (whatever it might be) which remained within the all-important realm of furthering training while building relaxation, consistency, and with-you-ness in the horse, there were no rigid rules in place to stop that from happening either. It is a great example showing how Harry's approach to colt starting is organic and not cookie-cutter.

I was thrilled to see Ty throw a leg over this colt on his very first session—not because he was pushing the envelope of the horse's training as is so prevalent in the very popular colt starting competitions these days where people race to see who can saddle and ride (and of course, stand in the saddle and crack a stock whip on) a colt first, but quite the opposite—because this colt was okay with a human sitting on him bareback during his first session within the parameters Harry has for horse work. Houston was not shut down

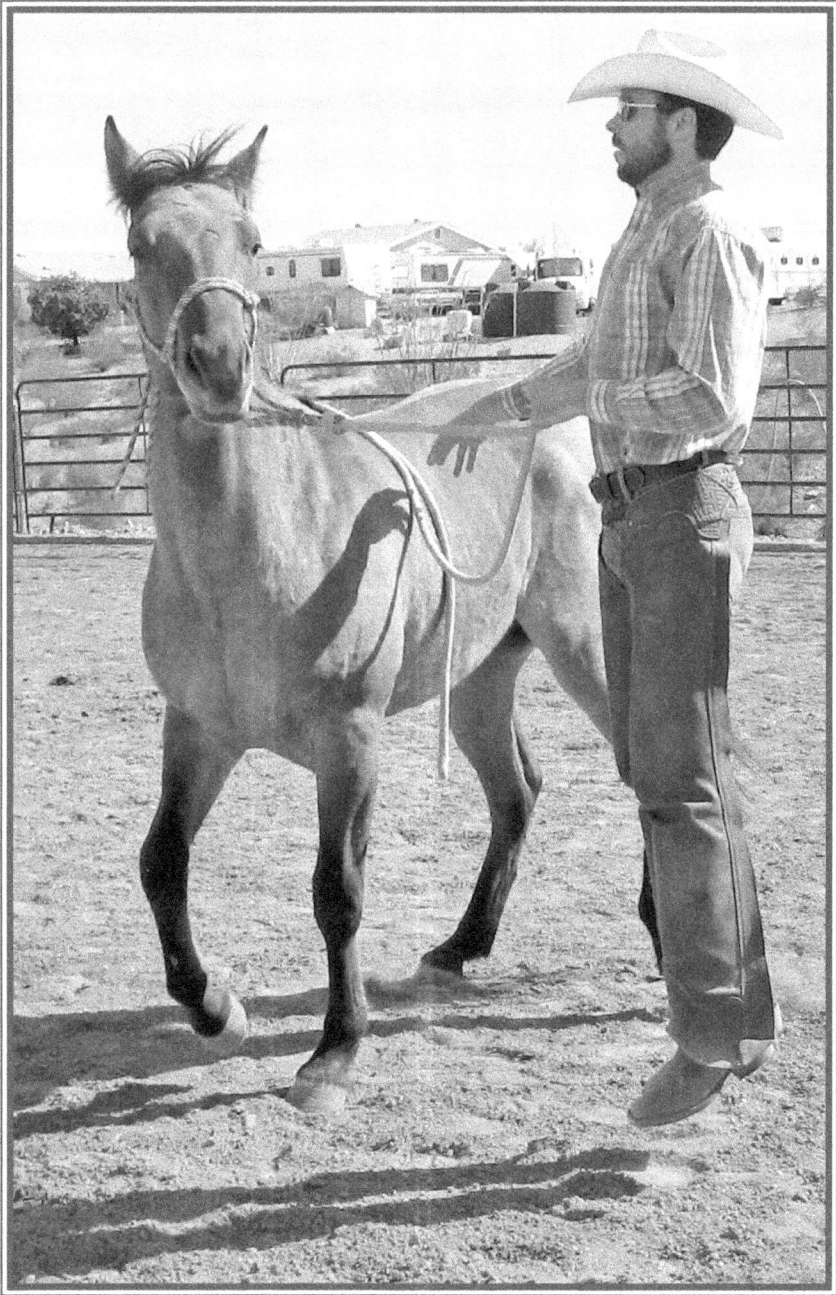

Ty seems to hover beside Houston as he jumps up and down next to the gelding.

(sacked-out) and merely tolerating Ty's presence on his back, but rather was awake and genuinely okay with this situation.

I was delighted for Houston, who was capable of advancing in this particular way because of who he was, and for Ty, who was able to play with the gelding in such a way (with Harry's coaching) as to unlock this unexpected opportunity straight away. The thrill for me is to see such potential in a young horse fostered. Indeed, I was there to study how people can build a super-positive relationship with a young horse without building in all the baggage that is seen in so many horses everyday—and here it was proven that there really is no rule as to what you can or can't do with a horse within a given time frame (depending on the horse). Rather, it is all about how you approach each individual horse working with where he is at any given moment that counts.

Ty in the "sack of potatoes" position on Houston during their first session.

Chapter Nine

Day Two, After Lunch Discussion
11 February 2014

*"It's amazing what horses won't
do if you don't let them."*
Harry Whitney

After lunch on day two, the bunkhouse clinic conversation got rolling. Early into the discussion, Kathy Baker from Tennessee had a question.

"When that filly [Bailey] came in, it felt good to her," Kathy said. "She was settled. You stroked her. And so, we think of that often as a sweet spot. You have talked about her feeling of you—there was a communication out there on the rope...and the horse is feeling back with what you're offering. How are you building that in on these young horses? There can be that sweet spot out there on the line because you're offering connection? Direction? Because, we all talk about them coming in and standing in a halter—they like being with us, but they're not doing anything."

"And that was so expressed, I think, with the little gelding [Houston]," Harry replied, referring to the gelding's session from before lunch. "If you just stand there and pet on him, he'd just hang

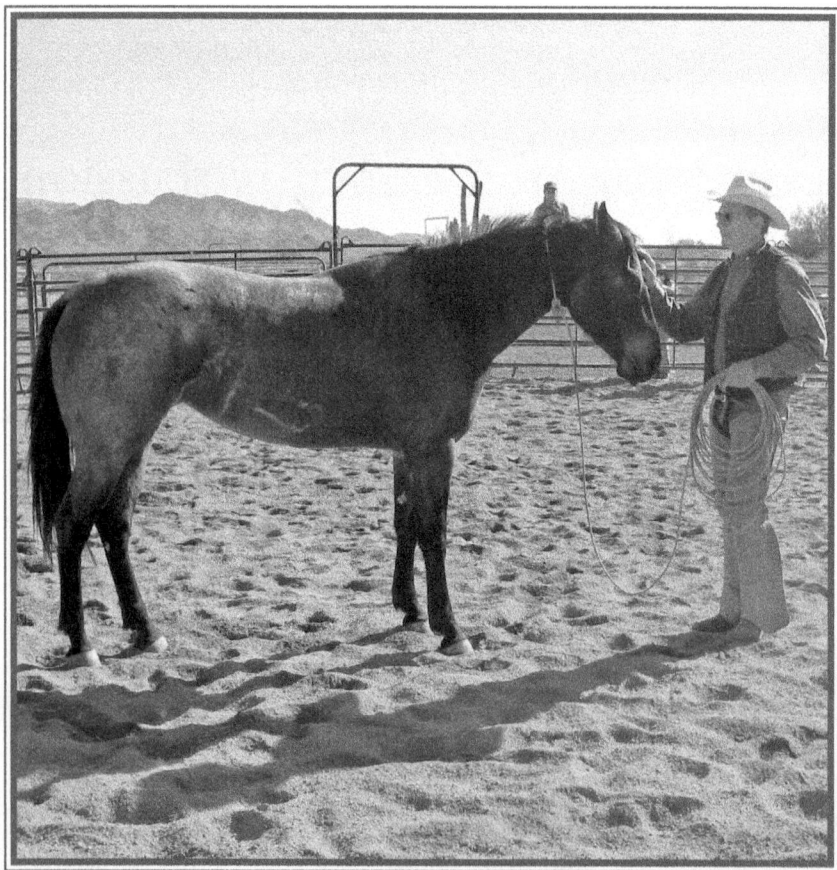

Harry strokes Bailey establishing a sweet spot between them during their session before lunch.

out all day. As soon as you start to ask something, he gets to pushing on you and resisting. Not in a big way, but yet it shows up. As long as he can just stand there with his head next to you and you petting on him, he's happy to hang out.

"Well, that's a good thing. You now have something to build on. You have something to come back to, maybe is a good way of saying it. So, if things didn't go perfect, you can come back to that good spot and start again. So, I think that's a wonderful thing to have in there. How you build that in there is just like with Bailey. Today, she was feeling good enough about this that maybe I could ask her to take her thought out there, and yet she'd want to be here enough that she'd stay connected. Thinking about, 'When can I just be there?' and yet feeling of me out there, and then you can begin to bring that up and let that down a little when she's out there and she knows when you let it down everything's going smooth and good—that she did the right thing."

This line of discussion got some things stirred up in my mind, so I entered the conversation.

"I had one of the fillies back several years ago going so well—I thought—leading up real nice," I said. "Everything was just super. And then one day, months into this deal, something happened where the filly wanted to go one way and I wanted to go the other, and it was up and over and backwards. I felt so bad about the way that went. But I know now that I didn't have her used to letting go of a thought.

"It was one of those deals where [up until the trouble] I guess we were wanting to go in the same direction. There was never, 'push came to shove.' But, when push did come to shove and it was important, boy, I was in a big wreck I wish I could have avoided. Is that wreck one of those initial experiences that's going to stick with them? I worry about that.

"I really like seeing this [colt starting clinic], because I would like to avoid having any of those wrecks, negativity...any of that stuff

ever built in there in the first place. So, a lot of what I'm trying
to soak up here is how do you avoid that? It comes back to that
thought, which I'm trying to pay attention to as with Ty working
on Houston. There's sort of a sticky spot. That horse is kind of at
a place where that little one went over backwards on me. Yeah, he
led fine, he went along, but then all of a sudden something happens
and he doesn't now. And you're kind of stuck, and you're holding in
there—and just seeing this unfold in these different horses is really
good for me, but I keep reflecting on those little ones that I had
where I made mistakes."

"So, we're setting things up to direct them," Harry responded.
"To send them off a little and bring them back in ways that would get
them where in their movement, if they get ahold of a thought, then
they can let go of it and make it back without those kind of things
taking place."

"And," I added, "I would have been lulled into thinking,
'Oh, they found comfort in me. This is so great, being able to love
on them.' But when it got down to it, it wasn't there. They were not
accustomed to letting go of their thought at all."

"We're lulled into complacency," Harry explained, "by
their cooperation that might just come from their lack of desire
to be doing anything else. And you see horses that are kept in an
environment where there's very little stimulation—not much to do.
And when the owner shows up they get real interested. They lead
them over here five feet and put them in a round pen. The horse
follows them around. There's something to think about, something
to do, and they really think they've got something working. Well,
they don't ever get it better until something comes along that's really
a strong draw mentally for that horse, and then the horse is gone and
there's no way to get him back because that's not been built in there.
The horse was just there out of lack of any other interest—you were
the most interesting thing in the environment. But something more
interesting comes along, too bad about you!

"So when those horses yesterday, a couple of them got to looking off somewhere, and I'd make a little move, and then I'd make a *big* move—kind of startle them, see. But that's thinking about not getting them in a spot where they're hanging onto a thought so tight that they end up doing something like you're talking about. And that's easy to get them in that spot. A horse like Bailey yesterday, as hard as she was arguing with that halter and stuff—one like her—if she had a strong thought and was going to go and you got in the way too strong with that, she'd go over backwards. You can see that possibility. I've seen too much of those kind of things. Those babies, boy, a lot of people end up tipping them over when it could all have been avoided."

Ty leaned back in his chair and looked at Harry.

"Back, kind of what Tom was talking about," Ty said, "Bailey the other day, had what I would call maybe some quivering, scary

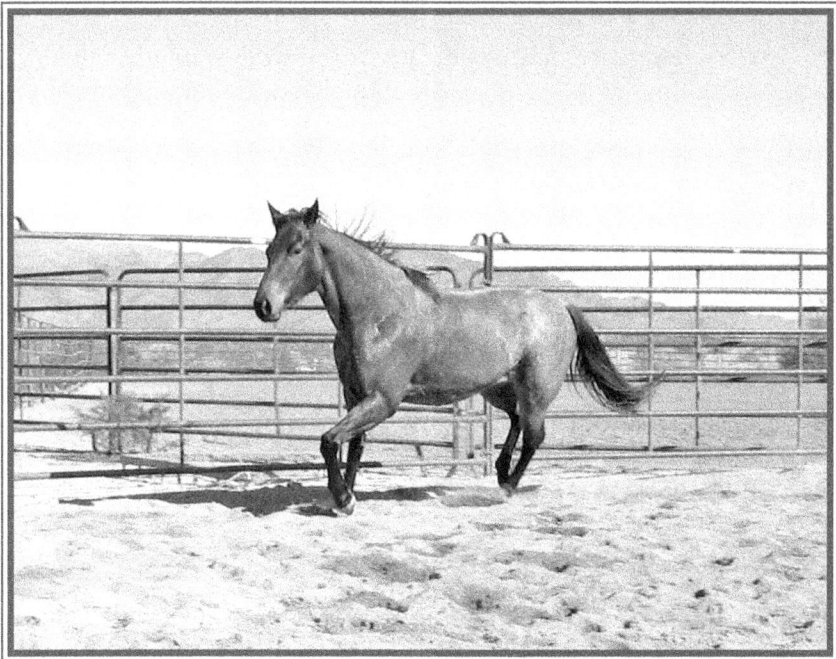

Bailey on the previous day having a moment where she was less settled.

type moments where you did get a little stronger and interrupted that thought. And you could just see that bundle of fear, the quivering and, 'Oh my goodness, what's going to happen?' How valuable is that? Because, I would consider they were pretty small areas where the horse was able to experience that, 'Oh my goodness, am I going to die?' moment, but in a very small way. How does that lead up to the moments that Tom was talking about—you know, those bigger moments where on a small scale where they're able to come through and deal with it, I guess? To figure out that it is possible that it can be worked through?"

"Is it small for them?" Kathy added.

"It may not be small to them," Harry answered. "And so, you just keep presenting—taking advantage of—every opportunity to get them to let go of a thought. And then, when the big thing happens, they're already in the habit, but if they're in the habit of hanging onto a little bit—a little bit in a few spots—when the big thing happens they're apt to do something pretty big."

"So yesterday," Anna said, "when you were asking her [Bailey] to move out around you, there were times where she would keep her shoulder on you, push into you a little bit on her way out—not physically—but today, that was looking nice. Now, you did attend to some of those, but, am I right you didn't attend to all of them?"

"I didn't make it a big deal, did I?" Harry replied. "I didn't really, really, work on it. We worked on it, but not enough you'd have thought there'd have been a difference today. But see, that was just symptoms. When the disease leaves town, the symptoms go."

"In her eyes," Anna continued, "was she using her shoulder in that way to protect herself?"

"Sure!" Harry replied.

"To keep track of you by leaning in on you?" Anna added.

"I talked about it yesterday, horses using their shoulders to push something out of the way that's in the way of a thought they're unwilling to let go of. So, she's already prepared, see? If she went, that shoulder is in there, she's looking out there a little, and especially on her right side. That's the side that she kicked out there that one time. That right side—I felt it today when I was on Big Easy. She brought that hip in there just a little and said, 'I wouldn't do that!' She let us know that we didn't need to be crowding in there or she might have to [kick], see? Well, that's a little protectiveness, a little defensive—whatever terms you want to put on it—but she was prepared there if she needed to. And so, that's stronger in that mare by far than it is in any of the others.

"If you were really interested in getting into a war, she'd be the one to pick," Harry added. "You could get in a war there pretty fast. ... [But] when they're that strong minded, when they get what *we* want that strong in their mind, boy, they won't quit you. That's one of the assets. I've said, their greatest asset is always their greatest detriment. She's got it pretty strong.

"I think Resa said she's second or third in the pecking order. But you see, that puts her on the defense a lot, when she's not up there. And so, 'I'm going to protect myself—I might have to get out of here, but I'm going to protect myself in the process,' see? Where a more confident horse would just stand there and say, 'No.' And they wouldn't be so quick to protect themselves."

Chapter Ten

Day Two, Flagging Tinker
11 February 2014

"When a horse knows how to respond to something, there's no need [for the horse] to worry about it."
Harry Whitney

After Ty wrapped up with Houston in the arena, Harry and Tinker entered the temporary square pen that was set up inside the arena. Harry began introducing the flag to the young mare.

"Ellen [Bartlett] made a comment that this mare didn't get very focused here yesterday," Harry said as he began working with Tinker. "I totally agree with that comment. So, I thought we would use the flag and see if we could get her mind here a little stronger with us, and at the same time, get her where the flag is not a big deal."

Harry stood facing Tinker. He offered a feel on the lead rope for the mare to step towards him. She was struggling to sort this out, so Harry began flagging to help break her mind loose from being stuck on other things and to focus and act on his request. The simple scenario that unfolded here is one I've witnessed many times with Harry and a horse, one I find particularly counterintuitive—that is, flagging in front of a horse when asking her to step forward towards you and the flag.

The beauty of its counterintuity is that it shows precisely how Harry works to communicate with the horse's mind rather than to drive the body. If Harry were driving the horse's body, then flagging in front of the horse would cause her to back up. Instead, as in this

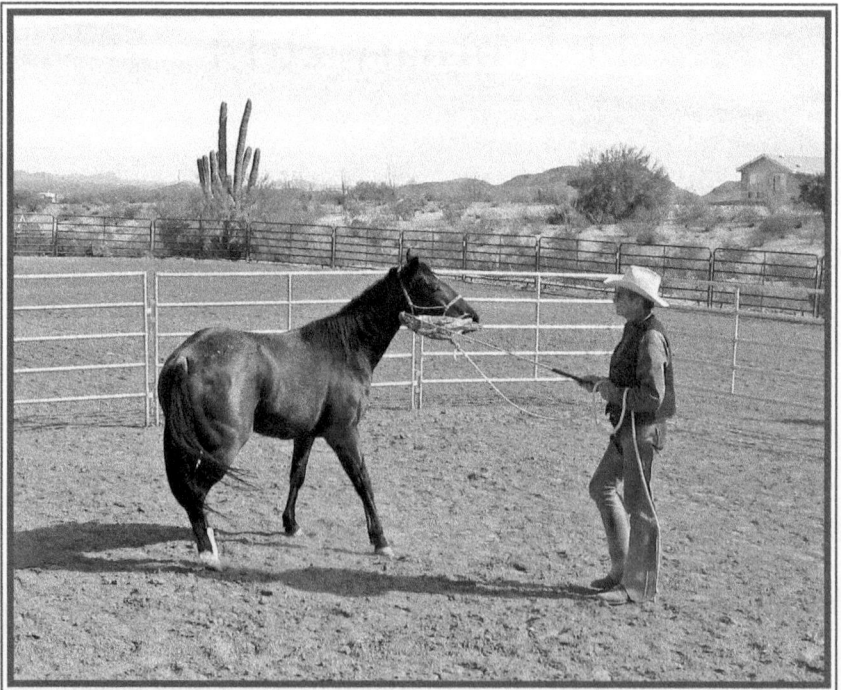

Harry introduces the flag to Tinker.

instance, flagging in front of the horse helped her to step forwards towards the busy flag which only can happen if the flag is used to instigate the horse to make a mental change to achieve a movement rather than to mechanically bring about a movement in the horse's body only.

"I'm just waiting here," Harry pointed out. "Pretty soon she's going to go more forward, no different than working off my horse. I'm just pushing on her here ['pushing' meaning flagging from a distance for a mental nudge, not literally pushing on her physically in any way] a little asking her to see if she could try going."

Tinker's thought broke loose and she stepped forward. Harry repeated that a few times and it improved with each one. Then he changed his presentation a bit to ask the mare to move forward out and around him as if to begin circling him.

"She's trying to keep track of that flag," Harry explained, "so it's hard for her to think about going forward."

As soon as he said that, she broke forward and took a couple of steps in the direction of the feel he was presenting.

"That's what I wanted right there," he said. "We'll just come over here and change sides; see if she could move off the other way a little."

While this was going on, Harry was not touching the horse with the flag. Sometimes I've seen Harry touch a horse pretty quickly with the flag, especially when introducing it to a fearful horse for the first time. With Tinker, however, he took an opposite approach and kept asking for changes with the flag near the horse but not touching her.

"I probably could have touched her there that trip," he said amongst the stepping forward and circling that began to shape up to some extent. "But, I'm going to see if she doesn't get a little more ready for me to touch her here soon. I'm using the flag to help her get more directable, and at the same time, get her more confident with the flag. And yet, we can direct her with it, too."

The scenario repeated.

"I could have touched her in there," Harry remarked, and continued. "I could have touched her right there—but she's tight. She stops, but she's tight. She's not stopping there with confidence. I'm just going to ask her to move...like that. [She did.] Good. Now, if she can let me touch her like that, see [Harry petted her lightly with the flag]—and she's a little unsure about that. She likes it back a little further; the more it came towards her front end the more it bothered her. We'll just ask her to go; she'll get a lot more confident here about going."

So much of what Harry explained to us when working with Tinker that day was not about *what* the mare did, but about *how* the mare did the things that she did. A big one, which manifested in a very tiny way, was how she looked away from the flag when Harry presented it along side her nose to ask that she tip her thought in the opposite direction and look out and away from the flag.

"That was about her just stopping there and looking away, see?" Harry began explaining. "She was looking away from the flag pretending like it didn't exist. So, I just whacked the ground hard enough that she couldn't ignore it. She just wanted to go away and pretend like it didn't exist. Awhile ago, I made a big issue of that because I didn't want that to come in there. They'll get real good at that, just mentally going away, and then they really don't take anything from the experience. And you might be petting them with the flag, you might be doing things with it thinking that you're really getting something done, but mentally they're not present. Tomorrow, it would look like you never touched her with the flag because she wasn't even experiencing it mentally even though physically she was standing there taking it.

"You can use that flag to start directing right from the beginning and they can get responsive with it. Or, if you think you need to, you can start with the flag by coming in here [he approached Tinker's nose with the flag's streamers held together in his hand], let them see it, let them smell it, and do these kinds of things—slowly let a streamer or two go. Pretty soon, you're petting them. But, I wanted to approach that just a little different so you guys could see that she could get this where we're getting her directable; we're getting her feeling of that, with movement. It's amazing—amazing!—what horses will take standing still that they can't handle with their feet moving."

When Harry said this, I immediately thought of the traditional "sacking out" process colts so often are submitted to. This typically involves snubbing them to a post or fence and making them stand still while spooky things like "sacks" (plastic bags, feed sacks, rain slickers, etc.) are rubbed all over them.

Often the result is that horses in this circumstance mentally shut down—disappear elsewhere in their minds—to be able to tolerate the overwhelming fright of it. That's the kind of thing Harry was talking about above when he said he was being careful with

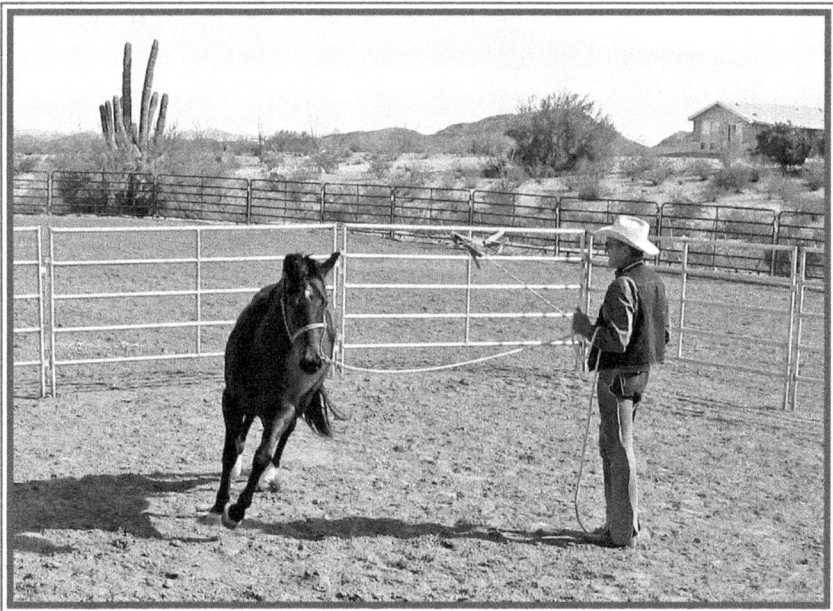

Harry continues working Tinker with the flag during this session.

Tinker that she not be "looking away from the flag pretending like it didn't exist."

A beauty of the approach Harry demonstrated was that it actively avoided such shut down spots from coming into a young horse like Tinker who could be an easy candidate for them by nature. Harry was on the lookout for moments when the mare withdrew inside herself mentally rather than stayed present and engaged in the conversation between them.

The spot Harry pointed out with the flag is one where it could be very easy for the person to accidentally build in some unwanted "training" in a colt. If the flag is used to ask a colt to take her thought in the opposite direction from it, he might actually look away but without really thinking out in that direction. What an easy thing to miss.

"All I wanted her to do was look over here, but she had that little brace in her," Harry continued. "I'd like to be able to reach out there, run that flag right up her face, and then come down her neck, down her back, and her be okay in there. That breeze made it just a little more difficult for her. But these are things that are going to happen in life. So, you go with that and you don't say, 'Well, the wind's blowing today, I can't flag her.' You can make use of those things and it can work out real good.

"I see people do these things and as soon as the horse goes they take the flag away," Harry warned. "Then they bring the flag in and they make the horse go—then they take the flag away. Pretty soon, whenever the horse sees that flag, she's wanting to get away from it. I don't want her to get away from it; I want her to respond to it so she could go forward. [Harry offered for her to go forward with the flag while we watched and she obliged].

"We're getting quite a few things done here at one time. Maybe not done, but we're sure enough working on quite a few things. It isn't long and they can keep walking right into that flag, drop their heads, and walk on. It's no big deal.

"If I come in there just a little firmer, see, she doesn't need to get upset—just step away from it. But, she's leaning on the right shoulder pretty hard there, pretty soon she'll get off of that. She's finding it a whole lot sooner. She'll get real confident. When a horse knows how to respond to something, there's no need [for the horse] to worry about it."

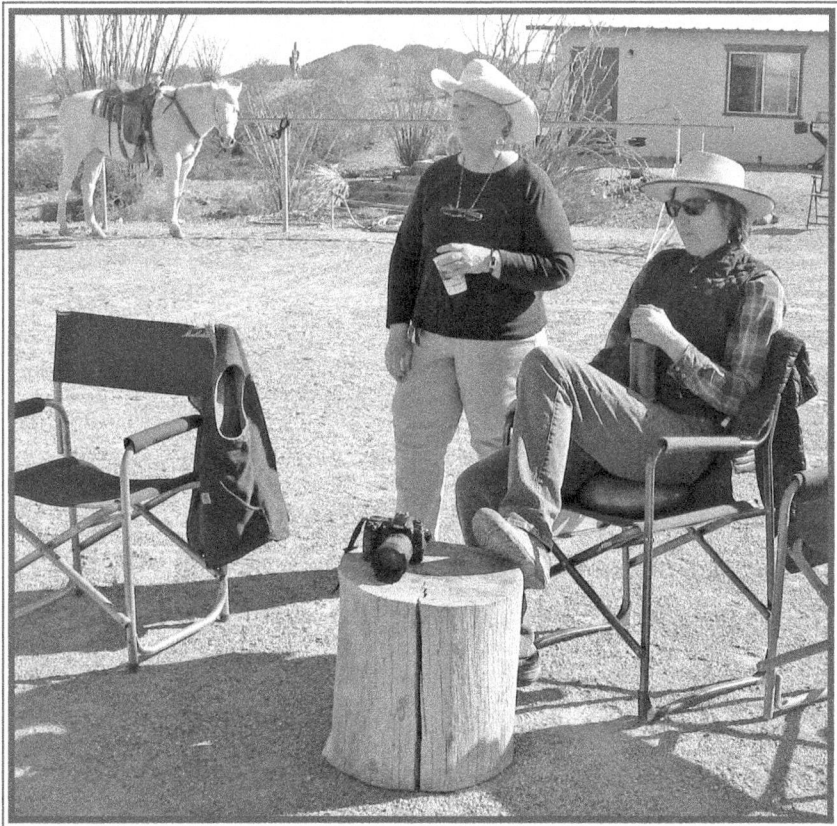

Auditors Claudia Clark and Libby Lyman watch the round pen activities as Big Easy takes a break in the background during day two.

Chapter Eleven

Day Two
(and Breakfast Discussion Day Three),
Working Towards Tying Smoke
11 February 2014

"Horses think like horses and people think like people and it's our responsibility to shift our thinking to try to view it the way they see it."
Harry Whitney

Having a horse that ties safely and comfortably is certainly convenient. True okay-ness at being tied means that the horse has been prepared to accept such confinement with relaxation and thoughtfulness. I had seen Harry work on this before with older horses who had trouble with being tied, but I had not witnessed Harry proceed with a youngster to make being tied an okay experience with the hope that it would remain so for life. I was delighted when Harry began working towards getting Smoke prepared to be tied on day two. For the record, I discovered Harry's approach to the youngster was the same as it had been for the older horses I'd seen him work with on this.

It was nearly 5:30 p.m. when Harry stepped aboard Big Easy and rode into the round pen to begin the last session of day two. Ty led Smoke into the pen and turned her loose. At first, Harry moved her around at liberty with the flag from Big Easy. Then, he put the

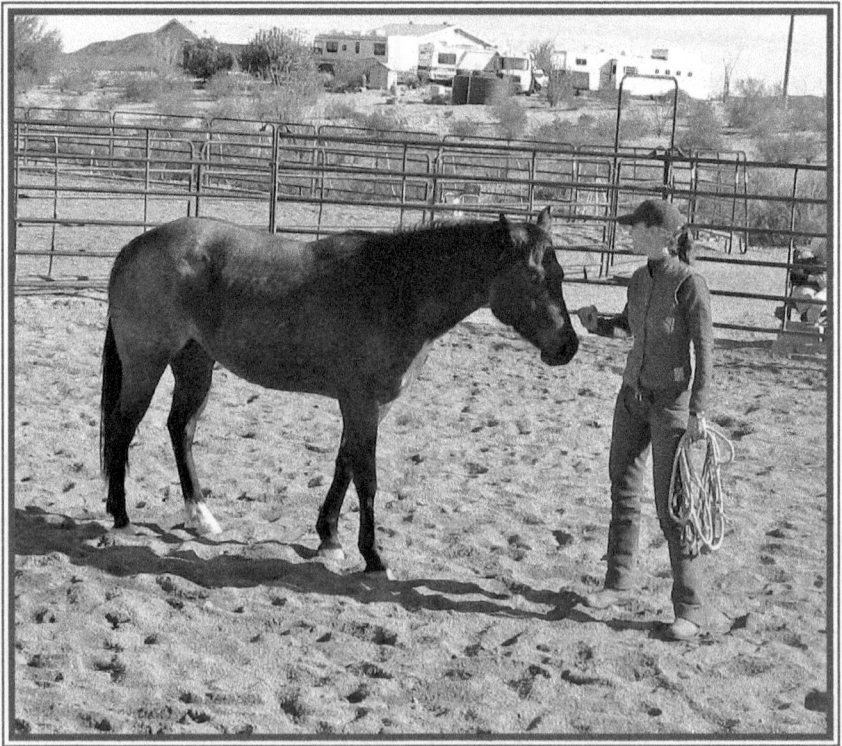

Mid-afternoon on day two before this session with Smoke, Anna worked with Sky in the round pen.

halter and lead rope back on her and ponied her, backed her up, and worked on the rigmarole.

Smoke's attention would switch from him to other things at times. She would get stuck sometimes when asked to move, or have her gaze elsewhere, for example, but Harry worked on getting her focus back with patient persistence and it always came back to him. She began to free up in her feet and travel along with Harry and Big Easy and focus her eyes on what was happening between them at the moment. She settled increasingly as they went along.

Harry dismounted and set things up to work on getting Smoke acclimated to being tied. He got a long rope—about 50 feet long—and passed one end of it from inside the round pen to the outside between the bars in a panel about chest high. Then he ran the rope along the outside of the pen (clockwise) the length of a panel and threaded it back into the pen.

Ty brings Chic into the round pen earlier in the afternoon.

Smoke still had a rope halter on with a lead rope attached to it. Harry coiled the lead rope around her neck so it would be tidy and out of the way and attached one end of the lariat to the halter. Once set up, Smoke was attached to the long rope facing the panel where that end of it came into the round pen. Harry then positioned himself where the other end entered the pen, the length of a panel (about 12 feet) to her left, near the gate. This arrangement allowed Harry to have quite a bit freedom to move around the mare while maintaining a hand on the rope attached to her. It also allowed him to run slack and reel it back in should the mare pull back.

The thing about tying horses, Harry explained, is that it can make them feel confined. This can cause them to experience a range of reactions from uneasy to full blown panic. The stronger reactions tend to be their pulling straight backwards with tremendous force.

Stories about tied horses pulling back so hard that they injure themselves or break lead ropes and escape abound. I've witnessed someone trying to teach a horse to tie by just tying them hard and

Harry spent some time ponying Smoke before working on tying her.

fast to an eye bolt in a barn aisle to "figure it out for herself." That fiasco resulted in the horse pulling back so hard that she sat down on her hind end, then fell and rolled over with her head held by the rope off the ground. The guy couldn't get the rope untied with the pressure of her head still pulling against it, and he had to cut the rope with a knife. I was amazed she came through without an apparent injury. More amazing still was watching the man fetch another rope and proceeded to do the same thing again, ignoring my advice that perhaps he try a different approach. I left the barn to work outside where I didn't have to see whatever came next. Not a brilliant method as far as I'm concerned. So, I was very keen to take in all that Harry had to offer on getting a young one okay with being tied without creating trauma.

The key to horses being okay to tie is to develop in them an understanding that they have room to move within the tight quarters where they find themselves tethered, Harry explained. The scenario with the rope he set up with Smoke in the round pen was a way for one person to work on having a horse tied while helping the horse to understand that she can move and need not panic. There was ample rope for Harry to keep the tail of it with him while he moved around at a safe distance from the mare. There also was plenty of extra rope he could feed out if Smoke retreated some distance from the panel as he worked with her.

Harry started off up against the fence panels to Smoke's left where his end of the lariat threaded back into the pen. He moved away from her and away from the panels a couple of steps. Smoke had about three feet of slack in the rope which drooped between her and the panel. She took notice of Harry's movement. He kept a hold on the rope, but his end also had a nice sway of slack in it at this stage.

Harry moved the flag a little. Smoke's head shot up, and she backed until the slack came out of the rope and she felt the firmness. It was not a panic or violent pull on the rope; rather, Harry was

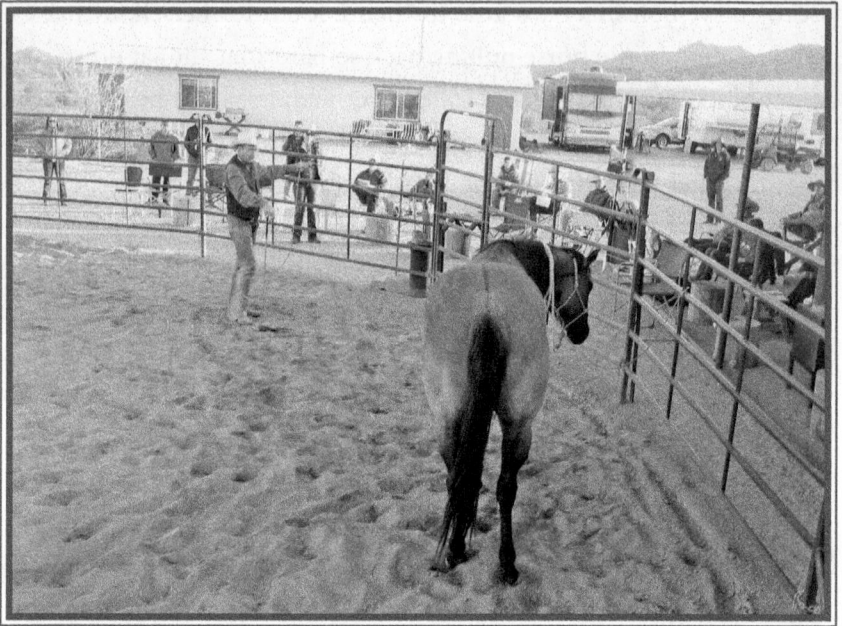

Harry prepares to work on tying Smoke by running the lariat attached to her halter through the panels to his hand at a distance from her.

dialing in his ask for her to try moving her feet with just enough energy to get a search and a change. He persisted with enough energy in the flag until the mare stepped sideways away from him. This changed her position from where it started at a perpendicular angle to the panel to where her hind end was further away from him. Her head was in roughly the same spot where the rope came through, but she succeeded in stepping her hind end over so she was at about a 45 degree angle now to the fence. Harry stood still leaning on his flag for a minute allowing a release from the flagging. He gave the mare plenty of time for the moment to sink in so she could begin learning that she could move laterally even with the rope holding her to the fence.

Next, Harry walked further towards the center of the pen keeping a hand on his end of the lariat. He walked slowly and began heading behind Smoke at a distance. The mare kept a keen eye on him, especially when he began crossing behind her. Once he was directly behind her—perhaps eight feet away from her—he stood still. He was at a balance point between her eyes. Then Harry slowly brought the flag up from the ground out towards his right while holding the lariat in his left. Smoke saw the flag out of her right eye which tipped the balance and she swiftly brought her hind end around to the left.

She was pretty concerned about Harry and the flag, so she turned so much that her left hind quarter was pressed up against the panel. She turned her head as much as the rope attached to her halter would allow so she could watch as Harry walked to his left towards her butt. Standing back a ways and still holding pressure on the lariat, Harry reached out with the flag towards Smoke's hind end.

She straightened her head bringing all of her body parallel to

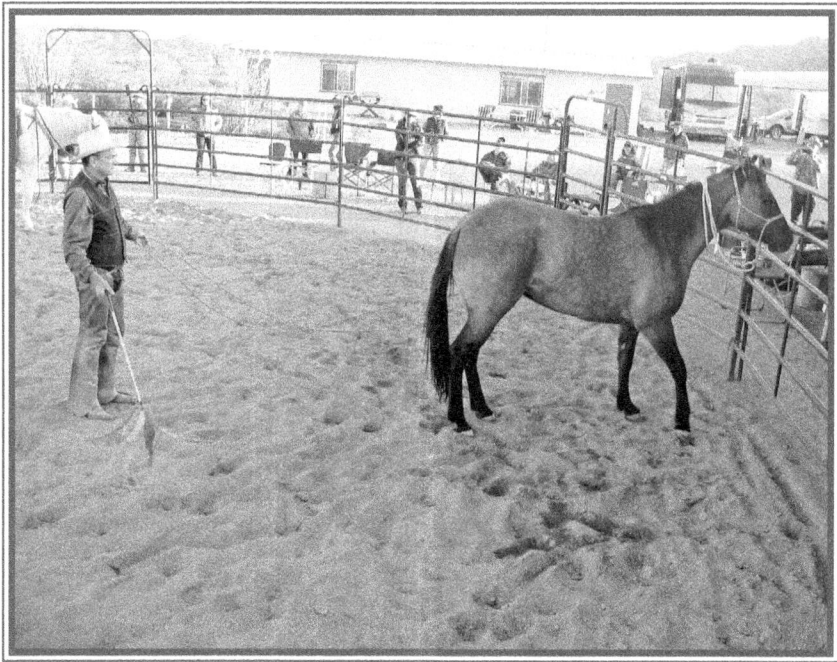

Harry moves slowly behind Smoke and eases into her other eye while keeping a feel on the lariat.

the fence panel along her left side. Harry kept a gentle but persistent flagging going. She seemed stuck there for a bit, not sure what to do with some fear and tension showing in her stance and eyes. Finally, she whipped her hind end around away from the panel and from Harry and switched eyes on him. The sudden movement prompted her to back hard and in a hurry looking intently at the flag which Harry had down on the ground at this point as she went. Harry allowed the lariat to run some slack out to her. She backed about 10 feet before she slowed and could regain her composure, still looking hard at the flag down low.

Harry gave her a few moments to regroup. He stood at ease not moving the flag, and she relaxed a bit. She began to let down, so he put a little feel on the rope and Smoke was able to walk calmly forward towards the panel and stand with her head low and without a high level of tension. Next, Harry backed out towards the middle

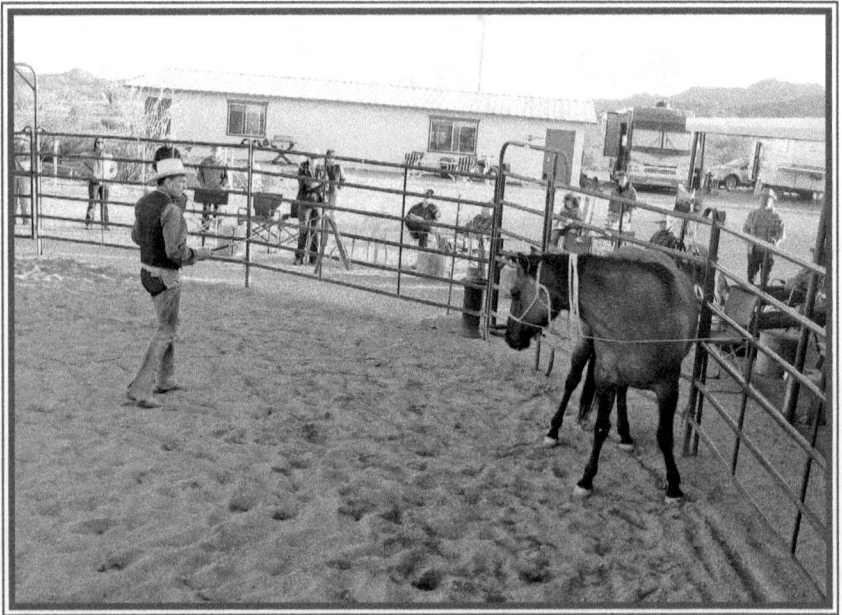

Smoke acts on her concern and attempts to turn around to face Harry and the flag.

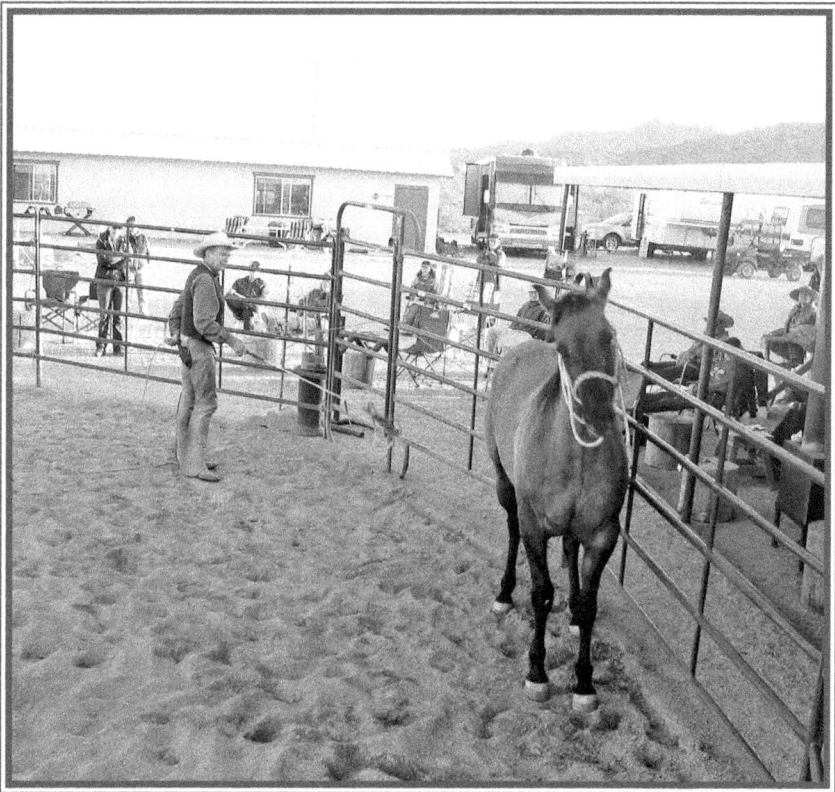

Smoke gets a little stuck and Harry keeps using the flag to get her to free up and move while he keeps a feel on the lariat.

of the pen again keeping his end of the lariat in his left hand and packing the flag in his right. He repeated the process of coming around behind the young mare, but this time she switched eyes and sides without needing to swing her bum so dramatically. She did not swing all the way up against the fence this time.

Soon, as Harry kept working on switching eyes, he was getting much more fluid changes as the mare moved from side to side. Increasingly, she was able to give up on pulling back very much and kept her head close to the panel when making the switches.

"She's coming through nice," Harry said. "There's frustration—can't blame her for that."

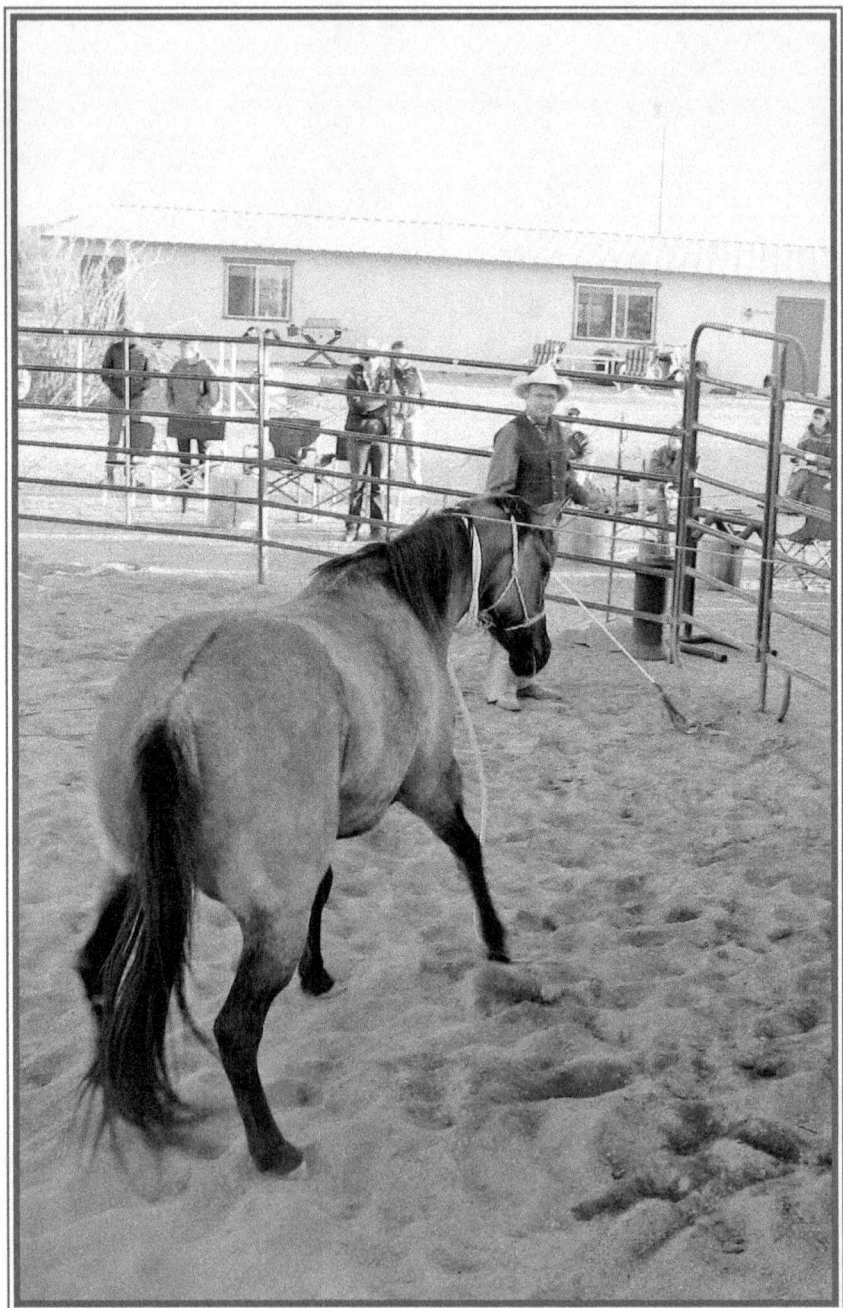

Smoke finally moves but with a worry about the rope which has gotten wrapped over her head.

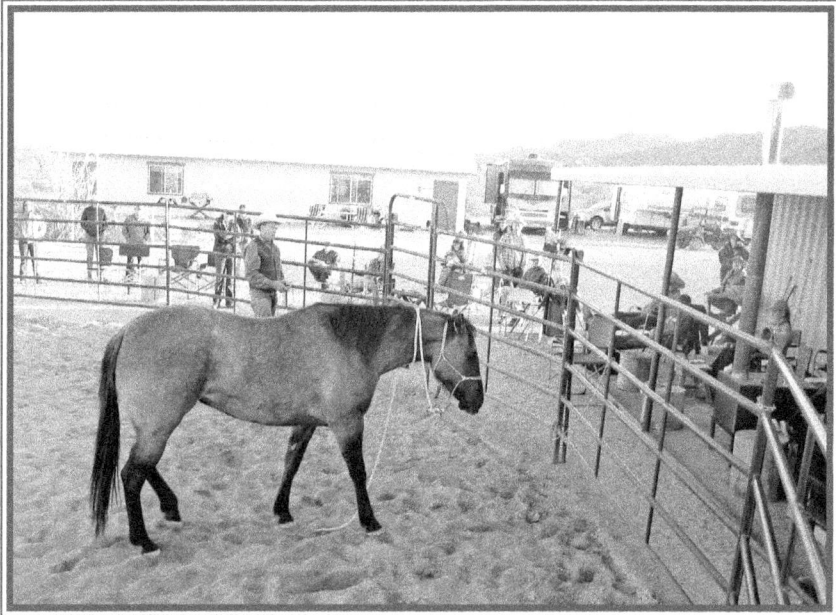

With Harry's excellent timing and feel, Smoke soon lets go of her worry about the flag and steps forward for a release with her head by the panels.

I noted in my clinic journal: *"In just a few times, she is getting it really well. (Switching her butt one side to the other and leaving slack in the lead rope.) In these tight quarters there is a place to move. Harry...holds the rope and moves flag. Encourages the horse to step over to the side rather than pull back. Moving feet vs. pulling back. Avoid wreck by running rope."*

When Smoke was getting really good at this and was quite relaxed with it, Harry ponied her for a few minutes in the round pen from Big Easy to end her session. As I sat perched atop a panel reflecting on the lesson, I was struck by how quickly Smoke came around to feeling better about changing eyes with Harry flagging her from behind. The demonstration clearly showed how getting the young horse mentally freed up to move her feet when "tied" made all the difference about how she felt being confined by the rope.

One thing I've heard over the years from folks like the guy

I saw tie the horse hard and fast is that you want the horse to never have any give from a rope or it'll ruin your chances of getting her to tie well. That, if you run the rope the way Harry did in this example that the horse will always pull back looking for that slack.

Quite the opposite was true in the scenario with Smoke, because the timing and feel of the lesson was set up so that she could have increasing confidence in the situation of being tied so that eventually she no longer would feel the need to pull back. She knew pretty quickly that she could back out a ways if she felt the need to, and with Harry's support, she quickly arrived at the point that she no longer needed to. It was much simpler for her to move a little sideways rather than to back a ways and make a huge sweeping gesture. I brought this up at breakfast the next morning....

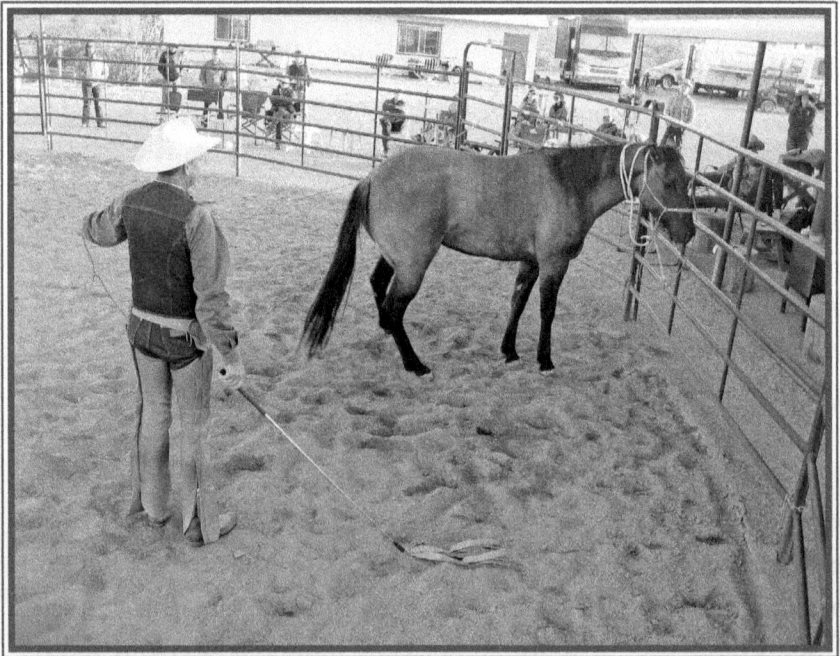

By the end of her first tying lesson, Smoke was able to stand relaxed and comfortable with Harry holding the flag walking completely around behind her and back even at close range.

From the Wednesday (Day Three) morning breakfast discussion:

"The very end when we were working with the tying deal," I said, "and you had the rope looped through the panels—at one point, that horse [Smoke] backed up 15 or 20 feet and you just brought her right back up to the panel. I know that I've heard in terms of tying, 'Oh no, if you tie them up you don't ever want them to have any stretch back because then they'll try the boundaries again, and again, and again.' It's not true. Clearly, you safely allowed the horse some rope, kind of kept the pressure on, and she just realized that didn't work out, [Speaking as if I were the horse,] 'But, if I go back up here and move my feet a little bit this way, then that works out better; that's okay.'

"You need to do it [run some line] for safety I think, but might that not be as good an idea for a horse like Bailey [who has a tendency to push and shove to find an answer] than another horse?"

"The thing I think of in there for safety sake," Harry answered, "you let it run, but when did it change with Smoke when she went backwards? It was when she let go of the thought and put a forward in it. And so, pretty soon she says, 'That just doesn't work.' And Bailey would figure out the same thing."

"With you, the flag was in operation too," I added. "And you were there to support that unfolding, so it wasn't like the rope was the only encounter that was dictating how she was going to feel about that situation. So, even though you were letting it run, you were keeping a little flag on her and that flag is not going to let up until she gets a forward thought; till she leaves that thought. I guess you have to think of that with all the components together, don't you?"

"Well, it's just like when she pulled towards Big Easy," Harry replied. "That was not solid—now someone mentioned last night I stood my ground a little, but she still gained a little towards him—it wasn't solid like tied off to a post. Yet, it didn't work out until she let go of that. They'll figure it out. Some of them take more time to figure that out than others because that could feel like they were gaining a little and they're convinced, 'Well, maybe it will work.' But pretty soon, they are sure it didn't work."

"It prevents total panic on their part," someone said from among the crowded tables.

"Yes, oh my," Harry agreed. "So, you've got to keep in mind the safety issue, and I say 'safety issue' because if you get too solid too quick they panic and then you've got a chance of something getting hurt."

"With Smoke," someone said, "I really like how her confidence grew when she realized how she's creating the pressure of either rambling into the fence by going one way or by setting off the flag by going another—when she realized it was [by] her own actions that pressure went away, how much confidence she gained. There was a real growing happening, a realization that I think she's going to take to other areas of her life. And, that was really neat to see that she figured it out, and that she figure it out early. She didn't even get so wound up before she started to move on her own."

"I've got to be careful how I say it," Harry prefaced, "because people will take it wrong, but the more times you can get a horse in a pretty tight spot and they can slow down and think about it and realize that there is a way out, then that applies to other areas and they get more confident in that. But the reason I say you've got to be careful is, I've been around some people that would set a horse up to get in a real problem—into a really bad spot—and they said that you've got to get them in some trouble there and find their way out of it.

"Well, I don't want to get them in the kind of trouble I've seen those people do, because they get them in some real trouble. Sometimes there were scrapes and scratches and dings and so forth that were not necessary for the horse to get in enough of a spot there for them to start to get confident that there's a way to get out of this without a panic. So, it's not that we're trying to get them in that kind of a situation, but now and then that comes in there, but the more times it does and they figure a way out of it that they own because they found it, then they get more and more confident."

"What's an example of the extreme pressure that you talk about that you saw these other guys [do]?" asked Bob Grave, who had traveled from England to audit. "Would it be something like flooding them?"

"Well," Harry replied, "tying them solid and flagging them until they quit fighting it. That's a pretty extreme example, but that happens. And they say, 'Well, they've got to get in some trouble and figure their way out of it.' That could have been avoided."

"Tying the hobbles on them and turning them loose?" I chimed in. "I see that all the time."

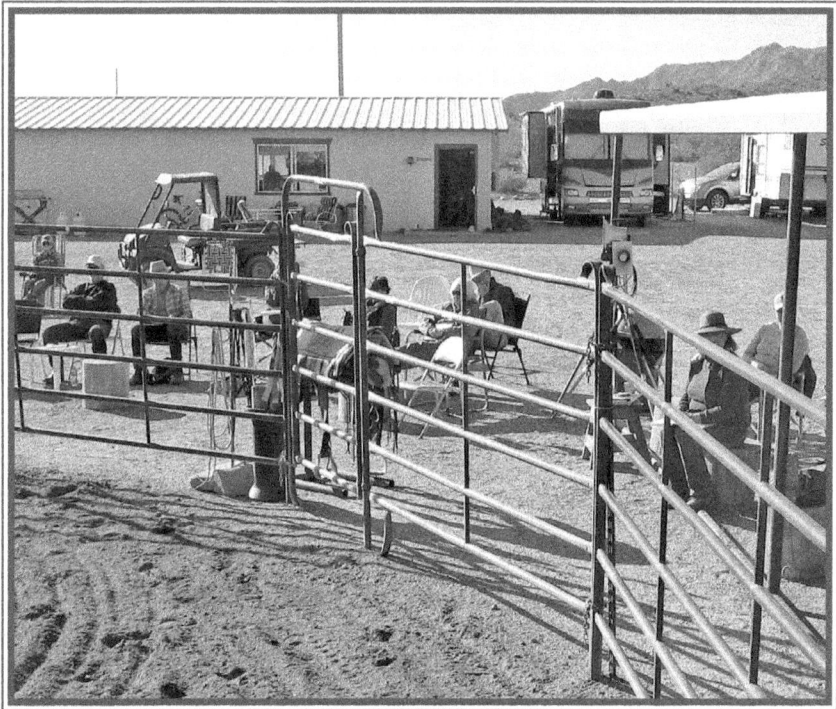

A view of the crowd at the round pen with the bunkhouse in the background taken from my perch atop a panel.

"If you're not real careful they know for sure you did it to them," Harry said. "And that's what I think about these other guys I was talking about. They would do something to the horse to get him in a little trouble that he had to find his way out of instead of allowing the set-up so the horse knew that they got her in that.

"Horses think like horses and people think like people and it's our responsibility to shift our thinking to try to view it the way they see it. I've said for years that the day the doorbell rings and I open the door and one of my horses is standing there saying, 'Let's go for a ride,' then I will expect him to make some adjustments in his understanding so it works out good for me. Because, it wasn't my idea he needs to help it work out good for me. But in the mean time, it's my responsibility to make the adjustments in my way of viewing it so that it works out good for him."

Chapter Twelve

Firmness and Clarity

Day Two, After Supper Discussion

11 February 2014

"Why do we firm up?"

Harry Whitney

      Referring to Tinker's session when Harry worked her in the square pen inside the arena earlier that day, Kathy Baker began the after supper discussion with the comment: "So, I noticed that you firmed up a couple of times with her, and right after you did, the change came through that needed to. There was always a big release."

Someone in the room couldn't hear Kathy's comment, so Harry paraphrased it for the group, "She said that each time that I firmed up with her [Tinker] pretty strong, then she made a change and there was a big release."

"So the firmness brought clarity?" Kathy asked.

"Absolutely," Harry replied.

"And that felt good to the horse?" Kathy concluded.

"You watch horses out in a herd," Harry said. "And, if it's not clear, it can get pretty firm. But, it's clear. So, the firmness doesn't have to be fearfully troubling to a horse. It can bring clarity so quick it's amazing."

Harry approaches a wary Tinker in the square pen on day two.

"On that same line," Linda Davenport, an auditor from Idaho, said, "that clarity, as long as they're searching, when's the time then you increase the request? Even though they're searching for an answer, trying something, sometimes you'll still increase?"

"Why do we firm up?" Harry posed.

"When their thought is elsewhere," Linda responded. "But, if they're trying different things—they're searching for the right answer—I noticed that today in some instances you would increase what you were asking and you'd get clarity."

"I'm going to say it again: what do you firm up for?," Harry replied.

"To block a thought," came the reply from a couple of folks and Harry in unison.

"I won't firm up near as quick as with a horse that knows," Harry said. "He's got experience; he knows. But, when a youngster like that keeps working at the same thought, sometimes you've just got to clear it up. 'Here's the boundary.' Now, within that, you can find something good, but here's the boundary. To me, that's just like the electric fence—boom! Clarity."

Harry uses the example of an electric fence sometimes to explain how consistency in one's firmness keeps it from being troubling to a horse. A horse can stand within inches of an electric fence and be perfectly at ease, leg cocked, taking a nap, he points out. He knows if he touches that fence it will light him up something fierce, but that doesn't bother him even standing right beside it because in his experience the fence is tethered to its posts. That fence never jumps over and grabs him, or chases him a distance to shock him. Therefore, the absolute consistency of the electric fence, even painful as it is if touched, doesn't cause a panic in his environment because it is always in the same predictable place.

"It's not that you're trying to make something impossible," Harry continued, "but they don't need to be going to that thought, and you've got to get firm enough that they say, 'Okay.' But, as with

Tinker, she had that little defensive feel come in there real quick. Well, no...I'm just not going to let that take place. When the clarity came that it wasn't going to work, big change, see?"

"I can't remember the specific horse," Linda said, "but it looked like she was really trying. She was a little nervous and trying a whole lot of different things, and you got right on it and it just like snapped her out of it, but she was still searching like, 'What can I do?' I was curious about that at the time."

"Again, if they're stuck on that thought of just how to get away," Harry replied, "They're not trying something to do here. They're just stuck on trying to flee the scene—'let go of that thought.' Sometimes you've got to get pretty firm. But sometimes, they keep trying, trying, trying the same things, same things, same things. Well, [we have to make] judgment calls. Ain't it fun!"

"That's not any different than when that horse, Smoke, was going around in a circle in the round pen with you trying to go towards Big Easy?" Ty asked.

"When she stopped when I was afoot?" Harry asked.

"Yes," Ty replied. "You were afoot and Smoke came around closer towards him and you got pretty firm there. That's the same thing you're talking about there, right?"

"Yeah," Harry said, "Because she was pretty hung up on that. So, to get her to try something besides that, it was going to take something pretty firm for her to try something different. That was such a high priority to be over there with him you could just feel her slap on the brakes and pull."

"At first didn't you just try to speed her up a little bit?" Ty Asked.

"Well, it came out stronger when I tried to speed her up," Harry said. "I didn't want her to speed up that high, I just wanted her to speed up a little. And when I was working on just getting her to make an up transition then she said, 'No, I'm outta here.' And, [Big] Easy was right there as a draw."

"It was kind of interesting, too," Ellen Bartlett said, "how you let go of the speeding her up—that was the original request—but you let that one totally go by the wayside while you took care of this other."

"Immaterial," Harry said.

"You really never got back to it," someone said, "but I have confidence that tomorrow she'll be trotting right off!"

The room filled with laughter at that last remark.

"Those are judgment calls," Harry added. "What's more important? There was no way she was going to trot a nice circle if she couldn't walk a nice circle. And, when she decided she'd had enough and wanted to go over there with [Big] Easy, then that had to get cleared up before we could do more. To me it was pretty clear cut

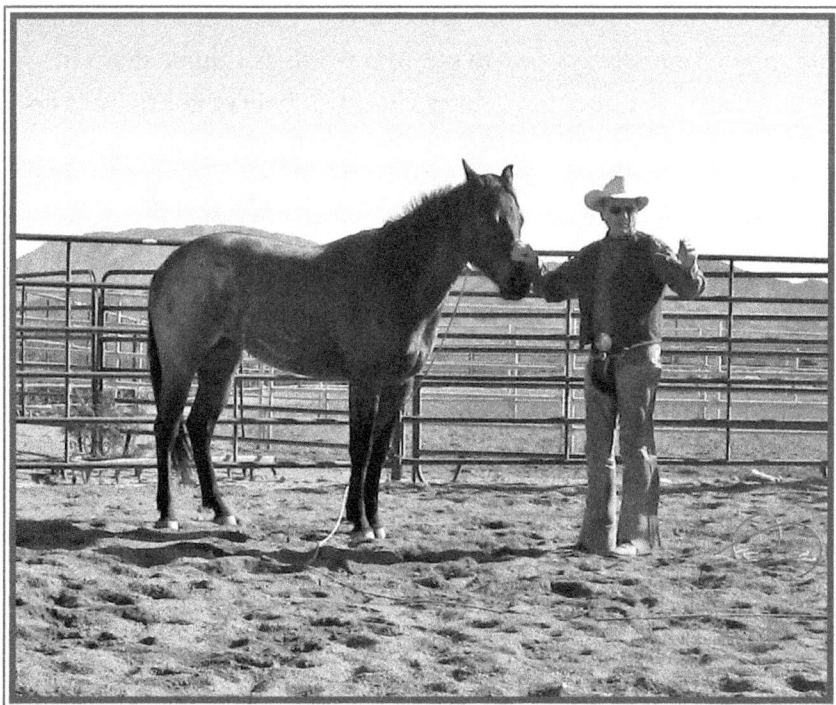

Harry answers a question while working Smoke in the round pen on day two.

what had to be worked on at that moment whether we got back to the other or not; she doesn't know."

An afterward about Smoke from Day Three, After Breakfast Discussion:

"She also asked how the horse thinks it's her idea and not you making it [happen]," Ellen said, referring to an earlier question in the morning's discussion. "So, let's hear about that."

"Somebody mentioned yesterday that I stood my ground when Smoke was pulling towards Big Easy," Harry replied. "If I set that up right, as she heads for [Big] Easy...well, the only reason that rope got tight is because Smoke was pulling away. She knows she created that herself. And yet, how it got created was because I stood my ground—is how that pressure got created. But she initiated that. She caused that. To make sure that that is in there within the things that we do is not always easy to put into words as I think about it. To not answer her question [Harry chuckled], you've got to set it up

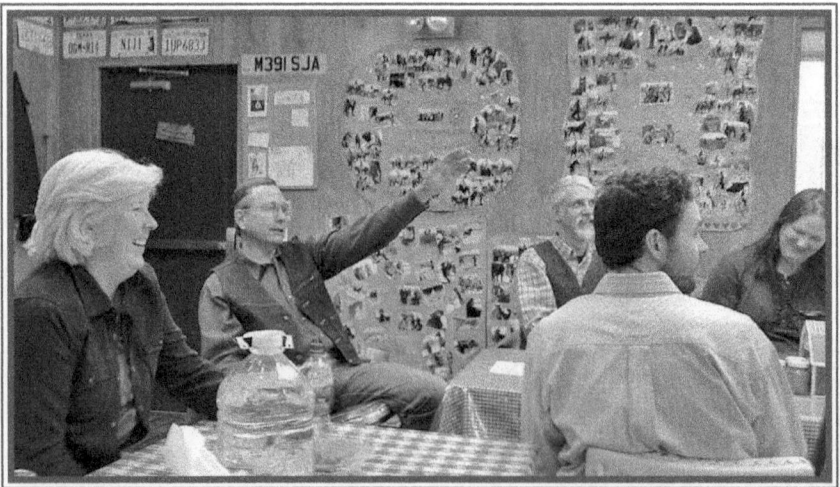

Harry, at the head of two long runs of tables in the bunkhouse, answers a question in his own particular idiom as Kathy Baker, Tom Moates, Ty Haas and Connie Crawford enjoy a chuckle. (Photo: Nancy Lawson.)

so they believe that they caused it. And yet, they know when you do something to them. They know it was done to them. And so, to try to time things so they're action causes this thing to be. That's where the timing of what we present is so important.

"When a horse is a little stuck, like that mare was stuck wanting to get to Big Easy and I slapped my chaps real hard with the rope, I didn't step in and spin the tail of the rope to try and drive her over there. I was just whacking my chaps saying, 'That's not working!' So, I didn't do anything to her, but I kept her under enough pressure that she would figure out that she needed to change how she's thinking or this is not going to feel good."

"Even if you had bumped," Ellen followed up, "if she's sagging towards Big Easy and you had bumped on your line, that would have been doing it to her, right? I mean, she would have felt made to come off of that and let that go, more than just whacking your chaps and holding your ground."

"More so, absolutely," Harry responded.

"It's so hard to find those spots where you feel like you're setting it up that they're doing it to themselves instead of you doing it," Ellen said.

"That was a great example so I kept using it this morning," Harry said, "because she was doing it to herself. I mean, I was just there, had the rope in my hand, but as she came around and pulled out to him, that rope got tight, then I whacked my chaps—well, why did that happen? All she had to do was walk on by. She definitely came into her own pressure there by doing that.

"You can have the feeling you've done it to them, but if you know you're doing it to help the horse feel better emotionally and let go of that thought of how to protect themselves and relax with that, then it's not like doing it to them in a way that's to criticize them, to punish them, to prove something to them."

Chapter Thirteen

Morning Session, Day Three, Bailey

12 February 2014

"If you're critical of something you might want one day, the day you want it you might not be able to get it."

Harry Whitney

"I'm just wanting to see a spot here where she really arranges her mind to go backwards," Harry said. "See, she's just avoiding things there. It ended pretty good, but then here she comes forward. Well, she wasn't asked to come forward. She could wait there a moment."

Harry was atop Easy, and watching him work Bailey late morning on day three provided a great example of how quickly a horse's mind can switch between following what a person is presenting and going to thoughts of her own.

"When I ask, she should just back up," Harry said while offering with the lead rope that she back. "It shouldn't be a big deal and it shouldn't get all crooked. See, she was going to go but she wasn't going backwards because her mind hasn't gotten arranged to go backwards. If I ask her to back up, she should just back up."

Harry offered again from where he sat in the saddle.

"That was better," he said. "See, one step then she's trying to go sideways, forward, something.... Pretty soon she'll take a couple or three steps and she'll wait there and she won't be thinking about other things."

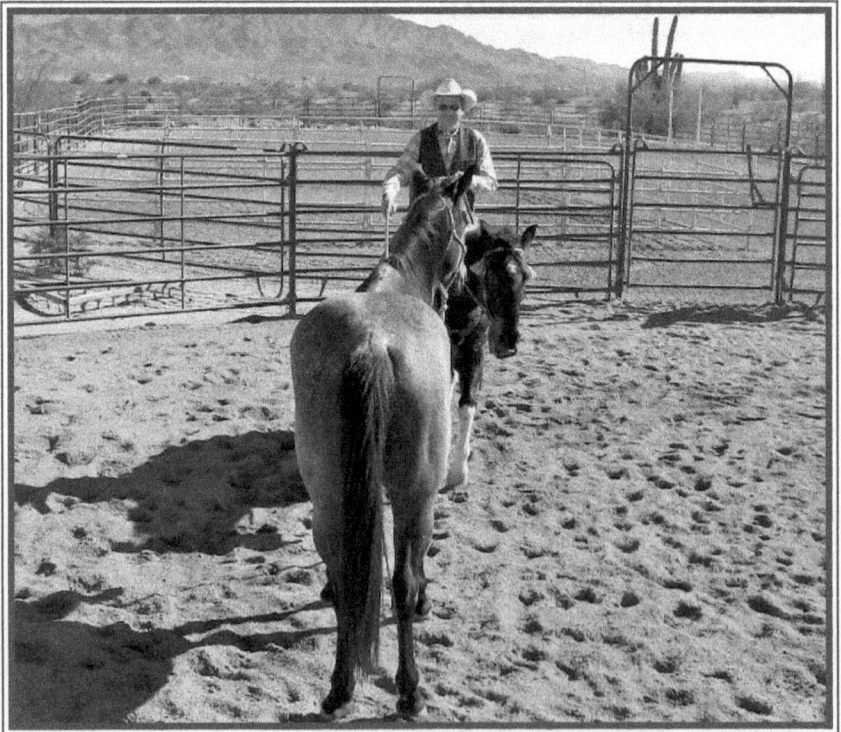

Harry begins to work with Bailey from atop Easy on day three.

Bailey managed to do just that, even if only for a few moments.

"That's better," he complimented her. "That was good! See her get ready [to move off], then she reconsidered—she was going to walk off, then she felt of what was taking place there between us. That's way better. She's got thoughts that don't need to be in there. She's backing up towards that stuff [a wash with bushes that dropped off just beyond the panels to one side of the round pen] behind her that's bothering her a little. Well, she could turn. She can swing her bum around the corner and back up [along the fence] but still be thinking about backwards."

The mare seemed suddenly to catch a breeze that blew her backwards.

"Those were pretty good steps right there," Harry said. "I'm not going to complain about that, especially with as tight as it's getting behind her there [to the fence]."

The beginning of Bailey's session exemplifies quintessential Harry Whitney. Harry wore a microphone (as usual) at his collar while working the horse. His words were broadcast to the audience over a portable PA speaker on a tripod nearby. The clinician provided a running commentary of what was happening between him and the mare. The audience of serious students collected there was captivated. We did our best to match up what Harry said to what we witnessed taking place in the round pen. That was, however, not always easy to do.

Always, more takes place between Harry and a horse than what we spectators can see or, I believe, what he can get spoken. It's not uncommon for his remarks to come after the unfolding action. Sometimes there simply is no way for him to speak about what is happening as it unfolds when each second includes myriad changes, exchanges of feel, and ranges of balance between the masterful horseman and the horses he works with.

Harry was working to get Bailey to back, but his focus, as

always, wasn't simply on getting the horse to take backwards steps. Rather, as he mentioned, getting the horse to think about going backwards was the objective. Harry was not settling for less than Bailey thinking about backing up and making a conscious effort to do so.

Once Harry got some nice changes with Bailey's reverse, he began working on ponying the mare along side of Easy and him.

"She went to go [leave Easy and go off on her own] and she found the end of the lead rope," Harry said, holding a dally on the saddle horn as he rode Easy in a circle with Bailey trailing along somewhat discombobulated on the end of the lead rope.

Watching Harry work one horse from another ranks as one of my favorite clinic experiences in general. The finesse with which

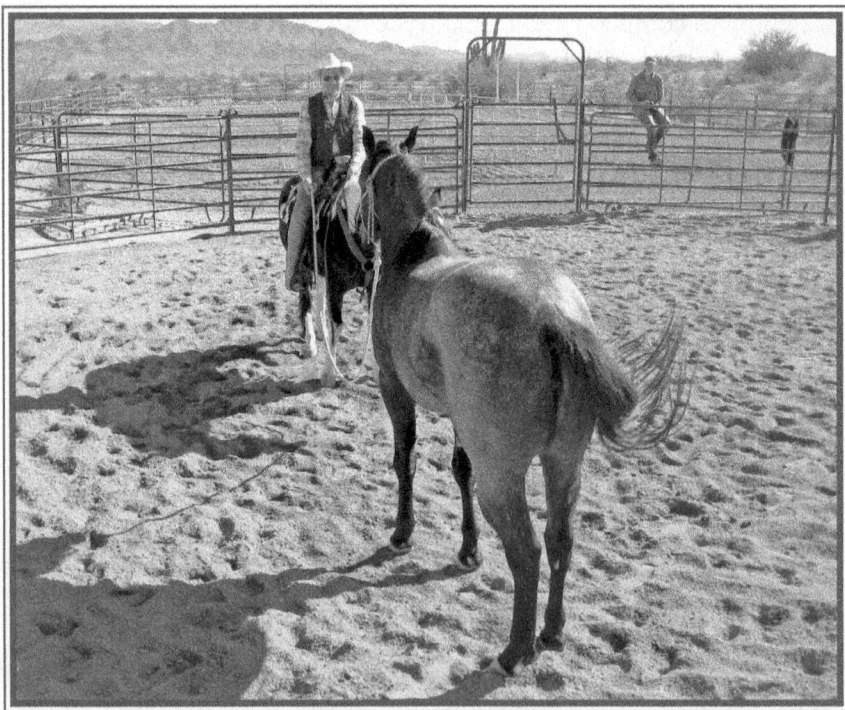

Harry got some nice changes in Bailey's backing and here he was able to back the mare with a slight request on the lead rope.

he handles the horse under him while working the other just amazes me. There are times where he will stop working with the horse on the line to tend to his saddle horse. Then he'll get back to working the other, present a place for her to be, and with great patience that horse eventually finds it and falls into the flow of the sweet spot that Harry offers. This was shaping up to be one of those sessions.

"It feels like she's starting to appreciate that little bit of slack she got there," Harry said as the mare began moving along beside Easy and Harry in a more thoughtful and willing way. "A little bit ago she didn't. Now she's struggling...and she'll find it again, see. They've got to go through that quite a few times sometimes before it really gets clear to them that *they're* the ones that created that slack. They're pretty sure that we should create that. She'll get that figured out here pretty soon. If she just comes on up here [along side of Easy], then there isn't all that pressure on her head. She's struggling there at the walk, isn't she? There! Now there was a change in her. Sometimes if you can get them to free up and make a bigger change—go clear to the trot—sometimes then the walk gets real good."

Harry made mention that the increased activity when asking the saddle horse to trot when ponying another horse can make the ponied horse think she's about to get kicked. This can cause her to drag a little harder at first and struggle more as she feels the need to avoid a kick she thinks is coming, but if you feed her a little slack in the line at that point then she may feel the freedom to break loose and come forward.

"Almost," Harry commented, working on this with Bailey. "She thought about it but she just couldn't quite come through. Her walk picked up, didn't it? Those feet came a lot quicker there and you say, 'Thank you!' That was a change of thought, see. There's some good slack in it. She's walking along there pretty good. Now we'll see what happens here if we hurry just a little bit."

Harry asked Easy to pick up the pace.

"She's not dragging near what she was earlier," Harry said, "but she's still not coming."

"Easy's trot is just a long walk for her," Linda Davenport said with a laugh.

"There!" the whole crowd said in unison with Harry when she broke free and had a real forward thought. The change in the mare was clearly visible; she broke loose and came forward with a soft, swiftness in contrast to the sucking-back drag she had been presenting before.

"Hey, Mr. Paint!" Harry exclaimed to Easy, shifting his focus to keep his saddle horse following along with the program. "He just had a thought and he was going!"

Harry rode Easy into a tight circle and got Bailey reversed so they were traveling head-to-tail on the circle. He then proceeded to work on the rigmarole—the move where Harry starts by circling

Harry ponies Bailey from Easy.

the saddle horse and the ponied horse head-to-tail and then offers
on the lead rope for the ponied horse to bring her head from the
other horse's tail forward past the rider's knee (the saddle horse just
keeps moving on the same circle) to a parallel position so she ends
up walking along side the saddle horse head-to-head inside the same
circle as defined by the saddle horse.

"The first day," Harry said about when they initially worked
on the rigmarole, "I had the feeling she might take a swipe with a
hind leg if things didn't go good. I don't feel that at all today. Much
better!"

After a few of those, Harry rode back out around the pen
ponying Bailey along.

"We'll see if she can hurry up a little more," he said. "She
ought to be able to out-walk Easy like he wasn't even trying to travel.
There's better. Very good. Pretty soon they can be trotting as soon
as your horse is trotting, and they'll walk as soon as your horse is
walking. It's amazing how accurate they can get in that area."

Earlier in the week I watched a situation unfold between
Harry and Bailey that proved to be one of the more memorable of
the two weeks of clinic for me. Harry roped the mare around the
neck and was working her afoot in the round pen. Bailey was rather
reactive and she ended up spinning around and got the lariat wrapped
completely around herself. Harry held the coils of remaining rope
and he let the slack run as she got wound up and moved about.

I sat atop a panel close to her facing Harry as the situation
unfolded. I braced for a huge wreck as Bailey began to panic feeling
the spooky rope on her hind legs, sides, front legs, and chest. I
distinctly remember thinking, "Something must be done!" If I were
Harry I think I'd be doing something to try and help her out and
prevent a wreck.'

Harry, on the other hoof, just remained perfectly relaxed,
holding the end of the lariat and following the troubled mare around
managing the slack in the rope as she increasingly freaked out.

I sat bolt upright and the other auditors stiffened their bodies, too, as it looked like Bailey was going to continue wrapping herself up in the rope. The mare seemed to be getting hopelessly tangled in a web and about to blow into a terrific terror-driven melt down.

Harry remained silent and just held the end of the lariat and kept calmly following along, watching things unfold.

To my amazement, Bailey suddenly hit a spot where she regained some composure. She began to think, and she began to sort out the predicament she was in. Then amazingly, she began to counter turn and get herself unwrapped. Before long, she had unwound herself entirely without a wreck. I was flabbergasted.

In retrospect, I realized that when I was thinking I'd be doing something if I were Harry, that he really had few options to intervene and none were good. Maybe he could have tossed the rope over her to help unwind it, but most likely any motion by him at that point— especially flinging the rope over top of an already distressed horse— only would have thrown gasoline on the fire. Harry knew that there was little, if anything, he could do to help at that point. Additionally, she was not quite to the point of harming herself, so rather than potentially push her over that edge by trying to help, he decided to see if she could sort it out for herself. He allowed her time to search rather than trying to make something happen, even as things looked quite perilous.

She did sort this mess out on her own, and by doing so she learned a very valuable lesson. The rope, even as bad a situation as it turned out to be for a little while, caused her no harm. In the future, if she got tangled in a rope the lesson hopefully would be one she could count on to help her out and she could be more confident in searching her way through rope troubles rather than panicking and making things worse.

"Y'all remember the other day when I had a rope on her and she got all tangled up in it because it was back behind her?" Harry asked. "Pretty short lead rope here—should have had the longer one—but we'll just see what happens here."

Harry now was dismounted. He walked towards Bailey's hind end reaching a hand over her back trailing the lead rope along the mare's side opposite him and positioned it high around her behind just below the top of her tail. Once in place, Harry presented a little feel on the rope. She felt the rope come to life with Harry's feel on it, but rather than show much worry she turned her front end opposite from Harry and unwound herself. She made about a 280 degree turn that brought her back around beside Harry who by this point was walking away. She followed along nicely and led like a dream.

"This is a little spot here I want to mention," Harry said. "You noticed I walked off. I see people do this, and they just turn the horses around to them and pet them as soon as their noses come around. Well, when we get ready to ride this beast, I'd like to think I could tip her nose, do a little something, and if she turns she'd think about walking off, not just turn around to turn around. So that's why I'm walking off, to get her thinking about how to come out of there.

"If you noticed, I didn't drop that down very low [the rope around her hind quarters]. I'm just trying to get a feel of this for her and then we'll get that rope a little lower and let her feel of that. The other thing I will make a little mention of there is that before I was done, if I thought I could just flip the rope down behind her I might do that, but if you're not careful what they'll often be doing is turning from the pressure of the rope against their side. They swing their bum. They're not following the feel on their head. So before I was done, see, I'd want to think I could get this."

Harry demonstrated the scenario again reaching out with one arm to keep the rope above her so that it didn't touch her. It was easy to see Bailey taking a strong look in the direction of the lead rope as she turned around. Clearly the mare was intent on following the feel on the lead rope and was not swinging around in a skittish attempt to flee the rope which was near her flank and hind quarters.

"It's like my reins, see?" Harry continued. "When we get on, we want her to follow this feel, so I'm not going to let it touch her bum—it may, but I'm trying not to, see? And get that to take place [have her turn around following the feel on the line]. That's much more real to how the rein is going to operate than when it drops behind her hip. I see horses that people drop it clear down low here and they think, 'Oh, that horse is turning so light!' Well, all he's doing is escaping his hind end from the pressure; he isn't following the feel on the rein. So then, when they get on to ride, they find out they don't have as much working there as they thought. So, just things that I've thought about, seen and experienced over the years, I'm trying to share with you there.

"I'm going to step over here [towards Bailey's hind end] to encourage her to think around here," Harry explained as she was sorting out the feel on the rope around her butt placed a little lower than earlier. "I see people and they, just as the horse turns away—and what I mean by 'turn away' is, if I have that rope around her and instead of turning the way I ask her to go she turns the other way [stepping directly towards him instead of following the feel on the rope and stepping away from him]—they just walk over there [forwards towards her shoulder] and pull harder and just let them kind of get in a wreck there instead of giving them a little support to find that.

"So, if I tip her thought over there any, just a little, don't need a lot, just get her to kind of tip her thought out there to the right instead of to the left here."

In her searching at this point Bailey began backing up to see if that might be the answer.

"And, that's kind of nice the way she's backing there," Harry said. "So, you notice I'm not criticizing that backing [even though it wasn't what he was asking for with the rope around her hind end]. You've got to be careful. If you're critical of something you might want one day, the day you want it you might not be able to get it. So that backing up, I just let her back. It didn't work out too good, but

I didn't criticize it. I'd like her to be looking over there a little more, but I just stayed with her. But now, if she looks over there any—I might cross the center line to help her look there and set it up for her to succeed. Pretty soon, I'd wrap it around her hind end with a 60 foot rope if I wanted and be out there and expect she could turn around with it. But I'm going to help her find these things without doing it totally for her.

"Now, I'm going to drop it down a little lower so she feels that against her hind leg more. We had talked about ground driving one or two of them before we ride them. Well see, this is setting that up, getting her ready that you could ground drive her. Not that you have to ground drive her—it's setting her up to ride; it's setting her up to ground drive if you wanted to.

"She could wait on me there—they get to anticipating, see? Well, that's not all bad. Now I'm not going to walk around there behind her so much and see if she can make it. Very good! Once she lets go of that resistance then there's just a smooth willingness to her that you wouldn't have thought was there Monday. The way this mare looked the other day you would have thought it would have taken longer here."

Chapter Fourteen

Morning Session, Day Three, Bailey (Continued)
12 February 2014

"I'll pick her foot up. I don't want her doing it for me."

Harry Whitney

You may notice right away that this is a *very* short chapter. It is so by design because sometimes during a clinic a little something happens that can provide a profound point on horsemanship in a flash. Sometimes the Ah-ha! moment is triggered by a bit of work during a session or the way something gets rehashed during a table discussion.

An instance that occurred at the tail end of Bailey's session on day three was so short that it could be overlooked by some as insignificant, but it is just the kind of thing that has clicked for me in the past. I thought it would be good to mention here as an example of a brief clinic moment that is pregnant with the potential to birth greater understanding. It was when Harry spent a few minutes working on picking up the mare's feet before we broke for lunch.

Getting a young horse good about picking up her feet is paramount to a lifetime of easy handling for the farrier and for the owner. It also is one more building block on the way to having the

Later during the first week of the clinic Harry demonstrated using a ring rope to help one of the young mares relax her leg before he worked on picking up the foot. (Photo: Nancy Lawson)

whole horse thoughtful, willing, and relaxed in all situations.

I appreciate how in Harry's clinics he stresses that with horses, "nothing goes unmingled." How a colt feels about having her feet picked up relates to the rest of what is going on with her, and little things like this aren't little to the horse and can be a barometer of how much with-you-ness you have or don't have built up with the young ones.

And as we were learning, "so they're started, so they go," so how we approach picking up their feet in the beginning of their training certainly will have an affect on how they feel about it for the rest of their lives.

"I don't want her to pick her foot up," Harry said, bending over beside Bailey to work on a foot while holding the lead rope. "I want her to relax her leg. If her leg is relaxed, I can pick her foot up. That's all I'm interested in is getting her weight off her leg and relaxing it."

Harry stood back up to address the crowd.

"I'll pick her foot up," he said. "I don't want her doing it for me. If I come down here, see [he ran his hand down her leg as he bent over again heading for the foot], and she'd just think about relaxing that and taking her weight off of it."

Harry gripped the lower part of her leg just above the fetlock putting some pressure on it.

"I don't know how much it would take there before she decided to shift her weight off of it, but when she does, that's all I need."

A moment later she shifted the weight off that leg and Harry released his grip at the moment she did and rubbed the leg gently.

"Now there came her weight back on it," he said, putting a little grip back on the leg where he had it previously. "So I said, 'That's probably not going to work out.' See her lean into that? So I'm doing just enough that she shifted her weight."

The session ended when Bailey could feel Harry's hand

moving down her leg at which she began removing the weight from it and Harry picked up her foot with ease, moved it around to show how relaxed the leg was, and then placed the foot on the ground on the toe of the hoof; she left it in that position while he stood up.

Then we headed to the bunkhouse for lunch.

Chapter Fifteen

Afternoon, Day Three, Flagging Tinker Some More
12 February 2014

"You rejoice with the change you got but you're not satisfied."

Harry Whitney

A flag can be a wonderful tool for training horses. But using it effectively, and without inadvertently creating ill effects, can be a tricky business. A flag often was used when working the colts during the clinic. In fact, later on in the clinic we had a "petting party" where about eight of us were in the round pen with one of the young horses, each with a flag or a long foam noodle, following Harry's cues to help one of the young mares get more relaxed about being around such things—but we'll get to that complexity later....

On day three, Harry did some extensive flag work with Tinker. I was struck, as always, by his excellent timing—that is, when he upped the energy in the flag to effect a change and when he released, (quieted it in relation to achieving what he was asking the horse to do). Also, the variety of ways in which he used the flag stood

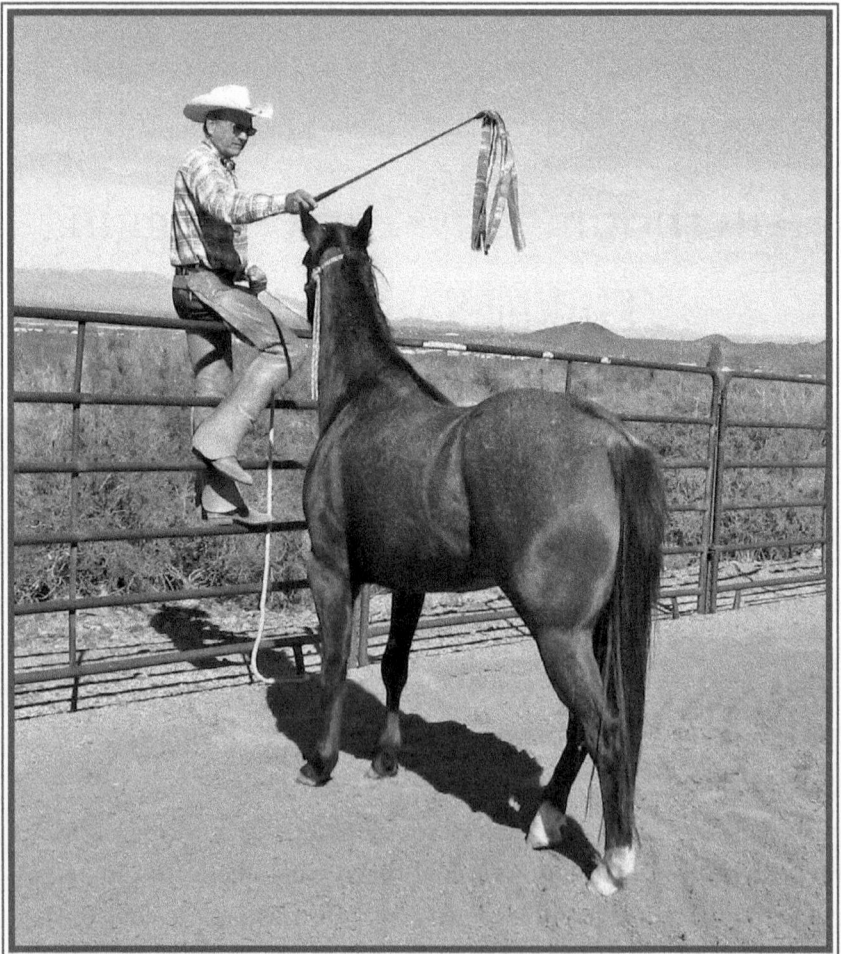

Harry flagging Tinker from the fence on day three.

out to me. For instance, he sat atop a fence panel to flag Tinker for awhile on this day.

Early in the session, Harry stood before the mare connected to her by a halter and lead rope. At first, Harry would suggest she back up by presenting her only with a feel on the lead rope. If Tinker was stuck mentally, he followed through by wagging the flag to break her mind loose and get her to move her feet.

"She hasn't backed up yet," Harry said to twenty-some of us scattered around just outside the round pen. "She's gone backwards but she didn't 'back up,' see? That's just a 'get away from,' but I want to see her take herself back, not just get away from something—to have a thought about *back there*."

He offered again for her to back up amidst the running commentary.

"There was a little better moment," he announced. "She got to thinking behind her a little there. So if I said, 'You need to think back behind you there,' I don't want her to think about completely turning and leaving, but to think back there somewhere [and back up with intent]."

In among the flagging backwards deal, as the mare hit spots where she was getting closer to giving what Harry was asking, he would release and give her a breather and she'd stand still and face him in an increasingly relaxed way. With some regularity, the clinician would reach out to stroke her once or twice on the nose before going on to the next request. I have seen Harry do this often when working horses. I've heard him explain it as a bit of a test to see if the horse is really centered mentally there with him.

Sometimes when Harry reaches towards a horse's nose to give it a pet, a horse immediately will turn and look away. In those instances, he sometimes backs away and makes a little noise—rubbing his jacket or making a quick slap to his thigh for instance—to regain the horse's attention. He will continue to play with that until he can pet the nose with the horse focused on him. Once he achieves that, he often will "tip the horse's thought" to one side or the other. This means he indicates by pointing in a direction with his hand, or sometime with a feel on the lead rope or even with the flag, for the horse to look and take an interest off to one side. Harry persists with that until the horse turns and has a good look in the direction he indicated, at which he releases the ask.

Occasionally on a horse that is really struggling to hang in there with a focus and wants to turn away as Harry's hand approaches, the clinician will catch the bridge of the nose with his fingers as the horse goes to look away. This can block the head from turning and likewise help keep the horse's attention from disappearing entirely in that direction. Usually when he does this, the horse gives to the firmness from his hand and in a flash relaxes and looks directly at him; then she can be petted on the nose. At other times, the horse looks completely past him in the other direction and he may follow the horse's head with his hand and switch his fingers to the other side of the nose and block that counter swing in the same way.

"So often right in the middle of petting," Harry said, "I tip that thought somewhere and I don't talk about it a lot of times. Like that right there [Harry caught the bridge of Tinker's nose as described above]; I just blocked that. Just another time of saying, 'Let go of that thought.' Just another opportunity to get her in the habit of letting go of thoughts instead of hanging onto them. She feels a little different than a couple of days ago."

Then it was back to flagging. Even though in the big picture Harry was working Tinker with the flag, his clinics always provide opportunities to pick up "little things" like the above. While something like being able to pet a horse's face without her turning away may seem a small thing, such a thing may not be small to the horse. If the horse dodges our approach, she isn't with us. If she isn't with us, then how will that little spot look when we ask for something more? And when it comes to starting colts, if these little things aren't attended to from the beginning it won't take long before avoidance or other unwanted by-products show up in bigger ways. By auditing, one can pick up on many helpful peculiarities that Harry has developed along the way which are unique to him that help one to see where horses are not with us in small ways and clear that up.

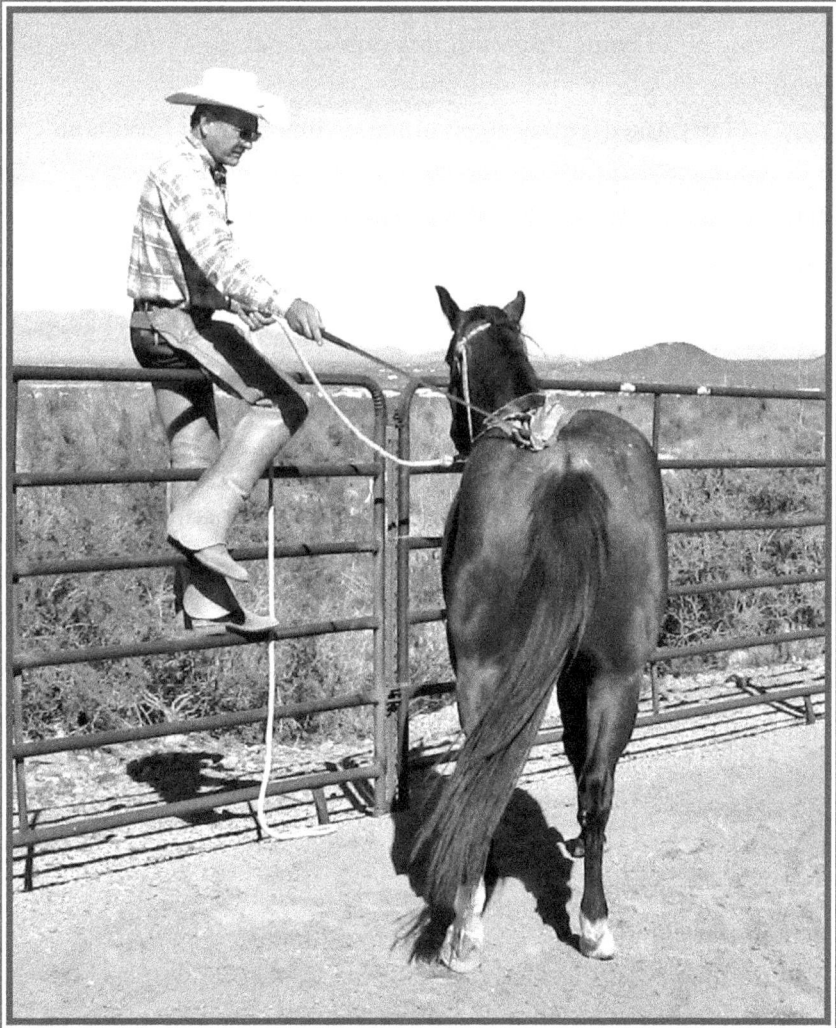

Harry continues to work on getting Tinker more comfortable with him and the flag from above her on the fence.

"Bumping them down in that area with the flag is just another means of getting them ready for our leg," Harry said as he used the flag to touch the girth area on Tinker.

He rather suddenly smacked the flag on the ground.

"Hey, you're not here!" Harry said. "What happened? Well, you were gone."

That was yet another quick moment where Harry addressed the horse's mind being wayward, this time by making a sudden ruckus.

Harry asked Tinker to go out and circle around him. The day before, she had pushed into the touch of the flag on her shoulder. Harry commented that the way she had reacted to that on day two had carried with it the feeling that he might get kicked if he wasn't careful.

"With this today," Harry said, touching the flag to her shoulder, "I don't have that feeling in here. Quite a little difference in how she's dealing with the flag today."

You don't have to be around Harry long to see how out-of-the-box a thinker he is. For instance, as happened with Tinker, I've seen Harry many times use the handle end of the flag on the horse, not just the end with the streamers.

Tinker was packing around quite a bit of tension as the session went on. Harry noticed the rock-hard muscles in her neck, back, and barrel and began poking her slightly with the handle end of the flag in these areas. The horse recoiled when the pokes landed in certain places and it was easy to see the tremors they caused reverberate through her entire body.

"Now I'm going to poke a little harder," Harry said, poking some more. "She's not twitching and jumping like she was."

Harry would poke, poke, poke in a bad spot and soon the mare would stop spasming so badly and begin to let down. Then he'd move and find another jumpy spot with his poker and the scenario would repeat.

"There are some spots in there that she could let go of and feel a whole lot better about," Harry pointed out. "What's the difference between this and giving her a shot? They would probably feel about equal to her right now. But there now, see she dropped her head a little and that same muscle that she was jerking [in her neck] is much softer and so that would help towards giving them a shot. We'll wait here a moment...she took a breath at least. She hasn't been breathing. See if she could let down a little more there. [Harry poked around some more.] There are still some little hot spots in there that she twitches from. Right there is where she was reacting more, and that's way softer.

"That right there [more twitching from the pokes] is kind of like a knee-jerk reaction but she's not leaning into me and she's not getting tighter all over. Pretty soon she'll let go of that knee-jerk reaction and I can poke around there and she won't have to twitch, but that has a different feel to it than when she leans into it, squints her eye, and grits her teeth

"When you say 'knee-jerk' do you just mean an involuntary reaction?" someone asked.

"Basically, yes," Harry replied. "It will go away here, see, but she isn't defensive about it. It didn't feel good. She can't help but react to it. That's better; even though there's a little reaction there you get the feeling that's just that knee-jerk type of thing and she doesn't feel the need to be defensive about it."

Harry got the poking business to a point where Tinker was much less reactive in all the hot spots he had found. He flipped the flag around again so that the handle was in his hand, and he proceeded to ask the mare to go out and make a circle around him.

"I'll pet her here a little [with the flag]," he said as she walked around him on line. "See that little rush come in her? That doesn't feel too good to her. We'll do that again. ... There that was better.

"They're often quite worried over there [referring to the side of the horse opposite him as the mare moved on a circle around him]

because they don't associate that with us. If they've got any trust in us whatsoever—they know these things are coming from us on this side—but it is often the off-side when you first saddle a horse he'll get to running around the pen and he'll look to the outside stirrup and get to running from it, kicking at it. It's almost never the inside stirrup.

"If we've done things to bolster their confidence in us, it doesn't bother them as bad if they can associate it with us over here, see? But when it's over there and she says, 'What in the world is that thing doing?' then it's a bigger worry."

Harry explained that he often tells people when they're playing with a horse that is really worried about the flag to take the flag off the horse and then put it back on. But, he's found it necessary to add, "Take it off *a couple of inches* and put it back on."

"If a horse is really worried about it and they're petting like this," Harry demonstrated by petting Tinker with the flag on her side, "and you say, 'Take it off and put it back on,' they'll do this [Harry removed the flag quite a ways away from Tinker and brought back in towards her]. Well, that coming back in, you saw a little tension in her when it came back in. They come clear out here [with the flag] and back, or they come clear out here and then wait to see what she's going to do instead of getting out there and getting back and reassuring them as quickly as you can. And that's kind of like I'm doing here with this. Come back [and touch her with the flag] and reassure her.

"Just get it up here where it's safe and away from her [near her top line]. Yes, going up there can be a worry to them, but at least it's getting closer when you're up here around their heads. If you come down here [Harry took the flag off Tinker and held it low near the ground] you're way more apt to get kicked than if you go up there. So to get it up there high, yes, that can be a worry to them too, but it's not near as dangerous for us. You come down here too quick to get it away from them, they'll kick at it or strike at it in a heartbeat.

And that takes the fun out of it!"

At this point, Harry began talking about a situation people get into when flagging a horse that causes him considerable concern. It happens when a person uses the flag to ask a horse that is very worried to move its shoulder away from him.

"There's a spot here that really puts the fear in me when you're letting people work with the flag," Harry said. "They'll go to reach in here [back along the side], but when a horse is really afraid of that flag she'll look at it. So, if she turned her head to look at that flag coming in here, then when she gets worried she goes to spin tighter around to get it at her nose where it's safer and her side comes into me and mows me down. And I see person after person do it. They're wanting a horse to move off, and they come in here and they shake it bigger to try to get the horse to move over.

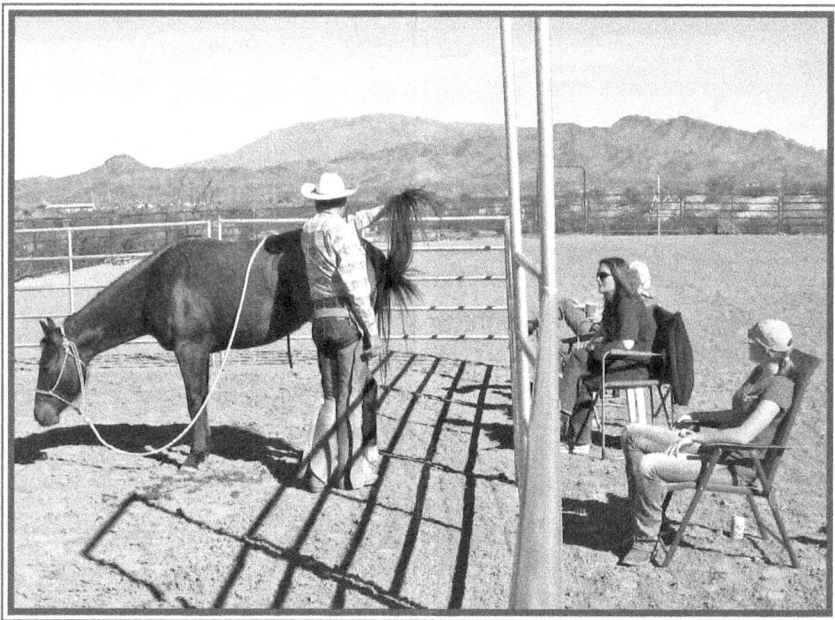

Another spot where tension can be evident is in a tightly clamped tail which Harry demonstrates on Tinker as Kathy Baker, Lauren Gruber, and Katelyn Praly look on.

"If I'm up here [high and by the shoulder] I can get that coming, but boy there's a spot there that you can get them to run over you in a heartbeat on a really worried one that has to look around there—wants to put her nose on it—and a lot of them do.

"That shoulder deal there that we worked on yesterday, and I'm playing with off-and-on here, is a very important spot. The reason I think that it's important is—I blabbered about how a horse uses his shoulders to push through something that's in the way of a thought—so, if a horse has some stuck spots mentally and she feels defensive about that shoulder, and so she starts getting real stuck about moving that shoulder, then she'll get where it's almost impossible to get her to move her shoulders. I'd like for her to step her shoulder off over there. Boy, you'll meet horses that that's just, you might as well tie your rope to a brick wall. That was good [Tinker moved her shoulder over as he worked with her while speaking to us]. So I think that's a pretty important little spot there that they get really stuck on."

We spectators had been quietly soaking in the scene and Harry's commentary. Tinker would come through and become visibly relaxed at times, and at others what Harry did with the flag again would bring up the tension and worry.

"She got really worried there," Anna said, noticing a sudden reaction in the mare. "I don't know, seems like something happened over there [I had moved while sitting atop a panel behind her which made a clatter]. It feels like they relate it to this other thing [the flag] somehow?"

"When you're on edge about something—you're unsure about something," Harry began, "it doesn't take much of an external stimulus to make you real convinced that could happen to you. I'll never forget when I first got a cell phone and my horses were living in an electric fence. Well, I put my cell phone on vibrate because of the clinic deal. I didn't think anything about it. I went through that electric fence and I hadn't stepped away three feet and that phone went off on vibrate. I liked to hurt myself! I felt the pain. I knew I'd been shocked—everything! Well, if I'd have been 100 feet from that fence it wouldn't have done that to me, but because that was there, then I just knew I'd been got, see? So she knew this flag was here—she's a little unsure—he shook, that rattled, and she thought, 'It got me!' But, oh no, it really didn't. But, I know the feeling!"

Harry went over to the fence, Tinker in tow, and took a perch atop a panel with his flag in hand. He began asking the mare to move with the flag from up above her.

"Now we'll see if she could just lead up here a step," Harry said.. "Thank you. Lead up here. Good! Very good. Now see, we haven't worked her from a horse. So those others, I got this done from a horse, but with her we can get it done from right here. Just a little tightness there but not bad. I'd like to see it as good on the other side."

Harry got a little aggressive with the flagging and she moved over.

"That was not about her stepping over," he commented. "That was about her sticking her head up there [in the air]. She was getting this shut down look instead of staying present and searching. We'll ask her to step up here a little. Ask her over there. Ask her to step up here a little without thinking about swinging away instantly—that just isn't going to work out."

Harry again flagged more vigorously to get a change in the mare.

"She doesn't want to step up on that side and just wait there like she did on this side," he commented. "Certainly not as good as that other side yet, but that's the best one I've had so you've got to rejoice in those things. Are you satisfied? No. You rejoice with the change you got but you're not satisfied. You're happy for today but you know there's better to be had, but that doesn't mean it has to be today, but you do know that's not the best she has to offer."

Chapter Sixteen

***

Late Afternoon, Day Three, Colt Starting with a Stock Whip
12 February 2014

"Sky came to Harry with
BIG YAWNS! Harry called it good."
From my clinic journal, day three.

I'd be hard pressed to think of a more potentially frightening tool to a horse in the hands of a human than a long, serpent-like stock whip. Not only does it move with a spooky, lively, whirring action in the air, but the gun-shot-like crack it emits when unfurled by the hands of a pro like Harry packs its own punch.

What role could such a tool possibly play in starting a young horse? It's a great question! It is one I might have asked when Harry entered the round pen with a nice braided leather stock whip to work Sky on day three if I hadn't witnessed him in previous clinics use the tool to help horses get beyond some troubles. One of the more impressive instances of this I witnessed was when Harry did a "free search" in the round pen at a clinic in Montana with Sunshine, a Morgan mare owned by Linda Davenport (the Linda who happened to be with us at the colt starting clinic). That search in Montana is described at length in my book *Going Somewhere*.

I enjoyed this moment with Sky and Harry in part because it again pointed to the fact that if approaching it properly, one can

Before cracking the whip for the first time, Harry takes care to be sure Sky is okay with being touched with a whip. (Photo: Nancy Lawson)

use whatever tack or tools are at his disposal to effectively get young horses going in a good way.

It is pretty obvious that cracking a whip near a colt to gain her wayward attention can work. But to successfully develop relaxation in the horse with such loud shots along the way is pretty counterintuitive. Watching Harry help Sky to settle down through use of the stock whip blasted through any belief spectators may have held that one should never do anything potentially "scary" around a young horse. It was a lesson in just how much such nebulous realms as feel, timing, intent, balance, and awareness are paramount to improving communication with a horse, and that it is not about the gear, or even the intensity of the potential spookiness of what's in the hand of the human.

"These horses are scared of guns and things like that—noises—and this mare has got a lot of blast in her," Harry said as he began to work with her. "You guys saw it there yesterday. So we're going to play with the whip here a little bit and see what takes place."

The "yesterday" situation Harry discussed was when Anna, who had been working Sky the previous day loose in the round pen, bent over and picked up a rock and tossed it out of the round pen. That action caused Sky to bolt. The mare reacted in a huge way and she ran, bucked, and carried on. Tossing that rock had been an innocent act on Anna's part; she simply was getting rid of a big rock from the footing while working Sky. But with the surprise reaction she got from the horse, Anna set about looking for more rocks so she could work on settling Sky around that situation. She did get the mare better about it but only after quite a bit of blasting around.

Crack! Pause. Pause. Crack!

"There's various things that we could look for here," Harry said, sizing her up. "She's already a little more attentive to the importance that I have in the pen because she was looking away both times that happened [when the whip cracked]. Well, she'll think maybe it won't work too good to be thinking about other things. I

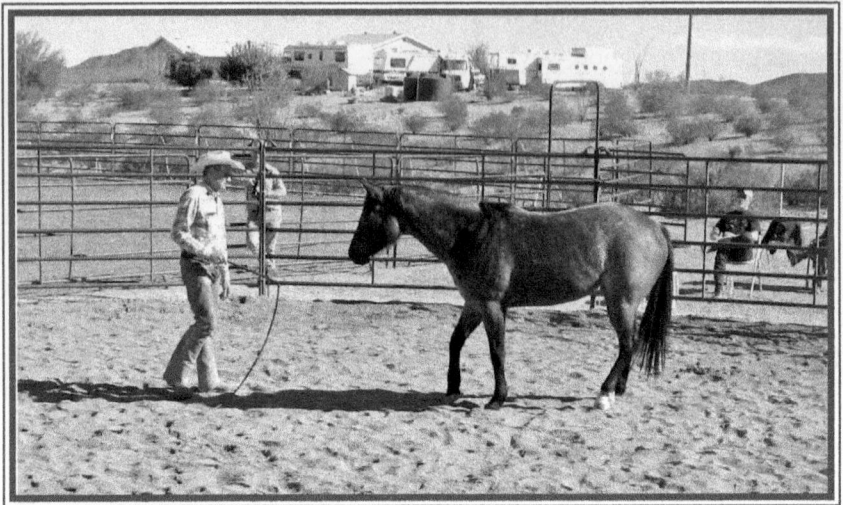

Harry approaches Sky with the stock whip.

could work here for awhile. It might take awhile before she came to me. I think it's great what already happened. It startled her but she didn't have to go smoking around here. I thought she'd probably get going and go pretty hard but she didn't."

"Harry, you said she had a habit of squirting out, blasting off; so this is going to interrupt that?" Kathy asked.

"It can," Harry replied. "But if she doesn't get any more smoking around here than that because of this, you wouldn't think that it would have to come in there for other things. But we'll see when we go to ask her to move a little—direct her—that might just show up again."

"Harry, could you talk about the timing of when you snap and when you don't snap, and what you're asking so I can be clear about it?" Ellen asked.

"She just left because I was playing with this," Harry replied, referring to moving the whip around her. "When she goes over there to the fence like this [Crack!], that's not going to work out too good. And yet every time that happens [Crack!] and nothing has really happened to her, she just gets more confident that that noise is not about something bad that's going to happen [to her]."

"So you wait until she gets all the way to the fence to snap?" Ellen followed-up.

"Probably," Harry answered. "Not necessarily all the way, but not too early, that's for sure. [Crack! Crack!] She's not totally convinced yet that this is about what she's doing. You'd like for her not to be worried about this. [Crack!]."

"She's putting quite a hardness into going which is why you're waiting awhile to snap?" Anna asked.

"Oh yes," Harry said. "See, that's not working."

Crack, snap, snap, snap, snap, crack! Harry began giving repetitive cracks of the whip and Sky began moving in a rather worried way along the fence around one half of the pen.

"That's just an opportunity to do it a little more so she'll find out it's not about her," Harry said. "It's not being done *to* her. And yet, when she decides—there we go, see [she stopped moving about]—she did get it to stop. But it still wasn't about her. She even came in closer [to Harry]. We're sure not going to quit now because she's still not feeling good. So, we're going to keep playing until we see if we can get her feeling better there...following through till there is a nice clear change, not just accepting the obedient thing, is probably a better way of saying that."

"But what do you follow through with?" Kathy asked. "I mean, that's a judgment."

"And how are you helping to make a change?" Ellen added. "I mean, we're watching it but are you doing more than what we're seeing?"

Laughter erupted among the crowd at Ellen's comment, the joke being that as long-time students of Harry's, we all had long ago accepted that Harry operates on a level only partially observable to the human.

"To answer that other question," Franny started, "would it be because you didn't settle for her coming in in a frame of mind that was still worried? You kept going with it [cracking the whip] until that frame of mind got changed?"

"Yes," Harry replied. "And I kind of alluded to that earlier, to continue till you get a real change. But how do you tell? How do you know that you're on the right track until the real change comes?"

"Instead of driving her deeper into the gloom," Ellen chimed in and chuckled.

"Yeah," Harry said, still keeping close tabs on the mare and snapping the whip periodically as the conversation continued.

Crack! Crack!

"That still bothers her enough that she had to go but she wasn't very upset," Harry pointed out. "She still couldn't stay, but boy, [she put] so little effort into the go. But I'm pushing my luck more on this right side that's causing her to have to go more than if I did it over here [on the left].

Crack! Crack!

"Harry?" Linda spoke up to summarize what she had seen unfold during the session so far. "So, the right thing's easy and the wrong thing's difficult and the right thing in this scenario is, regardless of what's going on, she's always going to be better when she's with you with her thoughts."

"There you go," Harry answered. "It feels better hanging out here [with me], doesn't it?"

After about 45 minutes of this session, it became a rarity for Harry to crack the whip. There became less and less reason to crack it as Sky became more and more with him and far less likely to be either off mentally on her own or worried about the whip moving about or making noise when it carried no directing intent from Harry.

"She didn't look very 'with me' in spots there," Harry commented, "but the instant I offered, she was here, see. She did not miss that. I like it that she hasn't really had to go. It could come in there, and if we go faster it may come in there."

Crack! Harry popped the whip for the first time in awhile.

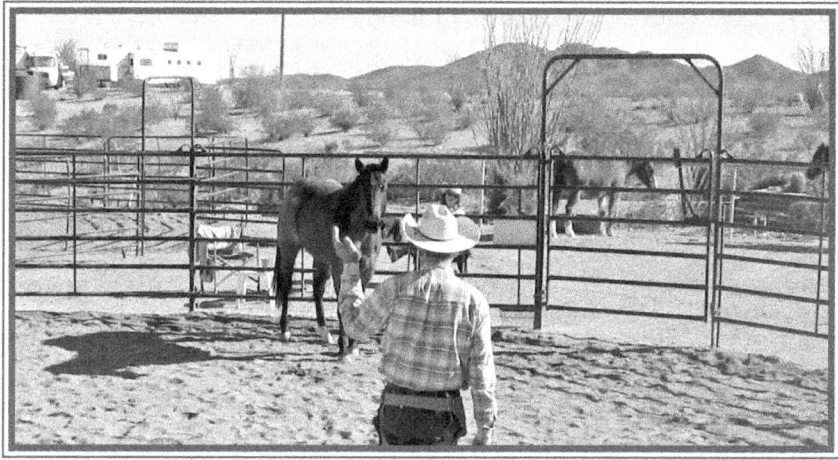

Sky becomes much less worried about the whip and more attentive to Harry as the session progresses.

"Now you see that pop drew her attention to me instead of her thinking about fleeing," Harry pointed out this change in her response. "She kind of lost me over there, but I popped it and instantly she was acoming."

"Harry, do you think the main reason she got so much better about not taking off, was it that you waited until she got right out there before you cracked it?" Anna asked. "I know there's lots going on, but I've felt it before, back home with something with me, that they'll try harder to get away [if you do something too soon]."

"Well, if you're not careful when you do those things..." Harry began, "that's why you've got to wait till they're a ways from you before you do it because you want to make the wrong *thing* difficult—it's not the leaving, it's where she is going when she leaves. Well, if we didn't have a fence she'd probably go to the barn. Well then, we'd make that not work out. But not the *trip* to the barn. That isn't going to prove it to her—she needed to go *to* the barn. That's why she made the trip. That's when you do something, right there.

"But after she got ahold of that [wayward thought], a little bit ago she lost track of me, I put a little pop in it, and she just [Harry snaps his fingers for effect] boom, she was there. Well then, if she was going across the parking lot you could make a little deal—you wouldn't have to let her go clear there when it's meaningful. But in the beginning you've got to let them go clear to whatever they think is the solution and experience that it doesn't work out."

"Is that the same then for a horse that rushes out of the trailer?" Anna followed-up. "Let them rush out?"

"Let them rush out," Harry replied. "Get out of the way and let them come out. But then this doesn't work out out here. Well, people are whacking and smacking on them on the way out—no, just get out of the way and let him come out, let him find out that didn't work. Then when he gets in, it works good. If he's flying out, get out of the way."

"Can you give any reflection on training a horse to lunge with a buggy whip?" Tim Thomas, an auditor from California, asked.

"Well, if you're not careful you're driving," Harry said. "You're giving them something to get away from so when they hear a crack like this, then they are scared. A lot of times I find horses [get worried] when they hear that whish. The pop doesn't scare them near as much. If you could just have a pop gun and go bang, it doesn't scare them as bad a hearing the whir because [they've learned] that's what came before something happened to them. We train those things in. We put that in them if we're not careful. But you can use it to guide a horse, just like I've been using my flag, but then you pet them with it. They shouldn't be worried and afraid of it. But people want them to be afraid of it because they want to be able to make them go with it. It could be done well."

Auditors Wes Bartlett, Ellen Bartlett, Ginna Ciszek and Tim Thomas take in the activity during a round pen session. (Photo: Nancy Lawson)

Chapter Seventeen

Morning Table Discussion, Day Four, Thursday, 13 February 2014

"...if our mind is not full of being present with them, what is there for them to be mindful of, really?"
Harry Whitney

"I like to use the word 'mindful' when dealing with horses," Harry said during the after breakfast discussion on day four of the clinic. "They should stay mindful of what we're doing and where we are, and all those things. But if our minds are not full of being present with them, what is there for them to be mindful of, really?

Then, we don't encourage that [mindfulness]—support that, help that be—and pretty soon they're everywhere else just like we are."

It was plenty obvious at this stage of the clinic that a colt's thoughts enjoy the primary focus of Harry's horsemanship every bit as much as the thoughts of the older horses I've seen him work

Cook, Lynn Wechsler, contributes to an after meal discussion.
(Photo: Nancy Lawson)

with in regular clinics. In fact (as you probably already surmised by reading to this point), the conversations during the colt starting clinic never really swayed from the topic of where the horses' thoughts were regardless of the immediate situations being discussed. Discerning whether a horse's focus was with the person or not was the crux to understanding many of the equine behaviors that presented themselves while bringing these young horses along in their training.

Anxious colts, and "difficulties" with them, pretty much always resulted from the horses not being with Harry, Anna, or Ty mentally. When working on an "issue," another important point Harry stressed was that one should not release simply for an obedient movement from the horse. Rather, one should hold out that release for a real change of thought which also goes hand-in-hand with increasing relaxation.

"When I first got out in the world doing clinics," Harry shared, "I ran into all these people talking about a 'one-rein stop.'

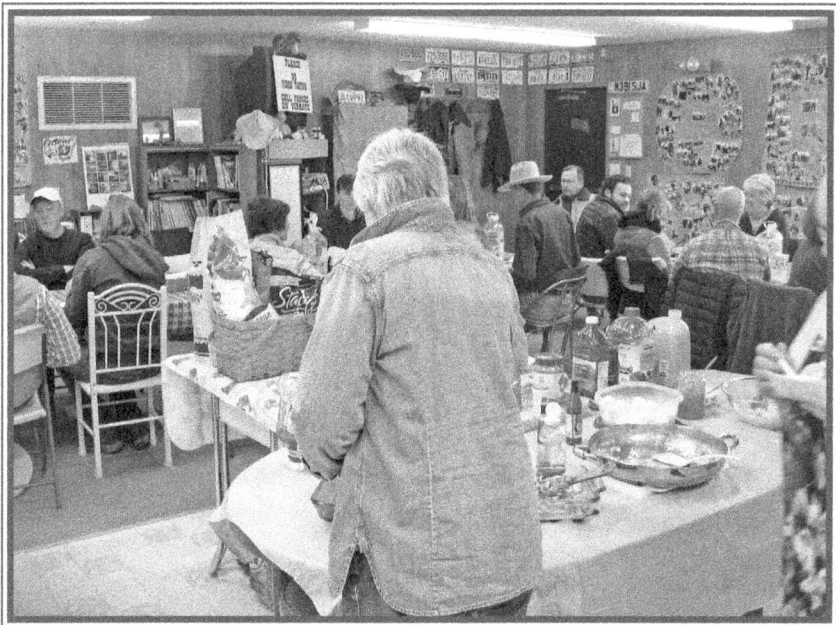

Breakfast in the bunkhouse.

And what I saw in horse after horse after horse was a rigidity—a stiffness—that was detrimental to getting a nice bend, making a nice turn, riding a circle. It seemed to me a lot of that was coming from riders doing so much of this one-rein stop. So I got kind of a pet peeve about not talking about that. Not because it's wrong, but because I saw what people took from that being presented and what they did with it.

"The presenter [horsemanship clinician] might have had it working in a useful way, but what people took and did with it, there was so much that was not good in there. What I saw was when they take ahold of the rein and they bend the horse around till he comes completely to a standstill, pull his neck over, and then they release the rein is that very shortly when you go to bend the horse, he'd just stick all four feet in the sand and flop his head over. That put a stiffness in him. As soon as you touch the rein he'd get stiff because it was about planting his feet and coming to a stop."

Harry acquaints one of the colts with the driving reins during week one.

Harry went on to explain that to get a horse to bend, one must get her to let go of the thought of pushing forward with her hind quarters and let that hind end step over, and that the release needs to come while there is still movement in the horse.

"Now, if you want a stop," he continued, "you just sit still and release as they step over. If they go to walk off, do it again. Pretty soon, they'll just step over and stop. But you're releasing before they're stopped while there's still movement."

I struggled with this idea at first. If you're looking for a stop, why would you release before you get what you're looking for? But then I grasped what Harry was saying. You essentially are releasing when the horse disengages the *thought* of going *forward*. She may still move those hind quarters to the side, but that commitment to going forward has ceased. If by contrast, every time you pick up a rein and bring the horse's head around it is for the sole reason of planting her feet firmly in a stop, then that will become your only option when using a rein this way.

Therefore, Harry was seeing horses become super stiff when the reins were engaged. But if you release the rein when the horse lets go of the thought of going forward, but *not* for planting the feet solidly in the sand, you still have a range of options available for the next choice of movements in the horse because she remains fluid. Floating to a stop can be one choice. Stepping the hind end over repeatedly can be another. Going forward again onto an arc can be one, and so forth.

"Then," Harry said, "when you're riding and you want to make a turn—you want to ride a circle—when you pick up the rein, they get ready to step over underneath themselves, and they can push themselves right around the turn instead of thinking about their hind quarters getting out behind them sticking in the sand coming to a stop, stiff and strung out. That's why I made an issue of it when Ty got that good one there. [Harry was referring to Ty working with Houston in their most recent session.]

"When he stopped, that little horse's hind feet were closer to his front ones than how he normally would stand. That's an important thing because then it would take very little to shift his weight onto his hind quarters and his front end is free to move. So

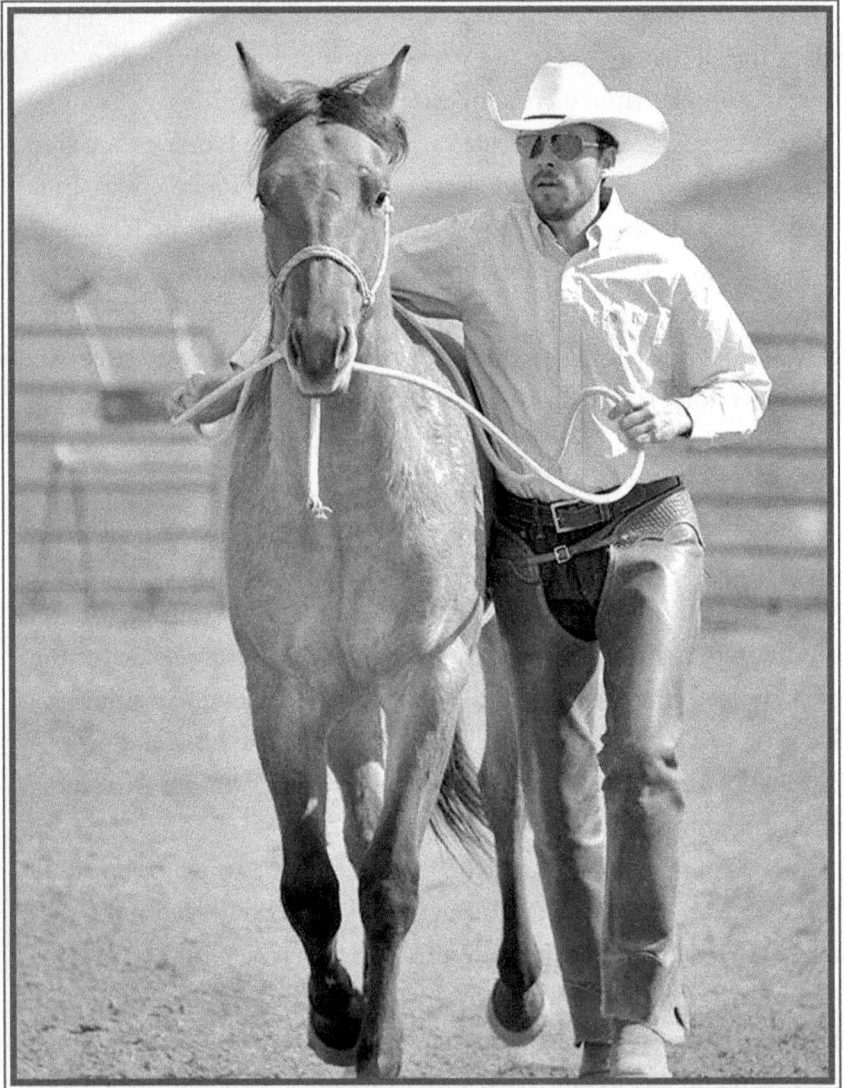

Ty trots along side Houston asking him to go forward while putting a slight feel on the lead rope reins. (Photo: Nancy Lawson)

he is getting himself balanced there by stepping across underneath himself, and yet you can get a stop within that, but you don't pull until they stop—there's a release as soon as that mind lets go of pushing forward and is ready to go there, you're releasing the rein and he'll just stop there.

"But if you wanted to follow through, if you keep some life in you and you offer, he should tip his weight back, bring that front end over, and away you can go! And so it builds in, and in the first ride—and if not in the first one, for sure by the second one—I want to be able to start to take ahold of that rein and have that young horse prepare to step his hind quarters over underneath so that he can bring his front end across, and he starts to rebalance real early there.

"Early, early in the program there's a rebalancing starting in there. Instead of waiting until you've been riding him seven years and then decide that he should be able to get himself in a better balance, a better posture, it can be starting right up front really early there. If the horse understands that when you go to take up on that rein that there's a way to balance because the only way he's going to get a release is if he lightens that forehand so it can move, pretty soon when you touch the rein to go to ask something you can feel him get ready. He just picks that front end up and rebalances himself instantly."

"So when he came through," one of the folks at the table spoke up, "and he was stopped and he was off balance, would you just continue walking through and ask again until he was balanced properly?"

"If there's a freedom and he's not pushing forward, take it," Harry replied. "But the better that gets then the more he'll arrange himself. Then on the ground and in the riding, you follow through with asking him to do something with that front end. That gives him a reason to get more balanced there. And that's the way with so many things that we do, we just try to make something be, but the horse sees no purpose in it—no reason.

"If you want your horse to be in better balance when you

stop—when you're standing still—then give him a reason to have been in better balance so later you don't have to get him balanced. You know he's standing there half asleep, on his forehand, he couldn't move his front end if he had to, but you ask for it. Then you put a little hustle in until he finds it. Say, 'Thank you!' Pretty soon he stops and he says, 'You know, I don't know when that guy might ask something, I think I'll wait here ready.' Well now, he took the responsibility. I don't want him standing there trembling in his little hooves. It's not about it being abrupt and rude to them, but it's asking something that will show them that later they would be prepared, not us have to get them there."

This discussion grabbed me because it covered a great deal in a short time. I appreciated that it addressed a very common maneuver that is taught zealously in clinics and videos which had come under Harry's scrutiny—the one rein stop. Many clinicians begin with new students and new horses by teaching this maneuver thinking of it as an emergency brake that they can use if they get into trouble with a horse. I believe that thinking of it in those terms contributes to a rider's anxiety and insistence that the horse STOP! when the rider bends him around with a rein—(this is the emergency brake after all!). It was a learning experience to hear Harry carefully dissect some issues that are often a result of its frequent mis-use.

I paid close attention to the fact that this example illustrated how easy it is to teach a horse an obedient response to a request while blocking a range of other possibly important options that the rider may need. If we create one conditioned response, as in a horse stopping dead in his tracks whenever we bring a rein around, how can we possibly expect the horse to be available to hear a whole range of other requests we might want to have with the rein? Subtle requests will be overridden by the autopilot we've instilled in the horse. And, developing an understanding of how this kind of problem can be avoided in young horses right from the start is priceless.

Likewise, concentrating on the idea that the horse take

responsibility for her own preparedness brought a clarity to my mind. Understanding that we can set things up so the young horse knows to balance herself in preparation for whatever we might ask was helpful to me to remember that we can get stuck in the habit of doing everything for the horse. There's a thin line between micromanaging our requests and driving the horse into everything, and neither is part of with-you-ness. But if we follow Harry's advice and can comprehend how to release for the change of thought rather than focusing solely on what the feet or the body parts are doing, we can set the horse up to find that sweet spot between us and bring herself to the role of a partner in our work together.

Chapter 18

Afternoon Session, Day Four,
Saddling Smoke
Thursday, 13 February 2014

"Nothing runs unmingled.
You work on this; it affects that."
Harry Whitney

Day four produced another beautiful, sunny high desert afternoon with an occasional breeze, low humidity, and temperatures hanging in the 70s. A remarkably blue sky stretched out overhead with wispy white clouds highlighting the heavens with faint brush strokes. The weather would have been perfect regardless of the time of the year, but for this Virginian, experiencing it in February was extraordinary.

About mid-afternoon, Anna led Smoke into the round pen and turned the mare loose. Harry led Easy, who was saddled, into the round pen, closed the gate behind them, and climbed in the saddle. The session began with Smoke turned loose and Harry using the flag to ask Smoke to move around the pen. The mare was sluggish and not the least bit eager to move.

"If she gets more responsive, she'll feel better about the whole deal," Harry announced.

Anna Bonnage and Ty Haas absorbed in watching Harry work Smoke in the round pen. (Photo: Nancy Lawson)

Easy wasn't following Harry's lead well either at first. I have heard Harry comment before that when working one horse from another there may be times where you need to turn your attention to the one you are riding and leave the other alone. Sorting out the saddle horse in general takes a priority. When Easy blew right through Harry's request that he stop, Harry let Smoke go on about her business and began asking Easy to back.

"His woahwer is broke!" Harry said with a laugh. "His goer works pretty good."

"Harry," Kathy began, "when you get the up-transition but you don't feel like they're thinking forward—as soon as they start thinking forward, do you let them come down or no?"

"Well, you might ease off a little," Harry replied. "That doesn't mean that you necessarily let them come down. But there isn't the pressure there was before that, which means they might come down when you ease off. I'd like her to feel of this [what he was presenting while riding Easy] and think about walking. She doesn't need to hurry. She could walk just the same as he's walking."

Harry next encouraged Smoke to move more quickly in a thoughtful way. The clinician rode Easy into a position on an inside circle and used the flag to ask the mare to move out forward. The words he spoke coincided with what he was offering for the mare to follow:

"Take your thoughts out there. Take your thoughts out there. Take your thoughts out there bigger. Now take your thoughts out there bigger. A little bigger...a little bigger...think out there. That was better. Think out there. Think out there...good!"

"Yea!," the crowd called out in unison as Smoke finally broke loose and moved freely forward. The change was obvious to us, evidenced not only by an increase in forward speed, but more importantly in an earnest commitment to going forward throughout her entire body—ears forward, head lowered from its previous position, and a newfound freeness of motion.

"That was way better," Harry complimented the mare. "Now she could find a walk there, maybe. [She did.] Now she could stop there. [She did.]"

"Harry," Kathy followed up, "does the horse that you're on ever make it more difficult because the horse you're working tends to be occupied by that horse? Would it be different if you were working her loose on the ground yourself?"

"Rarely do you see a lot of difference." Harry said. "If they're resistant from ahorseback, they're resistant on the ground; if they're resistant on the ground, they are pretty resistant horseback about those kind of things."

Harry decided to try to get the mare walking freely forward as well in the other direction before changing what he was working on. She came through but still with some reluctance.

"That didn't feel good [to Smoke] to have to do that" Harry said. "But it was not what I'd call a bad transition."

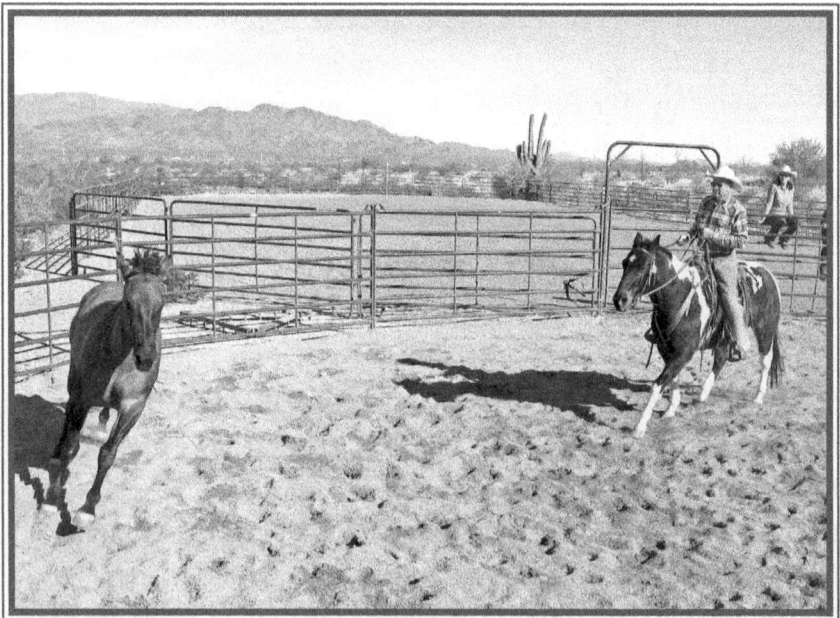

Harry encourages Smoke to move forward with a flag from Easy.

"It didn't feel too good because she felt made [to do it]?" asked Lauren Gruber, an auditor from Tennessee. "Because, it wasn't her thought? Because [why]?"

"Well, she's a little like Tinker," Harry answered. "She just doesn't want to put out that effort. Now if you scare them, trust me, they've got plenty of effort. But when they're feeling like you're directing it a little, to have to go faster and put out that much effort, [they can resist]."

As if on cue, Smoke punctuated what Harry was saying by bucking as he again asked her to get a more forward thought with the flag from Easy and take herself forward.

"We might as well get the buck out of her before we saddle her!" Harry commented. "Now we'll see if we can crowd her just a little; get her thinking forward, thinking forward, thinking forward. Thinking forward...good!"

Again Harry's words expressed his thoughts and actions for our benefit.

"Thinking forward—thinking forward. Good!" he continued. "Much better. Think Forward. Forward. Forward. Good—that's progress."

It may seem a bit daft to put some of Harry's repetitive verbal references from his horse work onto the page. However, Harry speaks these things aloud solely for the benefit of the onlookers—it's neither for himself nor for the horse, he says, and he does not verbalize any of these things when working horses alone. Including some of this talk helps paint an accurate picture of how things went at the clinic. More importantly, I hope it presents an opportunity for the reader to see how Harry is very persistent but not overly insistent when he makes a request of a horse, and how much time he allows these young horses to search for the right answer with the repetition of his requests.

"Was it pretty? No," Harry pointed out. "Was it progress? Yes. She's just not real pleased with the program at the moment."

Smoke provided moments of improvement commingled with plenty of reluctance to get on board with Harry's offers. But Harry and Easy just kept presenting opportunities for the mare to come through and get with them, and a sweet spot awaited her at any moment of breakthrough however large or small it was.

Harry dismounted and fetched a soft cotton rope that had a metal ring on one end. He made a loop by feeding the tail of the rope through the ring and situated it around Smoke's chest in the cinch area just behind the front legs. Harry stood off to Smoke's side holding the tail end of the rope; the ring was situated about half way up her side facing him. This arrangement allowed Harry to take up slack and tighten the choke around her chest from a distance, but if he fed any slack back towards the horse, gravity would pull the ring downwards and loosen the loop instantly.

A ring rope can be applied this way simply to "desensitize" a horse to the feel of the cinch that will come with saddling by tightening the rope in this area in stages. Horror stories abound in the horse world of first saddlings gone awry where saddles end up underneath horses' bellies, huge wrecks occur, and trauma gets put into them that can remain forever. To help avoid such a nightmare and to get a horse really thinking about this process, Harry takes the ring rope around the barrel a couple of steps further than simple desensitization by using the ring rope to communicate meaning to the horse.

"If a horse knows how to respond to something there's not much reason to be worried about it," he said as he began to demonstrate what he meant with Smoke.

Harry put a few bumps in the ring rope until Smoke took the hint and went forward, then he quit bumping (released the pressure), and they walked a circle together. When he wanted the mare to stop, he put a steady pull on the ring rope until she not only stopped but backed, and then he released. He worked at this with the rope in the cinch area until Smoke had it down pretty well and then he moved the ring rope further back down her barrel towards her back end.

He repeated the process and then went further back with the rope to the area where a back cinch would be on a western saddle. Finally, he did the bump-to-go, pull-steady-to-back deal all the way back by the hind legs. With each repositioning of the rope towards the hind end Smoke showed some new worry, but pretty soon Harry had her understanding the meaning of his bumps and steady pulls at each spot along the way, and she was able to calmly follow the feel he presented wherever the rope was located around her middle.

Harry removed the ring rope and asked Wes to hand him a saddle pad. He played with carelessly throwing the pad onto Smoke's back. He deliberately let the pad bump into her side, shoulder, neck, and hind quarters until he was satisfied that she was relaxed about it. Then he set the saddle pad into its proper position on her back, got a

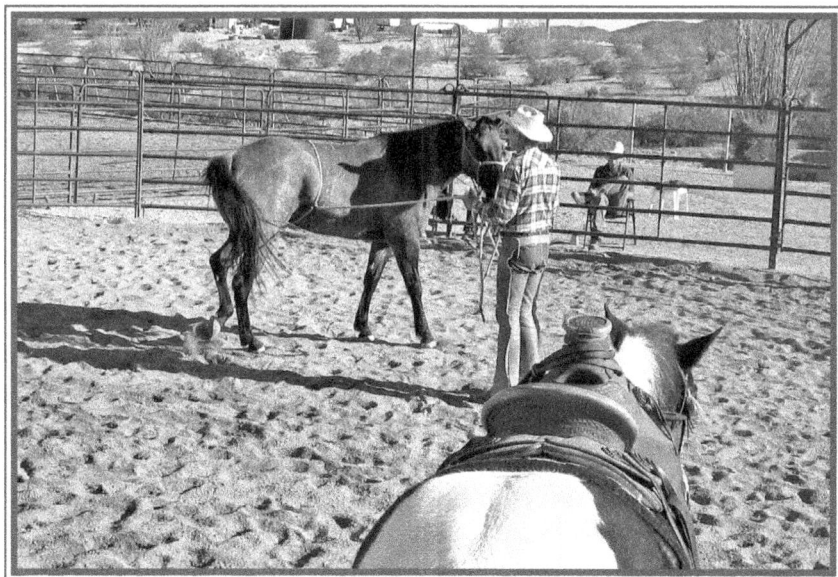

Harry works to prepare Smoke for having a saddle cinched on her by using a ring rope—he began with it cinched around her barrel up by the front legs and after several increments he has moved it all the way back against the mare's flank.

saddle, and, holding the saddle cradled in one arm and holding the lead rope with the other hand, he let the front of the saddle bump gently into her side and shoulder so she could get accustomed to the feel of it much as he had with the saddle pad.

In one swift motion Harry swung the saddle into place on Smoke's back. Without so much as a twitch she had a saddle on her back for the first time. He then dropped the rigging from its tethers on the saddle and deftly cinched it tightly in place without issue. The breast collar and flank cinch likewise were fastened in place as the mare stood calmly.

"This is called, 'Non-Event Colt Starting!'" Kathy said.

She wasn't kidding. The ease with which Smoke took her

With one fell swoop, Harry swings the saddle up onto Smoke's back for the first time.

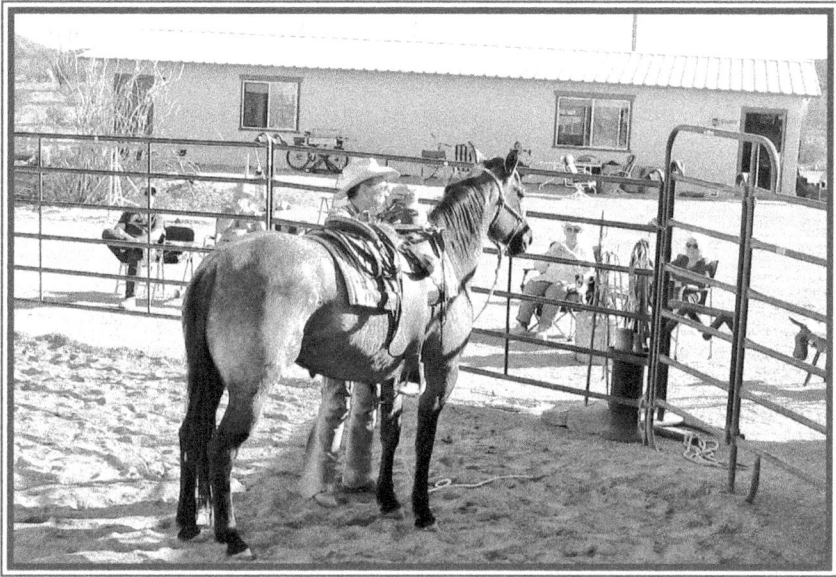

Smoke takes the saddle being placed on her back like a champ.

first saddling due to plenty of preparation was a joy to watch. If "so they're started, so they go" holds true, no doubt Smoke will go along fine with being saddled for her lifetime.

"So do you think there's a chance she's going to buck?" Harry asked as he prepared to move her around for the first time with a saddle strapped to her back.

"Yes!," came the reply from Linda and Ty and others at once.

"Here's where you take it off quick and think you were successful!" Harry said to his amusement and that of us onlookers.

While afoot, Harry used the lead rope and asked Smoke to move around a little bit. She wasn't completely relaxed, but she wasn't overly worried about the saddle either. It went well enough, so Harry climbed back onto Easy and began to pony the mare around the round pen. Soon he and Easy were working on the rigmarole with her.

"She has ill feelings about crowding her much with this other horse," Harry pointed out.

They spent some time getting that to shape up better.

"Things like that stirrup over there," Harry pointed out, "she just thought about it. That's good. At least she acknowledged that something was back there. It makes you wonder there for a little bit if she was really thinking about it."

"With this horse at what moment do you say, 'Alright now [that's good, we're done]?" someone asked.

"Remember what I said I wanted to get done here?" Harry replied. "I'm trying to help people see [multiple ways of working with colts], and if you didn't have a [saddle] horse you could have just gone ahead and worked her there [from the ground]. But what I'd probably do now—just for people to think about—is, if you didn't have a horse, if I'd've moved around on my feet and got it as good as it is right now, unsaddle her. Tomorrow—every day—it gets better, doesn't it? So, tomorrow come back and then crowd her up and she'll feel better about this. It just builds; you don't have to get it really, really good there, but if we wanted to get it better, see if we could get her feeling a little better about that, we'd turn her loose and move her around a little. She might have to make a few little bucks and so forth, but she'd get to feeling just a little better in there about that."

The session ended with Smoke having walked and trotted along side Harry and Easy. Harry dismounted, and Ty came into the pen and removed the saddle without any trouble.

There are obvious monumental moments when starting a colt—the first haltering, the first saddling as with Smoke this day, and the first ride. But every interaction with a human along the way before those moments affects the outcome of them on some level. Great attention to detail was taken with all of the colts during the clinic at all times—whether in the round pen for an official session or being led up the hill to be turned out at the end of the day—and the positive results were obvious when we got to the big thresholds.

Everything all along the way that week from how Smoke

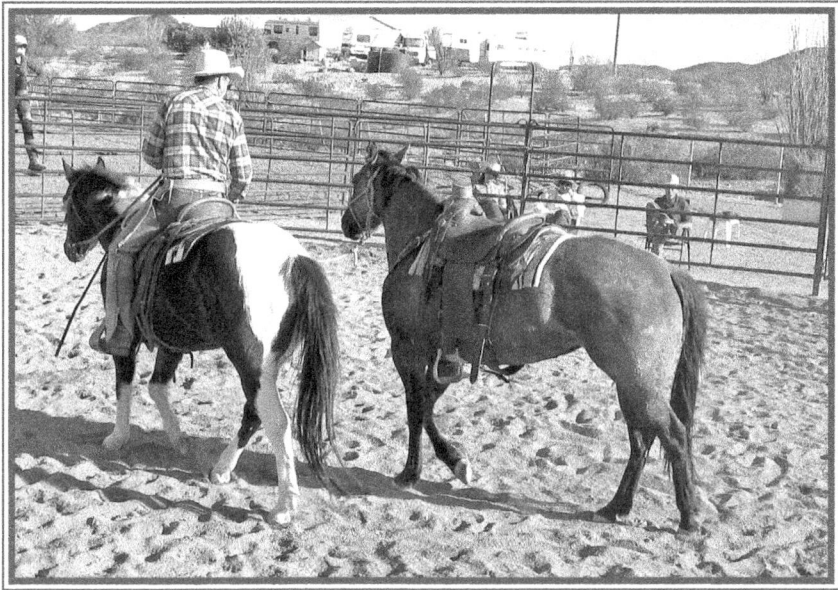

Smoke walks along side Harry and Easy following the feel on the lead rope packing a saddle for the first time.

was haltered and led to the round pen, how she was convinced to relax when doing this or that, and most importantly how she was repeatedly put into the habit of being mentally present when interacting with people contributed to the first saddling going so smoothly.

I can't help but think about the contrast of the mainstream, traditional methods of "breaking" horses like snubbing a frightened horse to a post, throwing a saddle on her, and having somebody climb onto her back without any preparation.

Nothing goes unmingled when working with these amazing creatures, certainly...and so they're started, so they go.

Chapter Nineteen

Last Horse of the Day, Day Four, Anna and Chic

Thursday, 13 February 2014

"I've got to be just as ready to let go as I am to firm up, but that's hard for people to think about sometimes, being ready to do everything in your power and yet ready to do nothing at the same instant should you need to."

Harry Whitney

The shadows stretched further across the rocky high desert ground as the day waned. The sun dipped so low in the western sky that the shipping container tack room blocked all but a small sliver of sunlight which hit the sand in the far end of the round pen when

Anna came through the gate with Chic and handed Harry the lead rope. Anna walked over to the gate and stood by watching as Harry began some ground work with the mare.

"She's really pushing forward with that shoulder and crowding me," Harry pointed out straight away. "So I'm offering here [that she move that shoulder over]."

Harry slid his hand up the lead rope and took ahold of the knot on the rope halter at the base of Chic's chin. Through his close grip on the halter, Harry began to have a conversation with the mare.

"As she runs forward, she runs into that halter," Harry said, referring to how he was presenting a certain sweet spot for her to find within his hold on the halter knot—if she pushed beyond the sweet

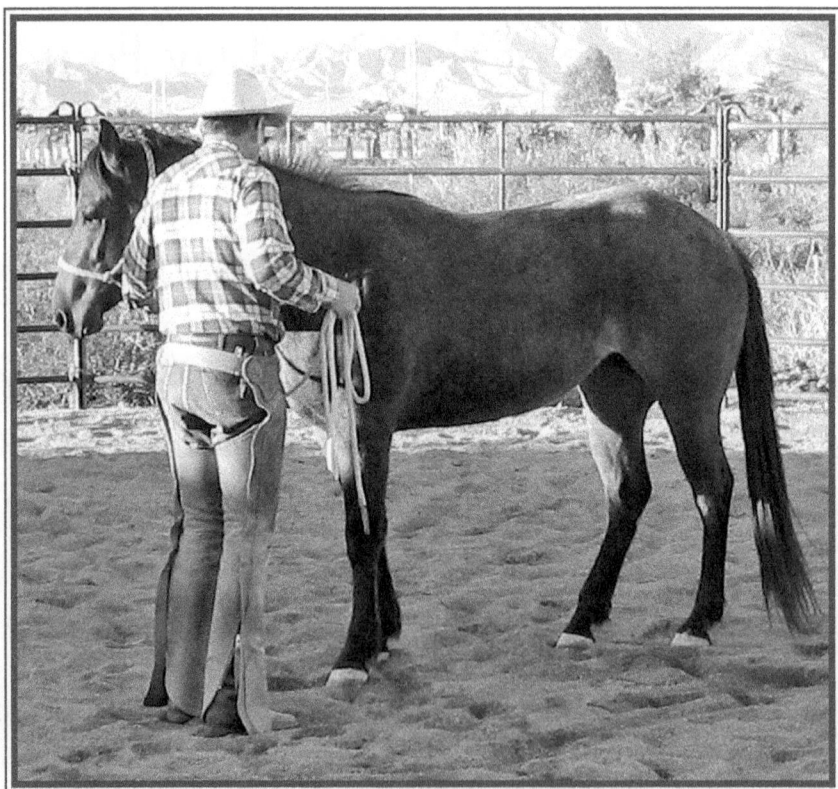

Harry prepares to ask Chic to move her shoulder over.

spot in any direction she ran into a firmness from his grip. "If she goes backwards, she runs into the halter. All she needs to do is step over a little like that, see. [Chic stepped her front end away from Harry.] Pretty soon that shoulder will step over better. [Harry kept presenting; she struggled but then stepped away from him again.] That's better. That first step [away from him]—there, that's very nice!—that's a big deal. I was letting her search a little there, see, but in a pretty confined area to find to take her thought out there."

Harry commented that earlier in the clinic Franny had asked about how he would get a young horse to work towards side passing.

"I think about that here," Harry said. "I'm asking her over there. [Harry was asking her to step over but instead she pushed straight into his grip.] It's that pushing forward that gets us in trouble there. She should feel of that halter and not push forward against it so hard, but, boy, she wants to push on that. So, all this junk [raising her head, shaking her head, tensing through her body, swishing her tail, etc.] comes in there, because there's a resistance in that. It doesn't feel good to her."

Harry asked Chic to back up.

"She's messing with her jaw," Harry observed, "and all that resistance comes in there before she can think backwards at all. To have those kind of feelings is not necessary; she doesn't know this yet. But it's my responsibility to let her know that that won't work. Getting upset about that is not going to work out."

Harry continued to ask her to back with the halter, but reserving his release for when she not only took backwards steps, but also began to think about backing and really begin to put some interest and energy into stepping in reverse.

"I've got to be just as ready to let go as I am to firm up," Harry pointed out, his hand still on the halter knot, "but that's hard for people to think about sometimes, being ready to do everything in your power and yet ready to do nothing at the same instant should you need to."

By holding the halter knot rather than the lead rope, Harry's connection to Chic was defined by a very small space, for lack of a better way of saying it. When a longer length of rope is used, many feet of distance can be involved in defining where the horse can move to explore where the person presents a sweet spot and what I might call an "imbalance," the discordance or firmness of some kind presented by a person on the rope to keep her searching.

But in this situation, there existed practically no delay in the feel between him and the mare because his hand was placed directly under her chin on the halter knot. Harry's timing between firming up and releasing had to be spot on (and was all but invisible to us onlookers) since there was not the forgiveness of any wiggle room between his hand and her. Yet even in such a small space, there was

Harry takes ahold of the halter knot as he works with Chic.

Anna and Chic get started. (Photo: Nancy Lawson)

plenty of room for Harry to have a full conversation—setting up a meaningful search—with Chic.

"She needs to stay mindful here," Harry commented as he continued. "Her mind is not here. I might stand here a minute and see what she does. She could just wait there. You see she's doing a little looking? I'm not going to criticize that. There's nothing wrong with her looking. But if I put a feel on this rope, or if I got ready to do something, she should be ready.

"Okay Anna. [Harry abruptly walked the mare towards the gate, handed Anna the lead rope, and exited the round pen.] Have fun!"

Anna didn't miss a beat when Harry sprung his tag-team-tactic on her, but we spectators were a bit surprised and had a laugh about it. Anna had been watching very intently and it seemed to me she already was thinking in her mind what she'd do with Chic next if she were Harry. Now given the chance, she began with some groundwork using more length in the lead rope than Harry had.

She led the mare to the middle of the round pen, stopped her, and got her mind centered up. Anna extended her right arm straight out in front of her with the lead rope draping from that hand to the halter and asked Chic to step her front end over.

Chic seemed to push back mentally when Anna asked her to take her thought off to one side or the other. Anna did a nice job of persisting with her ask until the mare let go of her mental backlash. This was evidenced by her eyes taking a strong look away from Anna and by her head dropping some as she relaxed when Anna released for the "right thing."

"I'd want her mind a little more centered with me before I went to mess with her feet," Harry said, intuiting where Anna was going with her ground work.

"Harry, sometimes when they push forward you just make some commotion with your chaps and let her run into the commotion," Ellen commented. "Other times, you bump the lead rope. How do you decide that?"

Anna asks Chic to think around her way with a soft feel on the lead rope. (Photo: Nancy Lawson)

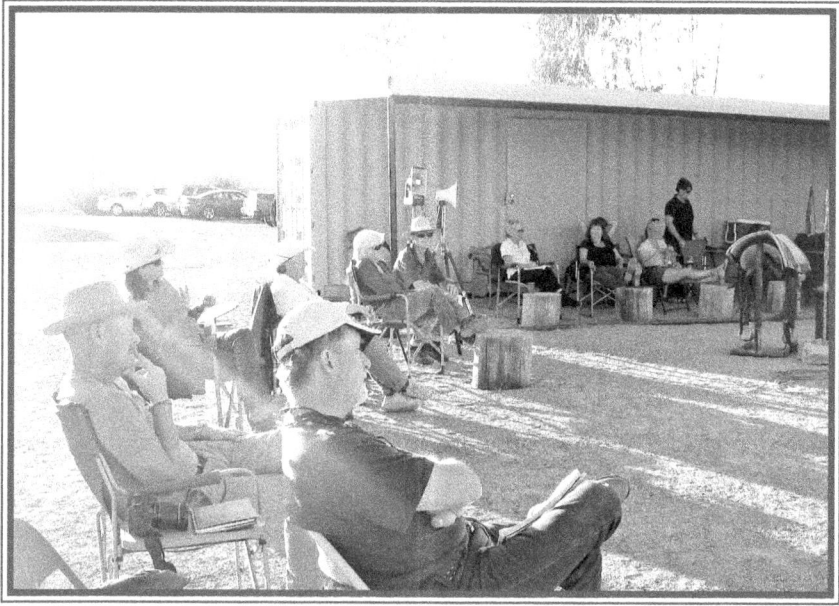

The shadows get long in the late afternoon as we die-hard auditors watch Harry and Chic in the round pen.

"Well, especially on these young ones that don't know much about backing off with the lead rope, I'll just create a commotion," Harry answered. "A horse that knows something about that—using the lead rope—then I'm apt to firm up with it."

Long periods of silence ensued as the crowd of us sitting in chairs and on stumps, standing, or perched atop panels watched Anna continue to concentrate on an array of ground work with Chic. The air cooled off, jackets came out, and the shadow from the shipping container crept to engulf the entire round pen as the sun dropped ever lower behind the tack room.

"Now just step in there and rub her on the side a little while she's moving," Harry instructed. "There you go. She'll get more confident. Let her work it out a little more, get a little more focus."

"She's really struggling to have her thought stay with Anna," Kathy said.

"Mmm hmm," Harry concurred. "I was thinking a little bit ago that it might help if we just turned her aloose and let her work it out a little more—get a little more focus."

"But that was a pretty good trip, though," Ty commented about the last circle the mare had made around Anna.

"Oh my yes!," Harry agreed.

"Carry on?" Anna asked. "Or would you like to come in?"

"No!" Harry replied. "Carry on. I was just going to say, try picking a foot up there and see what happens."

Anna stopped Chic and had her attention. Then she went over to her left shoulder, bent over, and ran her hand down the mare's leg as she asked the mare to prepare to have her foot lifted.

"Good," Harry said. "Good...good!"

"So Anna," Ty began, "did you feel any softening in her leg when he said 'good' the first time? And I guess the reason I ask is, what I saw was the head—her head stopped bouncing around and just settled. When I was out this morning, Harry had said 'good' in a few moments and I didn't quite feel everything."

"To me it felt a bit like, for her, things were really starting to feel good, and if I held on too long [to the foot] it might have gotten bad," Anna replied. "There wasn't a particular really good let-down, but there were a couple of them in a row that made me think to put the foot down...get it down while she's still got that good feeling."

"One of the reasons I say this is because if I'd have been on that foot, and if I didn't feel anything had happened to the foot, I would have completely missed what happened everywhere else in the horse," Ty said.

"Right," Harry said, understanding. "Those of you who have met Gus-the-mule [a little mule who has been a pasture mate of Harry's horses for years], he taught Anna a little something about picking up a foot—you don't present it right, it's not going to work out right. [Harry chuckled.] That's for sure.

"She was trying to pick Gus's foot up. Oh, she was having

a tussle! She asked me if I'd come up there and look at it—she was trying to pick his foot up. I said, 'Quit trying to pick his foot up!' I went over and picked his foot right up. That's one of those moments that my life expectancy was shortened for a few moments [because Anna was about to kill him!]. She'd try to pick it up and it wouldn't work, but she got to where she had a better feel of suggesting that maybe he take his weight off it and let her have that foot instead of *trying* to pick it up."

During the story, Harry continued to watch as Anna kept working on picking up Chic's feet.

"Good! Good enough!" Harry instructed. "That wasn't too bad."

"So what would you say was the major difference for what worked for picking up Gus's feet?" Ty asked.

"Not trying to pick them up," Harry reiterated. "Getting him to get his weight off from it and get ready for it to be picked up. But she was trying to pick it up—trying to get it off the ground. Well, the more determined she was to get it off the ground the more determined he got the she wasn't going to."

"Have you ever seen anyone else other than you do that, ever?" Anna asked.

The question went unanswered and hung in the air for a long moment giving it a rhetorical quality.

"See her shift her weight to get more balanced?" Harry asked. "Pretty soon she'd get herself more balanced than she did there even. And so this is another one of those spots where you put the responsibility on the horse. I see people reach up and they back the horse and step his feet around until he gets them placed just right and get it picked up quick before he moves. Well, you're doing it for them, see? Get them to take that weight off [of one]; they'll learn to get the other three positioned so they can take the weight off that foot. They know how to do these things."

Anna, with her gentle touch, ran her hand down Chic's right

front leg. The mare relaxed it fairly well, and Anna lifted the foot and looked at the bottom of the hoof.

"Just set it down," Harry said. "That's fine. She was kind of out of balance. She never did get her other three feet positioned good. So just let her have that and then start over."

"So for her right front, what would be the correct balance?" Ty asked.

"Well, the other three are really pretty good at the moment," Harry said.

As if on cue, Chic quickly shifted her feet around.

"Now they're not," he added. "You could go for it there, with that one hind foot forward and the other one back and they look pretty close together on the same line—her middle line—so they're not very wide apart. That's not very tripod-ish is it?"

"Tripod-ish?" Kathy said and laughed.

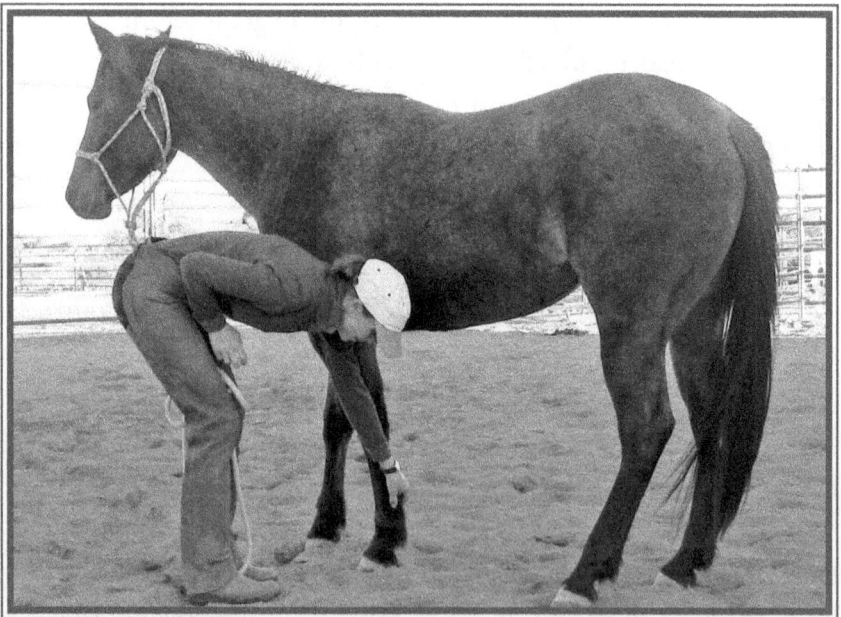

Anna slides her fingers down Chic's leg to ask her to relax it and prepare for it to be picked up.

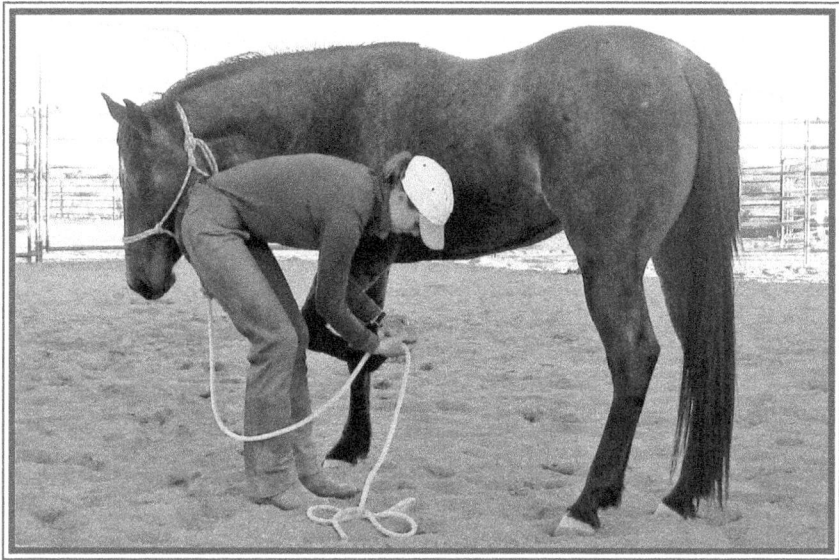

Anna picks up Chic's foot and is able to hold it and inspect it with no problem.

"You've never heard of tripod-ish?" Harry asked with feigned astonishment. "See her move that hind foot back? [Anna was again picking up the right front foot.] She got herself more balanced. Now I'd set that foot down as soon as I could. That was real good. We'll get that setting down even softer, but just the fact that she got herself more balanced and wasn't struggling, I'd be pretty happy."

Anna changed up and did a little ground work using the lead rope to ask Chic to circle around her.

"Good," Harry said. "When she stopped there her mind was pretty centered. That would have been a good time to come in and think about a foot."

"Should I play with these [front ones again] or go to the backs?" Anna inquired.

"Go," Harry said abruptly.

"Go?" Anna asked.

"Go for the backs," Harry confirmed. "You said *play* with these or *go* for the backs, so I said 'Go.'

"Now pick it up [the back foot Anna was thinking about picking up]. Just walk right on in there beside her," Harry said. "Just go right on down that back leg there [with your hand]; she's doing great. Good. Now see if she'll take her weight off from there."

Easy, who was tied to the hitching rail close by, chose this moment to vocalize.

"Earlier when Easy whinnied that had quite a meaning to her," Harry point out, "but it didn't matter much this time. There, that's all you needed."

Chic had relaxed her hind leg and Anna had gripped the leg bone just above the hoof to pick it up.

"Now you could take hold of her hoof and it would go better," Harry instructed. "When I take ahold of the hoof, I come in on the back side there so I'm not even touching any of her skin, just hoof. You can start clear up by their hip as you're coming down [with your hand]."

Anna began at Chic's hip and touching her with her hand, Anna slowly moved her hand down over the mare's hind quarter and down her leg. As Anna's hand got to about the stifle joint, the mare shifted her weight off that leg and she cocked it slightly. With the leg relaxed, Anna then reached down and, touching only the hard hoof wall, she easily lifted the foot.

"That's nice," Harry complimented. "That's real good, Anna. Now check the other side there—walk right around and check out that other hind foot. [She did and it went about the same as the first one had.] Very good. Her mind has gotten a lot more centered in the pen. You can work really hard to get their minds centered so you can do something, or you can work at doing something to help get their minds centered."

"Is that good enough for today?" Anna asked.

"Oh yeah," Harry said. "Anna could lay the lead rope on the ground there probably and pick that foot up. [Anna did so.] Now just pet that leg a bunch there—just rub up and down it. Now pick it back up and set it on your knee and then get to petting on it. Petting right in there; get to petting. There you go—[lift the foot] a little higher; let it come down a little, a little higher, take it back further, bring it forward further, all those things, see. That's real good. Now set that foot down and get out of there—what are you waiting on [Harry added with deliberate over-zealousness]!"

"Are you happy, Philly?" Harry asked.

"Oh, so much," she replied.

"Okay, you can put her up; Philly's happy," Harry said.

It was 10 minutes to 6:00 p.m. when Anna wrapped things up with Chic which concluded the horse work for day four. The smell of supper cooking wafted out of the bunkhouse. Then the evening ritual began.

A team of us haltered the colts and collected them in the driveway from wherever they were. Harry took Easy over by the tack room and removed his saddle. Soon, the crew of helpers—some walking, some sitting in the Kawasaki Mule holding lead ropes while Harry drove—led the colts and Easy up the hill to turn them out in their pasture. We fed hay, filled waterers, mucked out stalls, hauled bales of hay around on the Kawasaki Mule, and eventually gravitated back to the bunkhouse for supper...and more discussion.

Chapter Twenty

Evening Discussion, Day Four

Thursday, 13 February 2014

*"If we see no purpose in going,
they see no purpose in going. If it's
important to you, pretty soon they begin
to realize this is important."*

Harry Whitney

"So...interesting day, huh?" Harry said after supper as his way to launch the evening discussion. "Kind of fun that Smoke took her first saddling like she did. It was just apparent to me that she was not troubled about what was taking place—might as well go ahead and expose her to that. And I'm glad I went ahead and did it today because we're just that much further for tomorrow.

"We could have gotten some of the others there sooner—and I know you guys know all this, but it just keeps coming back to me that I want to take the time to let you guys see things as they unfold and talk about them, and hit on so many different things. We'd like to expose some of the other horses maybe to the whip and to swinging a rope and hobbling and picking up feet—but I'm not sure we're going to get all of them done on everything that's available. There is a lot of stuff you can do on a young horse that needs done at some point, so how much time could we spend with a handful of horses like this? Six weeks?"

"Easy!" someone in the group exclaimed.

"I was really having a hard time with Smoke," Franny said right away, "seeing what you were describing when she went with a thought forward. Can you describe the difference between what you were feeling when she wasn't [going forward with a thought] and what you were feeling when she just freed up and went?"

"On Smoke?" Harry asked.

"It was before you saddled her," someone commented.

"Oh, with her loose! I'm with you now, Franny. So you were having a hard time seeing...." Harry's sentence trailed off.

"Seeing when she started going forward," Franny interjected. "My understanding is there was a hold-back in her that I couldn't see. And then she would free up and go, and I couldn't see that."

"There was a tightness clear through her," Harry explained. "Her way of moving changed a little. More than the actual physical movement to me was the way she was feeling about it. There was a change in her expression. So when you put the two together, what you can see in the movement and the change of the expression, and you know that she had a better thought about it. Was it a huge change? Maybe not. But there was a change."

"Was there a feel to it?" someone asked. "Was there all of a sudden a drag that let go or something?"

"When she was trotting there," Harry continued, "even

within the trot, there's a feeling that if you pushed just a little more she would have just stepped into the canter, where right before that you felt like, unh, unh, unh [Harry repeatedly made a grunting noise]."

Franny shot Harry a look that seemed to say, "Have you lost it?" The group busted into a roar of laughter, including Harry.

"You don't know what 'unh, unh, unh' means?" Harry asked Franny, frowning, followed by a cackle. Then he recovered and continued, "That you really had to crowd her hard. There wasn't a freedom to flow into it and you'd really have to keep, keep, keep pushing on her to get her into that lope."

"Because she would just come down?" Franny asked.

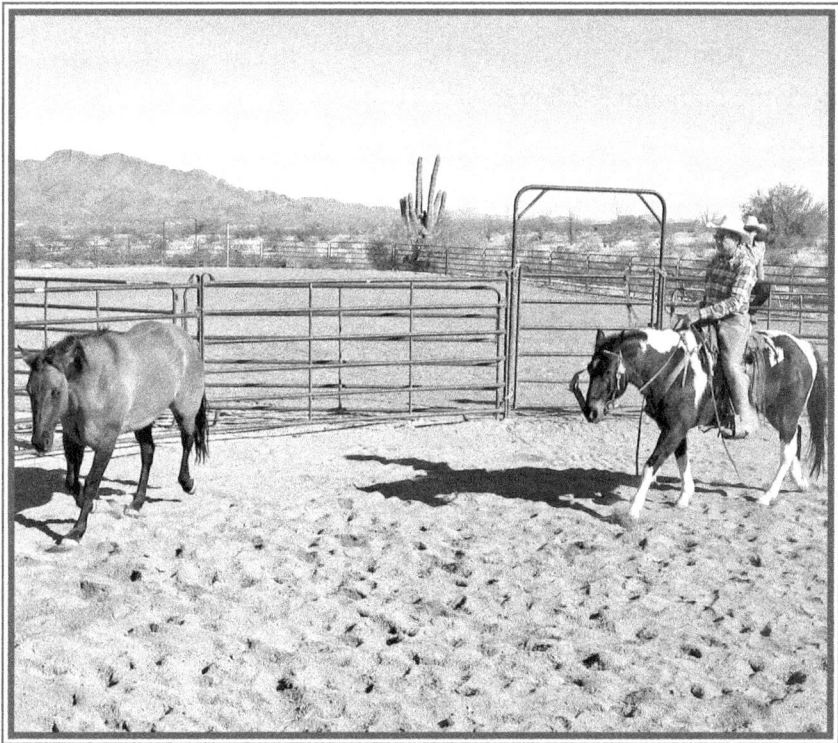

Harry working Smoke at liberty from Easy before her first saddling on day four.

"She was holding back," Harry replied. "But then when she freed up, you felt like if you did just a little more she'd go ahead and make that transition. Now I won't say that she would necessarily feel good when she made the transition yet, but she could have gotten there without it being that 'unh.' Some of that's not real easy to explain, what you're seeing there, but there's just a little freedom, a little surge forward, a little less of a snarky expression."

"If you don't see it, you missed it," Franny said matter-of-factly, causing the crowd to laugh again. "You know what I mean. That is a valuable thing to see."

"And that mare, I believe," Harry continued, "if you didn't handle it right, that mare could get more stuck and more stuck—grumpier and grumpier may even be a better word. She would get snarkier about having to go."

"And she'll get to feeling better about the going if you just block the not going?" Ellen asked. "Is that what helps her feel better?"

"Well, you just hang in there," Harry replied. "It's like I talk about my flies. [Harry explains sometimes that instead of training horses if he could just train flies he could then get a horse to let go of holding back and do anything he wanted.] You'll see a bunch of flies get a horse plum aggravated. And yet if they handled it right, that horse—he would think he was the smartest thing on the planet because he got ahead of those flies to be somewhere else. It would be his idea to go over underneath that tree instead of this tree."

"And how important is it, if she frees up to go forward, that you let her come right back down?" Ellen asked.

"Oh, not necessarily right back down," Harry answered. "And you don't want to let her come down too fast too hard. There was one time I let her there, on horseback, come down harder than I should have and I knew it. You want to be careful in there because even though they free up and go, if you let them slap on the brakes to stop a couple, three times then in the middle of trying to get the up-transition, they're in hopes that the next stride is the one that you're out of the way and they can slap on the brakes.

"So now you're pushing to get them to go up and they're holding back in hopes to slap on the brakes. You've got them holding back by having let them just crash. So once or twice you might say 'Thank you!' and let them come down to a trot or walk and then take them back up—and down and up—and then let them stop. Build that in so that they don't think that just because they loped three strides pretty soon they're getting ready to slap on the brakes."

"So the holding back doesn't feel good to the horse?" Kathy asked. "I don't see a horse cantering out in the pasture without thoughts forward, freely moving...."

"That's right," Harry replied, "because his thought is taking him. I keep talking about that. If their thoughts are not taking them then we're making them go, so they go with an ill feeling. They're being pushed into it."

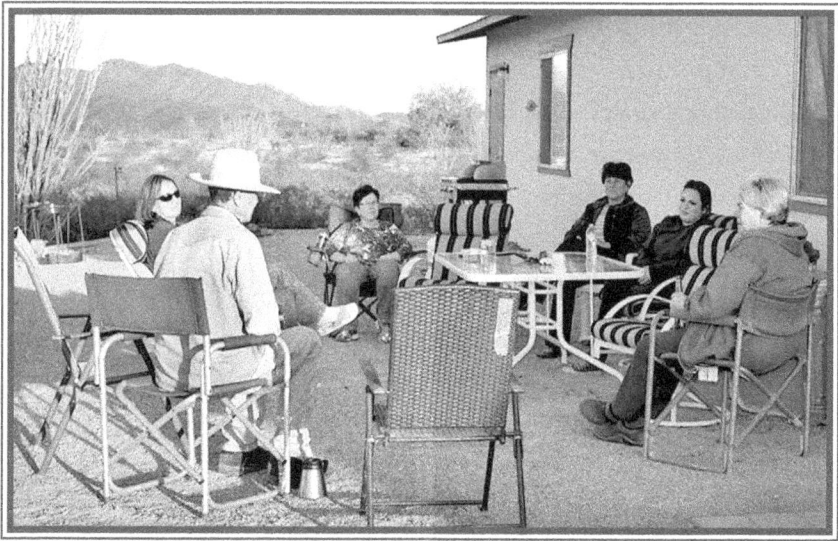

Auditors Tim Thomas, Lauren Gruber, Janice Guntner, Marcy Johnson, Danielle Gruber, and Frannie Burrridge take a few minutes to relax and visit before dinner. (Photo: Nancy Lawson)

"Two of the mares you mentioned, they just didn't like going," Lauren said. "They didn't like you suggesting that they go? But I'm sure out in the field they go, right? Just as Kathy said."

"Yes," Harry answered, "and yet you will see horses, and the whole group will want to go and here comes one loping along behind with his ears penned just mad because he has to keep up and as soon as he can he just slams on the brakes and then ambles up to catch up with the group. They don't even free up out in the field. They don't want to put out that effort out there even."

"So," Lauren followed-up, "how do you help a horse like that enjoy going? Because I see some horses enjoy going."

"It's way more difficult," Harry said. "You've got to really think about getting that mind to free up and go. But you're still striving for the same thing. You're wanting their minds to take them and feel good about it. And that's not an easy thing to get."

"So if you cantered him down to the end of the arena and got off of him?" Kathy asked, wondering about making a destination in the arena a sweet spot for the horse.

"Absolutely," Harry replied. "If you work at that, pretty soon those ears start to come up and they start to look out there with an interest and take you somewhere."

"So the one thing I noticed, Harry, with your horses," Kathy said, "they always have a look of interest on their faces, like they were involved in the process of whatever you're doing. They never were glazed-over, checked-out, looking out...it just seemed like they were involved in the process of what was taking place. They have nice expressions. So you think about going around in a round pen—boring, boring, boring—but it's not boring for them."

"I've met a lot of horses that people said didn't like the arena," Harry replied. "You take them out on a trail ride and their ears are up and they're going with interest, but in the arena, they just shut down—and I take them to the arena or round pen and in a little bit have got them freeing up and going with a little bit of interest."

Harry "hat breaks" Bailey during week one. (Photo: Nancy Lawson)

Harry explained that outside of the round pen or arena there often are features in the environment that help to get a horse's focus and get him moving out. Inside the insular setting of a corral, however, it can require something extra to establish that interest in a horse. One can construct that kind of interest in the corral by finding it in oneself, Harry says, (this may require some imagination) and then transferring the feel of it to the horse. Harry has the knack for getting this accomplished, but admittedly he struggles with how to help others bring that kind of purpose to riding in less exciting environments.

"But again, to me it's about sending that thought out there," Harry explains. "If that thought goes, they look like they have an interest in going. Yet part of that is us having a purpose. If we see no purpose in going, they see no purpose in going. If it's important to you, pretty soon they begin to realize this is important."

Harry tipped his head towards me sitting to his left and raised an eyebrow. That was all it took for the crowd to start laughing again, anticipating an instructive story involving some of my equine shenanigans was about to begin.

"I started to say, I hear people all the time...but here sits one," Harry said. "And I'll tell the story for him because I might embellish it in important areas that will make it more effective!"

"I'm recording it," I said, indicating that I'd have evidence if he got wayward in telling the facts.

"He was out on the mare that he used to have [Sokeri] that was sticky about going out. Well, he heard a calf bawling and he finally got the mare to take him over there where he could see over the fence. And here's four legs sticking up—the mother is dead. No wonder the calf's bawling; he's hungry. So, Tom rode to the neighbor's to tell them. After he got there he realized the mare just went. Well, what was the difference? The difference was in Tom, not what the mare knew."

"She saw the cow and knew it was important!" I said to an explosion of laughter. "It was clear to everyone involved—all two of us."

"But I hear story after story like that," Harry said. "Some people in Arizona—somebody fell off and bumped his head, and they ended up getting a helicopter, but the one person rode for help, and normally she couldn't leave the group and get away from the other horses but the horse just went. She realized later that she didn't even think about it at the moment but later she said the horse was no trouble to get to leave the group and go. Well, the intent is in us. I see people ride around in the arena, in the round pen, with no purpose and no intent to get something done—to go somewhere. 'Oh, we're going to make another circle,' [Harry says pretending to be the rider]. 'Yeah, I know...' [Harry then answers with drudgery in his voice as the horse]. But how do you put that in people? Every step is just as important to me as if there was someone in trouble that I needed to get help for."

This discussion was a good one for me because I come across many horses that have a problem going freely forward—and often that means I, or someone I am working with, has problems getting our intent lined out and presented to a horse. The story Harry shared about Sokeri and me is true. I told it to him just after the events took place because I was amazed that not only did the mare go, but that I didn't notice she'd quit not going until we were at our important destination. My mind was focused on the critical matter of what needed to happen right then and not on all the little technical details of trying to get Sokeri more forward that I'd been diddling with for weeks.

When Franny asked Harry what it felt like when the mare freed up and went forward, I understood her inquiry. What does it feel like? How do we precipitate such a change on a horse?

Sometimes I'm certain that Harry is here on earth in this horse business by Divine design as an example to others to show

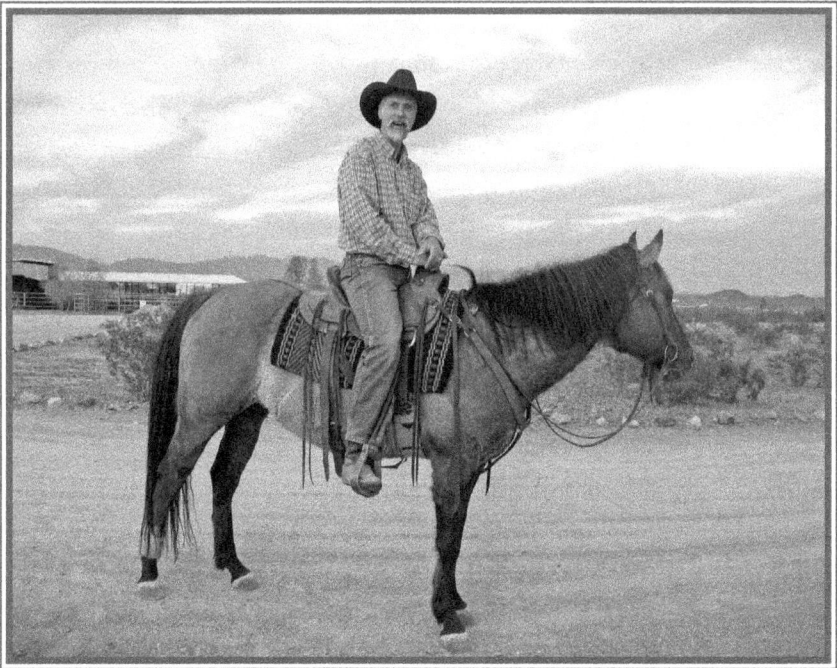

Tom Moates riding Alex on Friday evening of the first week. Alex was a gelding who was traveling with auditor Ginna Ciszek. (Photo: Ginna Ciszek)

what can be achieved through horsemanship so that they might seek to achieve a kind of horsemanship that is truly helpful to the health and welfare of the horse. Were it not for my witnessing his abilities with horses, I might consider these things impossible—or simply not consider them at all—and go about shopping for a harsher bit to accomplish what I want to get done with a horse.

Perhaps what I like most about this discussion is that it shows the great gulf between what is visible/tangible and what is experiential between human and horse and thus cannot be taught per se. Harry has difficulty sharing how folks might bring interest and importance to tasks in the round pen because there isn't a way to download such information into another human's brain. As a teacher, he does a great job of drawing a road map of sorts—this is how a horse looks who isn't forward, this is why outside the arena has a different effect on a horse than inside, here is an example of how Tom found a moment of forwardness in his mare, etc. But ultimately Harry cannot explain what it feels like or just what it is that he projects to a horse in the round pen that makes the horse feel an urgency to get forward *with him*. That is, with him and not fleeing from him. It is, after all, all too easy to get a horse fleeing forward.

And, as a final note, since it was Smoke who instigated this conversation, it brings to light that a colt who has not been worked with much can have a propensity to hold back and it isn't always the human training that creates the entire problem. If we see such a reluctance to go forward in a colt, as Harry said, if not handled right from these early training interactions with humans a horse can get worse and worse about it—snarkier and snarkier. What a great opportunity it was to share in and learn from such moments as this, and to then realize we weren't even half way through the two weeks of clinic!

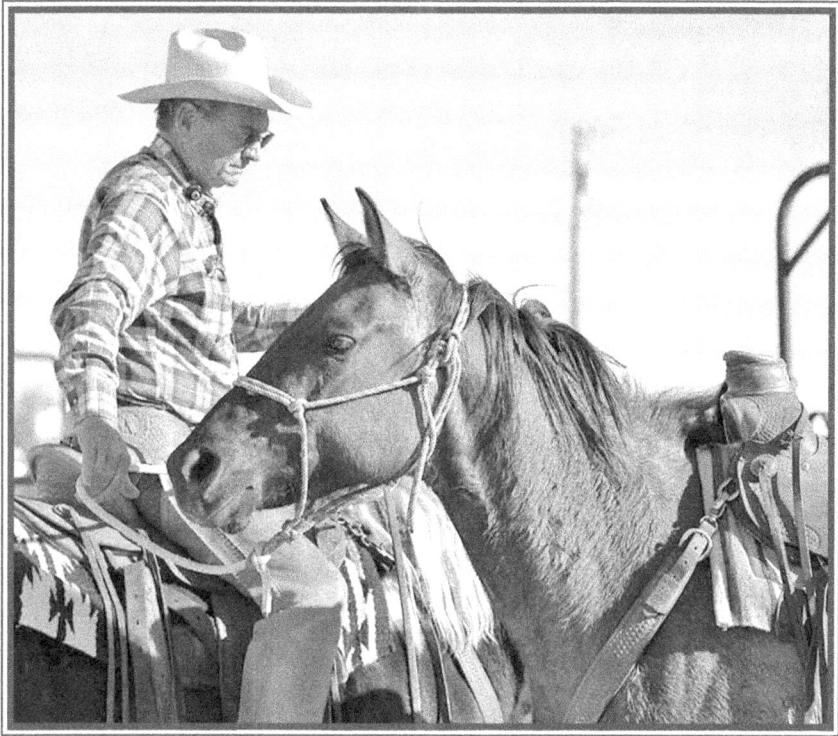

During her first saddling earlier in the day, Smoke follows Harry's feel forward on the line.

Chapter Twenty-One

Day Five, Morning, First Horse,
Sky Gets Wound Up
(or, What's a Numnah?)
Friday, 14 February 2014

"You have to be careful in a case like this where she had that little flee deal...I don't want to tip her back into that, and yet, I don't want to have to be so careful here that I can't get much done."
Harry Whitney

Day five began for me as the others had. I woke very early, spent some time writing quietly in the bunkhouse, started fires out by the round pen in two of the woodstoves, visited with Anna when she got up to run the sprinklers in the dark, and watched the sunrise over the desert as a crowd congregated by the fires for a morning devotional outside before breakfast.

The sunrise began in the distance as a slight glow, existing elsewhere (way over there) across the vast expanse of high desert. Soon, it traveled across the land and arrived to be with us. The sunlight flooded our spot by the round pen in an amazing orange glow that warmed and surrounded us as if its radiance emanated from right there in our midst.

Already, I sensed our time together in Arizona was slipping by. That is the way with the busy rhythms of a long clinic. It begins, and then there is a sort of time warp with breakfast, horses, supper, discussions, breakfast, horses...then rather suddenly, the final day

The moon rivals the mercury vapor light for the brightest orb at the mare motel. It is well before daybreak and already preparations begin for the final day of the first week of the clinic.

Ty Haas warms up by the fire before leading the daily devotional which was offered each morning for folks who were interested. (Photo: Nancy Lawson)

arrives and the clinic ends. In retrospect, it all seems like a time capsule that doesn't abide by the normal laws of the universe.

I considered the clinic being nearly half over and was grateful to have another week to watch the progress of these colts with Harry, Anna, and Ty. So many great steps forward had been made in their training, but at the same time there was so much left to be done with them. I longed to absorb every bit of Harry's approach to get them each under saddle and going great. Already, I was wishing I could watch Harry take this bunch of youngsters through another couple months of progress.

The first horse on the final day of the first week was four-year-old Sky. Harry began the session by entering the round pen with a lariat. Daylight was then fully-fledged and the sun was in its position high overhead. The mare was loose in the round pen, and I tried to nail down in my mind just what color she was. From a distance, her grayish tone prevailed—a gray roan. Up close, as I watched her from my perch atop a panel, the sunlight struck her coat revealing reddish highlights on her nose and along the backs of her hind quarters—a red roan, at least in part.

Harry built a large loop and nonchalantly flipped it all around himself. Sky quickly sized up Harry and the lariat and expressed her opinion of them both by taking off for a romp around the pen.

"It still worries her for me to play with that rope," Harry said. "Not near what it was the other day, but it's still a concern or she could have just waited there or come over instead of blasting off in the first place."

Harry walked around dragging the end of the loop on the ground. Sky followed nicely behind him. The clinician then flung the loop around over his head, launched it, and it landed perfectly over the mare's butt. She took this new arrangement more-or-less in stride, moving around just a little and holding her head high with tension, but then settling to a stop with the rope draped over and around her backside.

Harry fiddled with it for a few moments, exploring the extent to which it might bother her. When he was satisfied she was more relaxed about it than at first, he removed the loop and continued walking around the pen, flinging the rope about with deliberate carelessness. Sky readily followed him. He stopped, turned towards her, threw the loop, and again roped her hind end.

This time as Harry drew in some slack, the loop tightened around her croup until it was about the size of a dinner plate, at which point it fell from her butt to her side opposite Harry and hung there against her ribs like a noose. Harry pulled it across her back towards him until it slipped over her spine and fell to the ground. In a swift motion, he again tossed it across her back. The loop went over her shoulders, landed on the ground by her right foot, and at that very second she happened to pick up that foot and step into it.

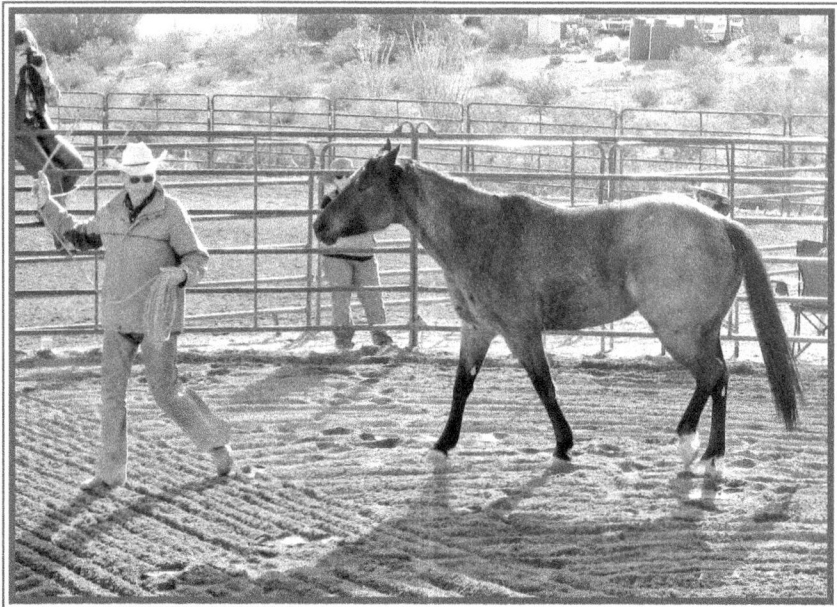

Harry swings a loop around carelessly as Sky follows.

"That loop won't pull tight enough to tighten around her foot," Harry explained as she stepped free from the loop due to a knot he had tied in the lariat which acted as a stop so it would only cinch so tight, "or, I could have snagged her foot and impressed you guys with how slick I did that. Yep...do it all the time! [Harry put on what I might call a swashbuckler's voice.] Missed twice in my life."

Harry's feigned big-shot-ness sparked a round of laughter.

I was especially interested in this session so far because of Harry's use of the unfolding scenarios between Sky and him to

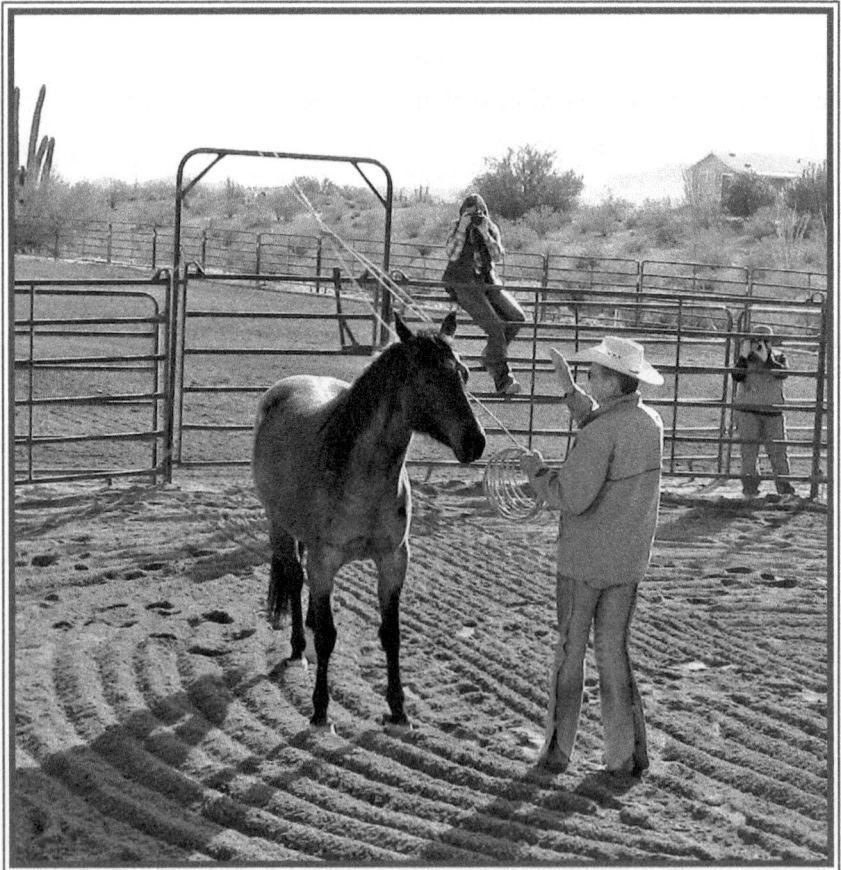

Harry tosses the loop over Sky's rear end.

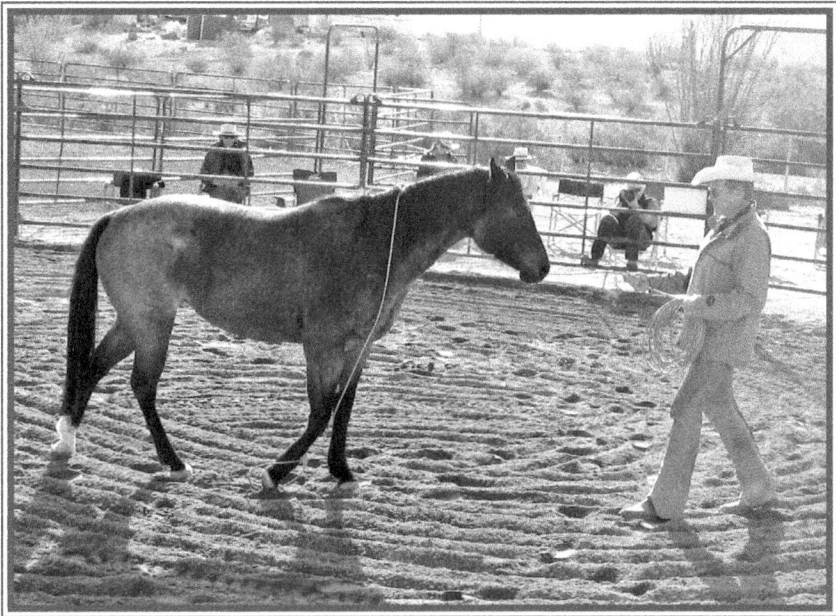

Harry skillfully (that is, inadvertently) ropes Sky's front right foot.

explore where she was or wasn't okay with the rope or things in general. Clearly, we were not witnessing a 27 point check of pre-decided tests to be done with each colt as if they were used vehicles going onto a pre-owned car lot. There was ad-libbing going on here, and it again stressed how each individual horse is different and how many varied situations can be used to ferret out spots where a horse needs some help.

"I was in a place that had some pretty flighty Paso Finos," Harry began a story. "We were playing with a hoola hoop a little bit. The owner takes the hoola hoop with this real sensitive mare. As soon as he got where he could touch her with it, he rubbed right up her face and let it slip over her head. She went to turn away, so he just hung on. Well, of course that panicked her even more and it pulled the hoola hoop from a circle to kind of an oval. That mare took off as panicked and desperate as you ever saw a horse. Leaping in the air, she could have cleared this fence trying to get through that hoop.

"I run and grab my rope, run out there in their little arena, and I threw a loop out there. Man, I threw a pretty loop and she was just running right into it. I was so anxious to get her stopped, I jerked my slack because everything was perfect and it pulled across right there [he pointed at Sky's forehead]. If I'd waited another instant it wouldn't have [and would have been around her neck]. The rope slid down her face.

"She was so traumatized, her nostrils were so flared, and her little chin was so tight that it stuck right there [Harry indicated on Sky that he meant around her snoot just above the nostrils]. So I held up and just took off running around her and bent her nose around and got her stopped and walked up to her, petted her, and slipped that rope over her head.

"When it was all over, he [the owner] says, 'I've never seen anybody rope a horse like that!'

"I said, 'Neither have I!' Dumb me, I should have said, 'Oh yeah, I do it all the time!'"

We enjoyed another hearty laugh. While telling the story, he had kept an eye on Sky. Now he moved the rope around a little and occasionally approached her, reached out, and petted her face.

"She still had to go when I first came in, but a big change there," Harry said. "She feels a lot different about it. It would be real nice if one day we could walk in with that rope in our hand and swing it a little and she'd just drop her head and walk over to us instead of getting so worried. I wouldn't have to do much here to wreck this, but I can still do more than I did the other day without wrecking it. But even right here, it wouldn't take much. If I just crowded her an ounce she'd be gone. So, I could bring out some flee pretty quick there."

"How do you balance that with telling them to not be so fearful?" Ellen asked. "You have to be careful...[her voice trailed off as she waited for Harry to complete the thought]."

"You have to be careful in a case like this where she had that little flee deal," Harry answered. "Well, I don't want to tip her back into that, and yet, I don't want to have to be so careful here that I can't get much done."

"What do you call it...careless with...?" Kathy asked.

Harry focuses on answering a question in the round pen during week one. (Photo: Nancy Lawson)

"Careless with caution," Harry answered.

Harry walked another trip around the pen swinging a loop here and there as he went. Then he stopped and threw a loop over her hind end again.

"Good, she didn't get near as troubled over that one," he said.

Harry reeled in the rope and then slipped a small loop over Sky's head again and began playing with some ground work. The mare got a little worried and spun away from Harry. She spun a quick counter-clockwise 360 and stopped facing Harry with the rope now draped around her hind quarters.

At this stage with some slack in the rope Sky stood relaxed, but then Harry put some firmness on the line to see if she could search things out to unwind herself. The horse hit flee mode and

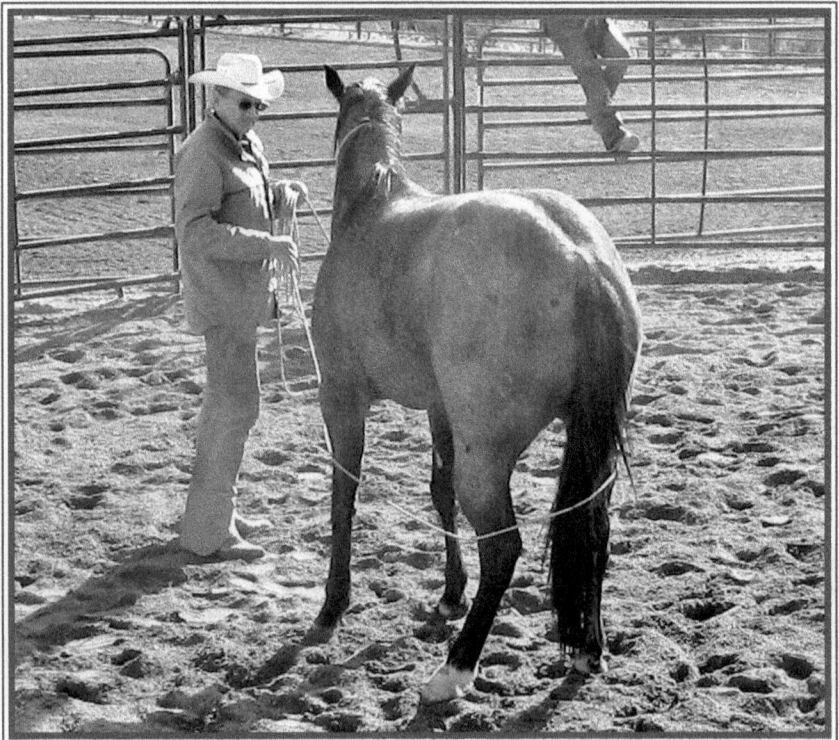

Sky is wound up in the lariat but relaxed at this point, facing Harry.

took off like a bullet in a small counter-clockwise circle around Harry. The clinician managed the rope that was still running from her neck along her side opposite him and around her hind end. He kept a firm feel on the lariat to keep her searching for a fix for this predicament. She went bigger. Harry fed out a few coils as she ran a larger circle out close to the rail of the round pen.

"She might make it around to unwind that pretty soon," Harry said. "And it doesn't matter if or when, see? This right here [Harry indicated the tail of the rope that he held], I could undo it

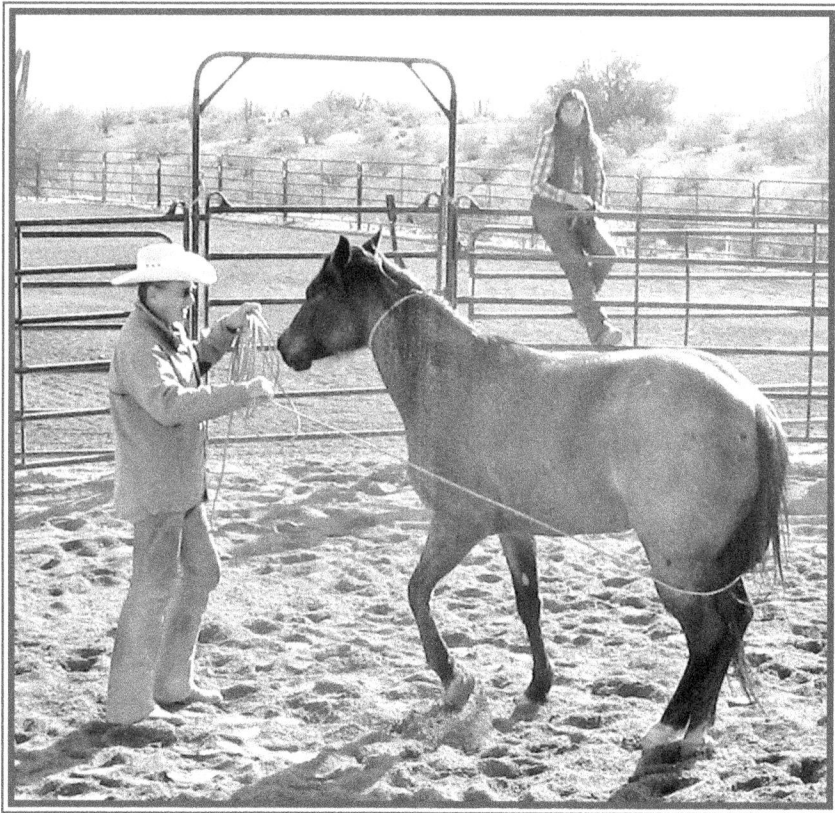

Harry puts a feel on the line to see if Sky can search out how to unwind herself, but she turns in the opposite direction causing more tension to come in the line between her and Harry.

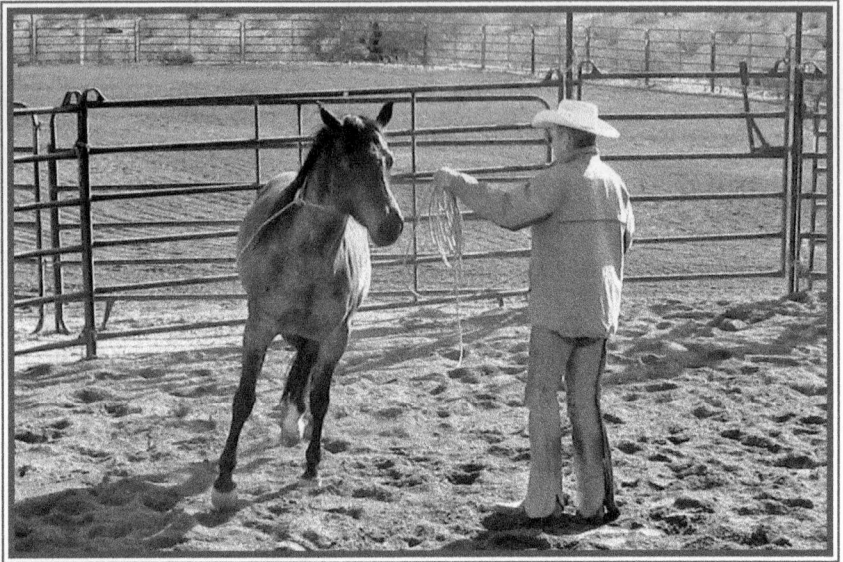

Things with Sky get a little panicked but Harry remains the eye of the hurricane.

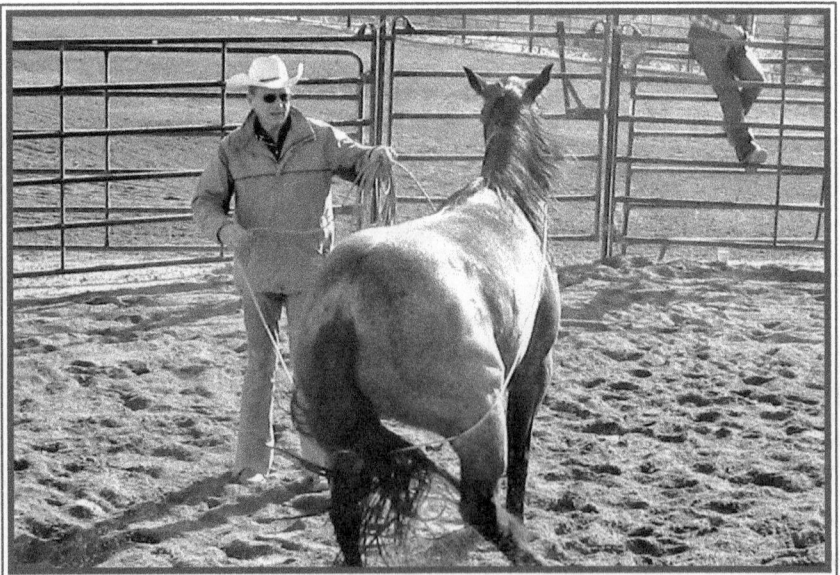

Sky takes off in flee mode around Harry, still wrapped up in the lariat.

and quit. She doesn't have to turn around there—we could get that working later. But, that's not the direction she likes to turn, so it's something she doesn't think about."

In other words, turning clockwise which would unwind her wasn't on her list of options because, as Harry pointed out, she doesn't like to turn to the right, so she simply doesn't. Harry, kept a firm feeling on the line which kept her searching. Soon, Sky quit running around and changed her approach by slowing and then stopping and facing Harry. Even at a standstill it was easy to see the mare struggling quite a bit with the rope still wound once around her. Then she finally thought about it and turned around in the direction she did not favor and unwound herself and stood quietly beside Harry.

"I love it!"

"That was lovely!"

"Oh my gosh," came the comments from the crowd all at once as Sky worked out the answer to her dilemma.

"Whenever she looked to her right you gave her a little release until she searched that out?" someone asked.

"Yes," Harry confirmed. "There's a spot a lot of people would have kind of panicked when all that broke loose."

The crowd burst into laughter at Harry's use of "a lot of people."

"I didn't say some of *you*," Harry responded, causing a jolly crescendo.

"It's another one of those spots," Harry said. "I didn't set that up, but her turning around there got that set up. Well, she had to think her way through that. No different than when I cracked the whip, when I swung the rope, she had to think her way through that, so a great, great opportunity in there. But, I wouldn't intentionally go around trying to get that set up. It set itself up, so we just took advantage of it."

Anna asked why the situation that had just been resolved with the rope all around and behind her didn't provoke the same level of rushiness she showed earlier in the session when Harry had just brought out the rope.

"Well, this is different," Harry commented. "She wasn't getting away from me [like she had at first]. So, that was a different deal. And, she recovered [from getting wound up in the rope]. It took her awhile, yes, but she recovered."

"I keep thinking what you said, Harry, about their biggest detriment can be their biggest asset," Linda said. "Then envisioning her down the road using that mind. Wow!"

"Yeah," Harry responded.

Linda's comment certainly sums up much of what we observed with Sky in this session. Early on, she was taking in everything and reacting big to many things. But, as Harry worked with her, she was able to let more and more of the buggers around

Harry provides a sweet spot as Sky relaxes even though she isn't yet fully unwound.

her go so she could be more with him. That led to an improvement both in how she responded to Harry's requests and her own ability to relax—but with that came the ability to then turn her sharp mind on searching out an answer to being wound up in the rope. Her active mind, as Linda inferred, was both her biggest hurdle and greatest asset in this situation.

Sky getting herself wrapped in the rope, Harry's cool, calm, collected response to that, and allowing Sky to use her quite active mind to get herself out of the predicament was similar to the situation that occurred with Bailey that was discussed back in Chapter 13. Bailey had been much more wound up—she had made two or three revolutions and had been in quite a pickle. Sky had made only a single round, but that one bit of rope across her hind legs was all it took to bring up some life-size panic in her. As Harry said, he could have lifted the rope clear off her hind end to released her from the grip of fear and been done with it, but it turned out to be another golden opportunity for me to consider an alternative to that natural instinct in people (in me) to get the horse safely unwound rather than let her figure out how to unwind herself.

By unwinding herself and getting free, the horse grew in understanding many times beyond what she might have if Harry had taken care of the issue for her. By realizing that she had the power to sort out a mess that involved a human and a rope for herself, her confidence was able to grow in that department. Hopefully in the future she will be less inclined to panic in such a situation.

As a side note to this happy ending, even though working through trouble spots can be of huge benefit to a horse, I think it is super important that Harry stressed he does not get a horse into deep trouble on purpose. Having a colt wrapped up in a rope, or some similarly bad scenario, certainly is a potentially dangerous situation and, among others, can have the unfavorable outcome of a horse sensing that we put them into that predicament. That can work against building trust with the horse.

However, if the horse gets herself into trouble, it may be worth letting her search out the answer if the situation allows. And, to reflect on another aspect of Bailey's earlier incident as I mentioned in that chapter, I believe as badly wound up as she was, any attempt at that moment to unwind her may only have served to intensify her worry and panic and really caused a wreck.

This session with Sky provided fabulous learning experiences for me to think about the balance of letting a horse search at something versus fixing a problem for her. By watching Harry work

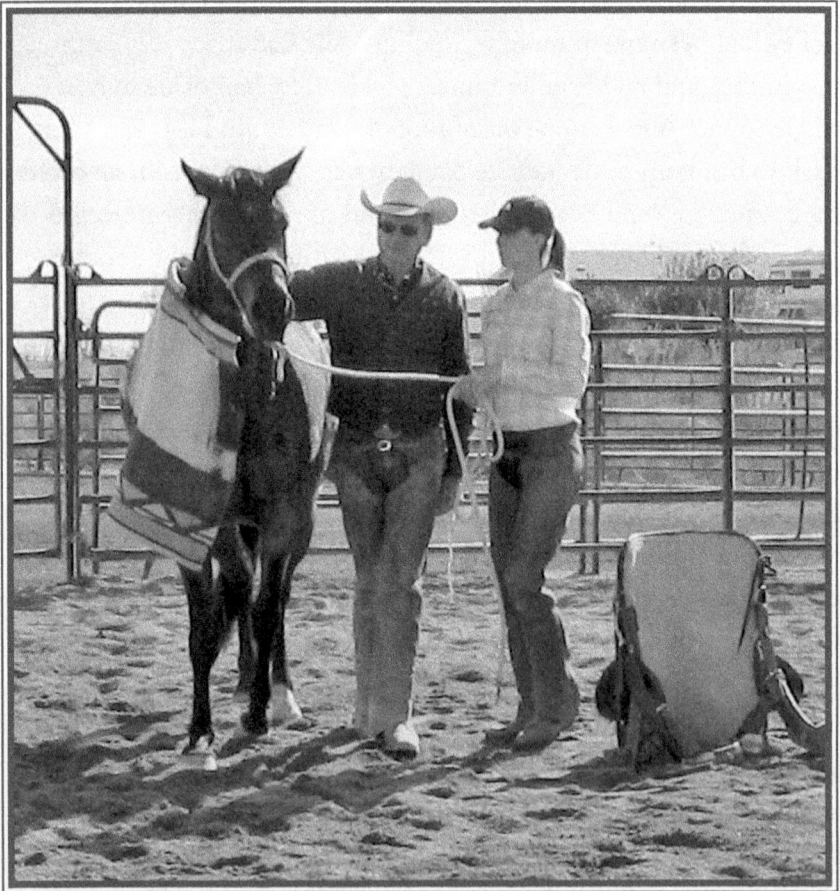

Harry and Anna work side by side getting Sky okay with the numnah*. (*See the afterword to this chapter for more on the numnah.)

With Sky now saddled, Anna proceeds with a little ground work to see how she does.

in this way, I definitely have become more inclined to let horses work at sorting out matters than I was before.

Towards the end of the session, Harry again placed a large loop around Sky's hind end. He took a hold on the rope where the honda was on her back which was roughly where the cantle of a saddle would be. He put some pressure on the rope which draped across her hind legs and then asked with the halter rope for her to back. She did and he released. After another few repeats of this there was no need to support his request with the halter rope, and he was able to put some firmness on the butt rope and Sky was very willing to back up. This was a matter of adding some meaning to the rope by using it to request something of the horse increasing her need to search and think about what was happening rather than just reacting to it and panicking.

To round out the session, Anna entered the round pen, tacked Sky up in a saddle pad, and did a little ground work. She removed the saddle pad and then worked in the girth area by wrapping the lead rope around her barrel. This all went great, so she saddled the mare up with Harry's treeless saddle. After a little more groundwork without issue, Anna mounted up and rode Sky around. It all looked relaxed and great and was a very nice end to a session which had begun with the horse showing plenty of flee and concern.

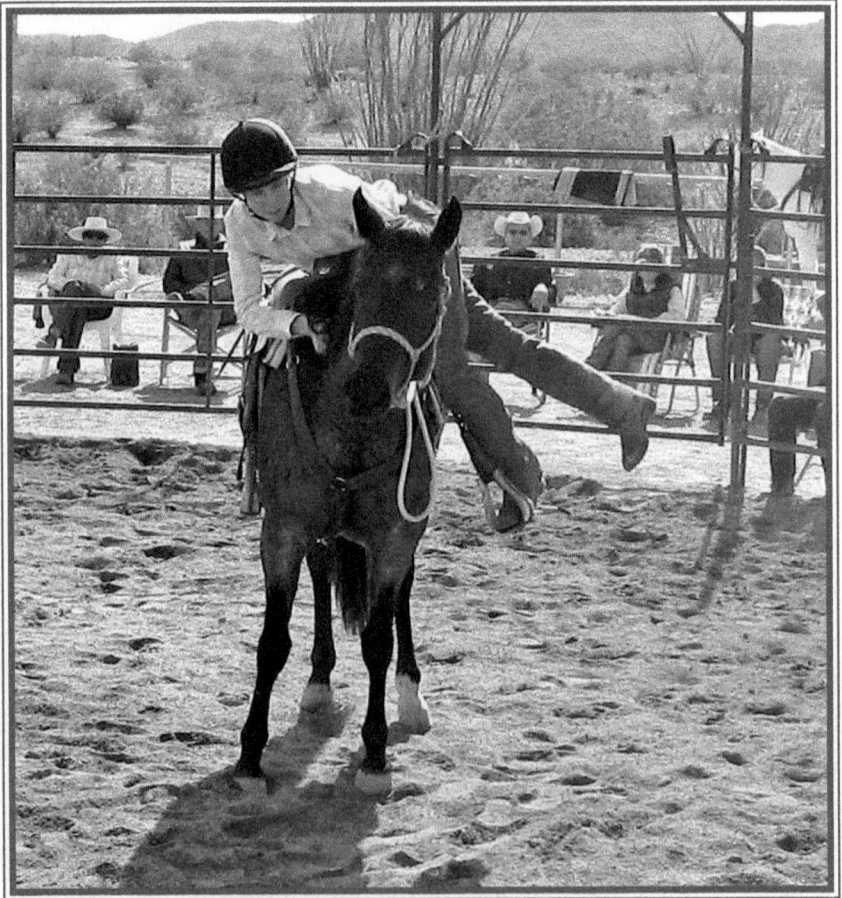

Anna goes to the sack-of-potatoes position and takes her time rubbing Sky to see how she is feeling about having her up there.

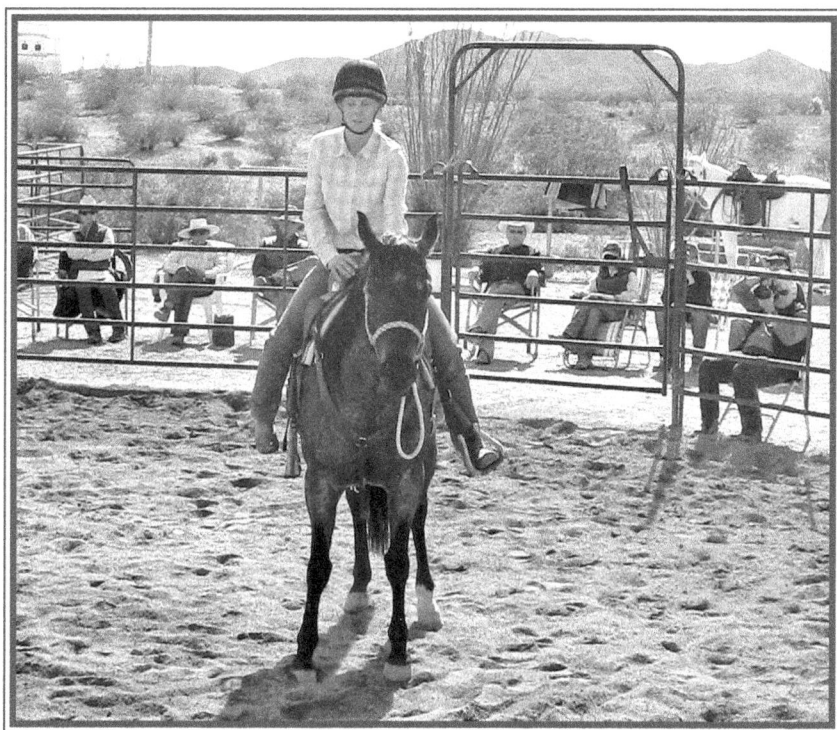

Anna had no problems throwing her leg over Sky, and once aboard she had a nice ride on the mare in the round pen.

An Afterword: Numnah

All kinds of things can be learned at a Harry Whitney clinic. That Friday morning was no exception as we watched Anna saddle up Sky towards the end of her session. But we got our equine vocabularies stretched when Anna said something about a "numnah."

Many of us thought she had said something else—perhaps something about "your numbness"—but couldn't quite figure out what she really was saying or what she was talking about. After some confusion and discussion, and Bob Grave's input as another Brit acting as an interpreter, Anna's story was corroborated and we were satisfied that "numnah" is a legitimate Britishism for saddle pad.

Chapter Twenty-Two

Day Five, Morning,
Smoke's First Mounting
Friday, 14 February 2014

"Confidence eliminates grumpiness."
Harry Whitney

Smoke was up next for her first session since her premier saddling experience the previous day (discussed back in chapter 18). Resa led the mare into the round pen on a halter and turned her loose. Harry, shaking things up once again, stepped into the pen with a saddle horse who was new to the operation, Miss Muffit.

Miss Muffit was owned by Ginna Ciszek, a regular Harry clinic rider and auditor who splits her time between Washington State and Arizona. Ginna was auditing both weeks and had three horses with her since she was stopping at Harry's on her way back to Washington. Miss Muffit sported a solid white coat, or as Harry put it when he stepped into the saddle: "This is a Paint that ain't."

"She's 13," he continued. "She had a little bit of a rougher start than we'd like to think, and Ginna acquired her and has had a little bit of a project all along. Really quick, sensitive mare. So I've always liked the mare because she's kind of sensitive."

Harry reached down from his perch and grabbed a flag from a stash that stood in a holder just outside the gate. With the flag in hand, he rode the mare around the round pen. He introduced the flag to her face, ears, jaw, and neck to make sure she was okay with it before the two of them set off to address Smoke with the flag.

By this day, day five and the final day of the first clinic week,

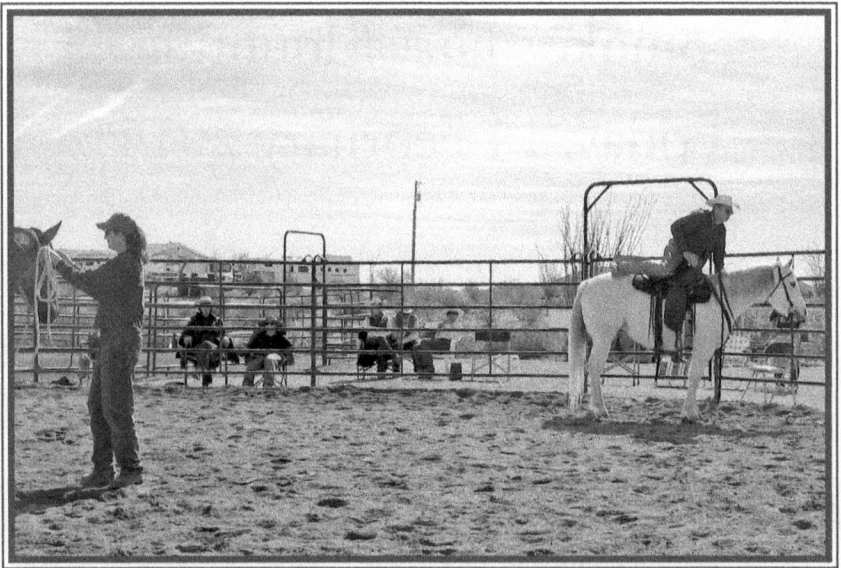

Resa Underdown unties Smoke's rope halter as Harry throws a leg over Miss Muffit.

many of us were struggling at times to keep track of just which colts had done what in their progress. For one thing, clinicking with six young horses 10 to 12 hours each day is enough to get anyone wayward as to just where each is in the course of things. Add to that how similar these sisters looked to each other and it is even easier to understand how we might confuse them.

Linda had kept good notes on Smoke's previous session and she read them aloud to help refresh our memories as Harry got started.

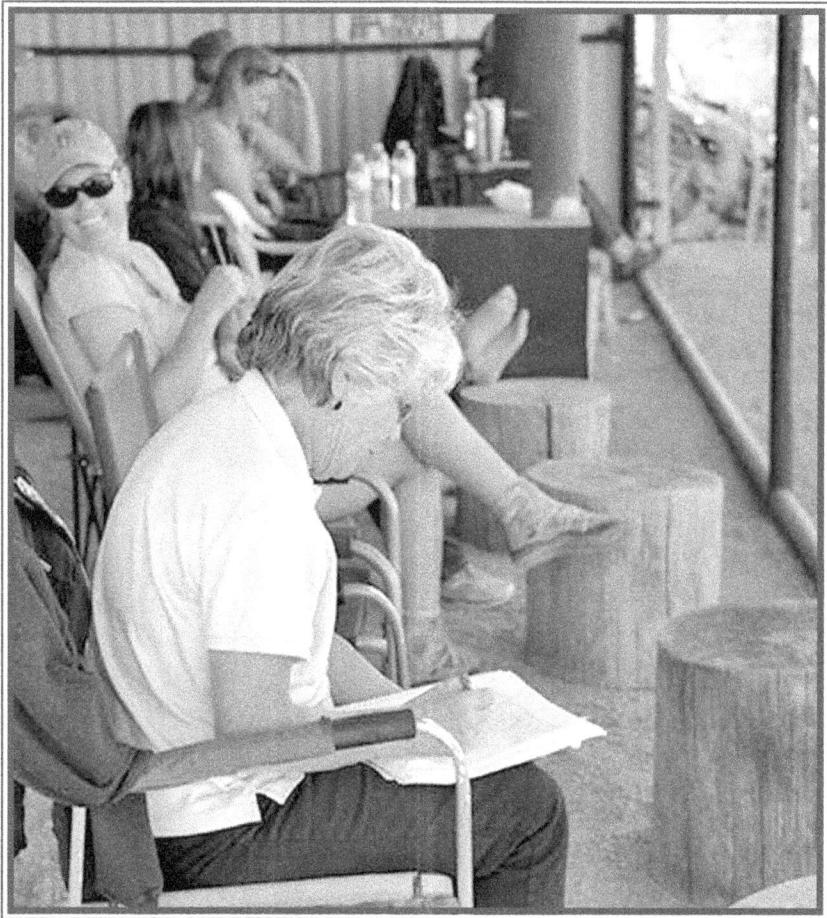

Linda Davenport getting down some of her extensive notes. (Photo: Nancy Lawson)

"[Linda read off a list of things that had happened]...and then you went with the rope back to her flank and she was okay," Linda concluded the review. "Then you saddled her and you moved her around off of Easy and up into the trot—not a flinch. No buck. *Nada*. No dust!"

"No dust," Harry repeated.

"I'm getting so disappointed," Linda pretended. "Not like any colt starting I've ever been to—there's always *dust*!" [Linda punctuated that last "dust" with a slap on the arm of her chair.]

"Stop watering the pen and there'll be plenty of dust," Harry answered with a chuckle.

Harry began the session by working Smoke loose in the round pen with the flag from Miss Muffit. The mare made a few trips around the pen, sniffed at the freshly dragged footing, and then dropped to the ground for a nice roll in the loamy sand. Then she hopped back up, shook, and stood carefully eyeing Harry and Miss Muffit.

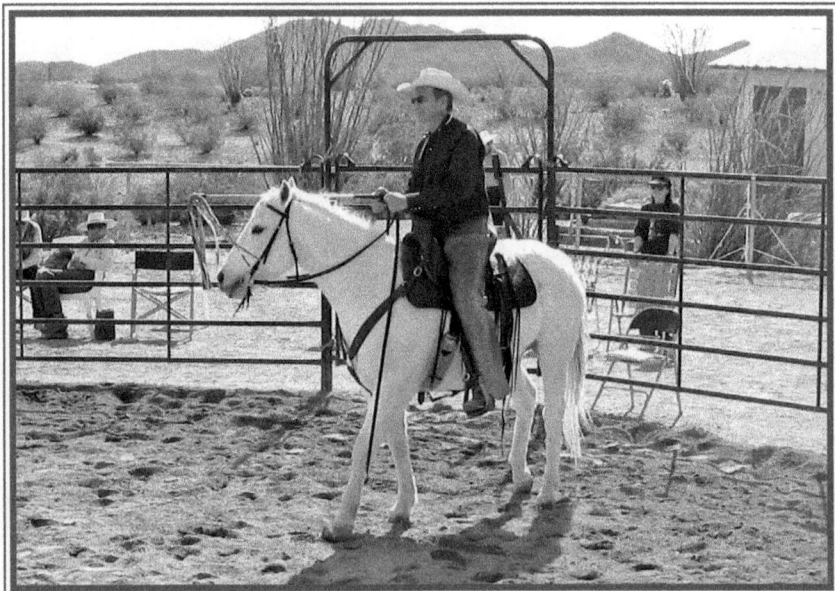

Harry and Miss Muffit with the flag at the ready.

Harry asked the mare to move around. She showed improvement over the previous day regarding her stepping off in a relaxed way, but still there remained a general unwillingness in her to go forward.

"This is what we were talking about yesterday, about she wouldn't free up and go," Franny said. "And that was when I was saying I had a hard time actually seeing it...I can see it *now*. I can see the hold-back."

"There! Now there's a better moment," Harry said as he continued working on getting her more forward. "Her ears are still back, aren't they? But see that one [step] loosen up then right after I said 'there?' Now she's struggling, she's struggling, she's struggling. See her want to turn in, then after she was struggling a little ways? There's a better moment."

This was another instance of Harry speaking rapidly about what was transpiring between him (riding Miss Muffit) and a horse (Smoke) to try and help us see what he was seeing, feeling, and doing. It drew my attention tighter to the micro-changes in Smoke. It also stressed just how important the slightest change is to a horse. And for me, it was a reminder that horses don't miss even the most minute detail of what occurs in our interactions with them. It is our duty to try and see the slightest change in our horses and acknowledge it when we have set up a search and are helping them find the answer. And that answer should be, regardless of what we ask their bodies to do, that they come through to be feeling better, be more relaxed, and eventually be willing partners.

Harry eventually found a good stopping spot with the liberty work with Smoke and got a halter and rope put on her. He then proceeded to do some ground work on-line with Smoke from Miss Muffit.

"Struggling. Struggling. That's good. That's good," Harry continued with quick insights as he rode a circle (the horses were circling head-to-tail). As things progressed, Smoke was falling in or

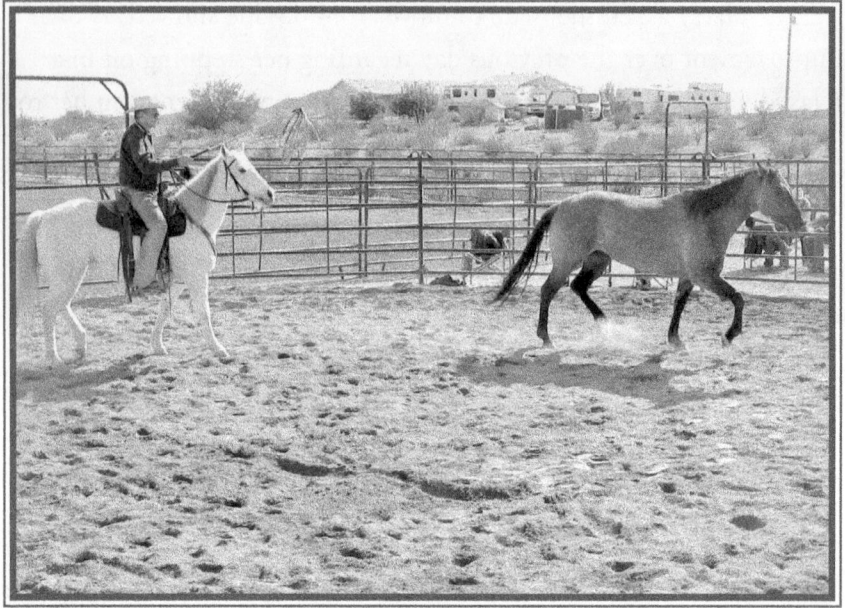

Harry and Miss Muffit work on Smoke's forward.

out of synch with him and Miss Muffit. He continued with this play-by-play reporting of what he was feeling and seeing for some time. "Struggling. She's trying a little. There we go. This is way better than yesterday. Not good. Pushing back. There's a change.

"You're fine, Muffit!" Harry said among the running commentary, which made me think about how he was not only focused on improving things with Smoke but taking care of his saddle horse, too.

"Some people are unclear about what a circle should look like," Harry said as he circled the horses. "When a horse is really on the circle—walking a circle, thinking about it—her inside hind, the one closest to me, should be reaching towards the center line of the horse. The inside front should step in towards me, not towards the outside, so the inside hind will track further away from me than from the inside front if she's really on a circle here like she should be. She's stepping a little deep there because she wants to turn in here, but that's pretty good there, see? I'll ask here that she get a bend and step her hind quarters, take that thought right on by me. That was real nice—I'll take that."

Harry then reversed the horses and got the circle shaping up in the other direction.

"If she's really thinking on that circle she'll have an arc to her body," he said, "inside hind stepping over underneath her walking around here—that inside front stepping in towards me ever so little."

When Harry got some noticeable changes in Smoke's willingness to go forward and to track correctly on the circle with some semblance of a bend through her body, he stopped and let the horses stand still. He called for Ty, who grabbed a saddle pad and saddle and entered the round pen. Harry and Muffit held the lead rope as Ty got Smoke tacked up.

Smoke's second saddling was completely straight forward and

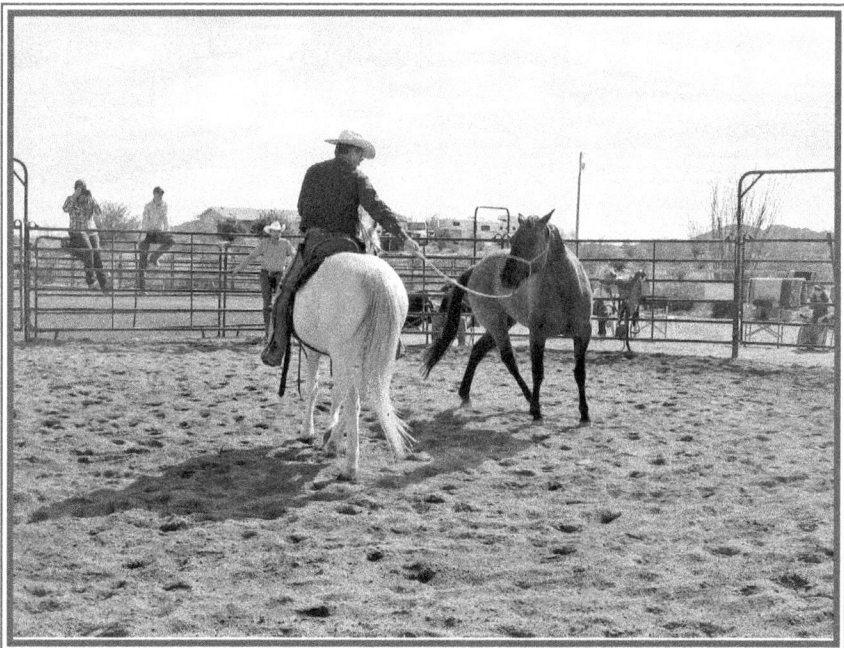

Harry has Miss Muffit circling head-to-tail with Smoke.

Ty throws the saddle on Smoke for her second saddling.

uneventful. All the work done earlier in the week clearly was paying off with very smooth transitions for these colts as they progressed. Smoke's second saddling was certainly testimony of that.

Once Smoke was saddled, Ty withdrew to the panels, climbed up, and sat directly opposite from where I was perched. Harry began again to work Smoke on the lead rope from Miss Muffit.

There were times earlier in this session when Miss Muffit had penned her ears, swished her tail, and generally "grumped." Harry had addressed this while continuing to work Smoke. He had commented that "confidence eliminates grumpiness," and the way he worked on Miss Muffit's grumpy attitude was by bolstering her confidence.

The best way to describe what I witnessed regarding this was that he urged her on when working with Smoke with his own confidence. His self-assurance seemed to be contagious to Miss Muffit, and he combined it with asking her to perform actions that were relatively bold for the mare. The more Smoke yielded to Harry and Miss Muffit, the less grumpy Miss Muffit felt.

As the groundwork proceeded, in what at first seemed a

counterintuitive occurrence, Smoke became a little more aware of and worried about the saddle rather than remaining relaxed about it as she had been at first.

"She doesn't have Muffit grumping at her," Harry explained, "so she can think about that saddle a little more."

By getting Miss Muffit to feel more confident, she became less grumpy. Interestingly, even though it was Smoke who was getting moved around. She was affected by Muffit's improved confidence to move her around and so was better able to relax about the situation between them. But that in turn allowed for new thoughts to filter into her head, and she then began to focus on this new thing strapped to her midsection. It was a situation that again made me note in my head that I must pay close attention to where horses are focused. The horse's momentary focus dictates how she feels and what she does.

When things were going well with Smoke being worked on line from the other horse, Harry removed the halter, got his flag

Harry and Miss Muffit pony the now saddled Smoke and work again on her forward.

again, and worked her loose in the pen. She walked out fine. He played with transitioning her up to the trot and back down. It didn't take long before Harry moved Smoke up to the lope, and she bowed up and bucked a little bit as she entered it.

"She didn't want to buck there," Harry said once she smoothed out, "but that first lope just didn't feel right. So she got a little hump in her. But it sure didn't amount to much. [Harry played with moving her around more at liberty.] She was saddled yesterday but I didn't do anything loose. That was really good."

Harry stopped and looked across at Ty who still sat on a panel.

"Get the halter on her; what are you waiting on?" he said in a phony hurry.

Ty scurried down into the round pen and put the rope halter back on Smoke. Harry turned his attention back to the crowd.

"That was just because of that first initial feel of it [the saddle at the lope]," Harry continued, "and you just interrupt that [concern about the saddle] a couple times and she'd be done where another horse might need to try to experience it [really bucking]. On a horse that's really not that panicky scared but needs to put a little effort into that and try it, then you might just let them."

Ty handed Harry the lead rope and after some ponying work with Smoke saddled, Harry stopped and looked at Ty again.

"Good luck, Ty," Harry said, indicating that he should be the first person to climb in the saddle on the mare.

Ty approached Smoke. He stood there momentarily sizing up his assignment. He gripped the saddle horn and pushed and pulled at it rocking the saddle to check the girth tightness and see what kind of reaction she'd have. All systems looked like a "go."

"Raise your foot up there and pet her with your knee," Harry instructed. "Mess around just a little there. Good, now put your foot right there in the stirrup. Pet her over here where this other stirrup is."

Ty played around on her right side first. He bumped her with

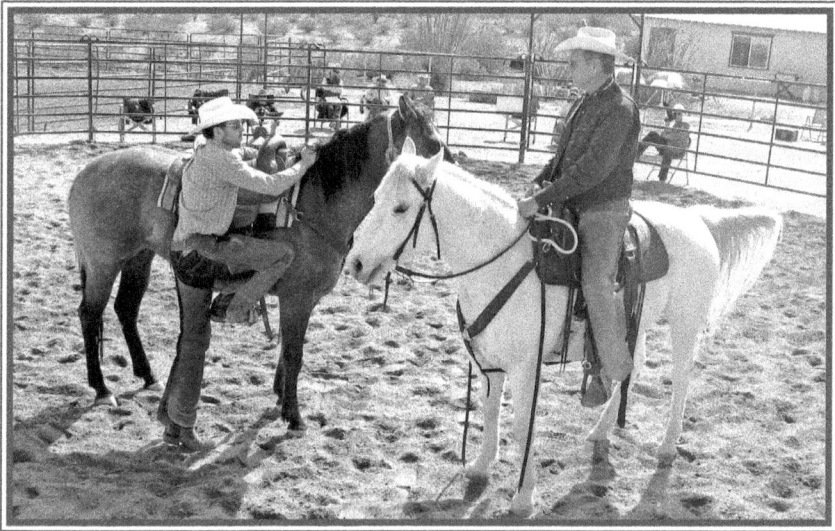

Ty raises his knee and puts a foot in the right stirrup to see how Smoke reacts.

his knee deliberately in the shoulder. He flopped the stirrup on the opposite side. He touched her all around her side with his hands. Then came the moment we'd all been waiting for...Ty pulled himself up with his right foot in the right stirrup and he lay across the saddle in the sack-of-potatoes position. Harry had a short hold on the lead rope and it looked to me like he even had a dally on Miss Muffit's saddle horn just in case, but those precautions weren't necessary. Smoke stood there like a champ and never flinched.

"Now just get down," Harry said. "Now I'm going to move her a step or to; you go around to the other side and do the same thing."

Ty repeated this scenario on the left side with similar results. "Now just raise your hat up there and pet that mare," Harry directed.

The hat activity went pretty well. Ty then stood beside her sizing things up as he prepared to really get aboard.

"Hang on tight, anything could happen," Harry said in a way that I was sure was both serious and kidding at the same time. "Put

Ty steps up and puts his weight on the left stirrup for the first time with Smoke while Harry keeps a feel on the lead rope and Tom snaps photos of the historical event from his perch on the rail in the background. (Photo: Nancy Lawson)

your foot in the stirrup and raise right up, swing your leg right across, and get up there."

Ty did just as Harry said, made it into the saddle with a smoothness, and settled there. Smoke never flinched. Thus the first time a person sat on her was another quiet non-event. It was going so well, Harry began telling a story to us while sitting there assessing the situation.

"I didn't tell Ty, but it's kinda like a guy I was helping," Harry said. "He was cowboy to the core. He was raised on a big ranch. His dad ran them broncs up in the hills till they were four or five, bring them in, snub them to a post, get on, turn them loose, and if you were still on top 20 minutes later you were going across the desert. He had a horse that he'd had a lot of trouble with bucking, so he wanted me to look at it. So I was helping him. I had that Turbo horse, and Turbo, he didn't handle a lot of activity well. This guy got on.

"Just as he settled in the saddle I said, 'Now I've got good news and bad news. The good news is, I've picked up a lot of broncs—a lot of rodeos—I don't care what happens at this point, I'll be there for you, man. The bad news is, Turbo won't!'

"So that's what I thought of here. I don't know what Muffit would do if she blew up and went to bucking. I might join in, for all I know."

Harry ponied Smoke and Ty around slowly. Smoke adjusted

Ty deftly swung in the saddle and sits atop a very quiet Smoke while Harry maintains a feel by petting the mare's face.

a little awkwardly to the new balance of having a rider at first and floundered slightly as she sorted it out. The nice thing was that she was thinking about how to accommodate having Ty on her back rather than panicking about it or otherwise trying to remove the problem. Things went well, so Harry pushed the envelope more and began working Smoke and Ty in circles again from Miss Muffit. Ty rubbed her all around on the bum and the neck and shoulders while Harry was moving her around. The mare remained very calm and the first ride went beautifully.

"Okay, get off this side," Harry said.

Ty slipped down.

"Okay," Harry continued, "take her, lead her over there a little ways; step up on both sides."

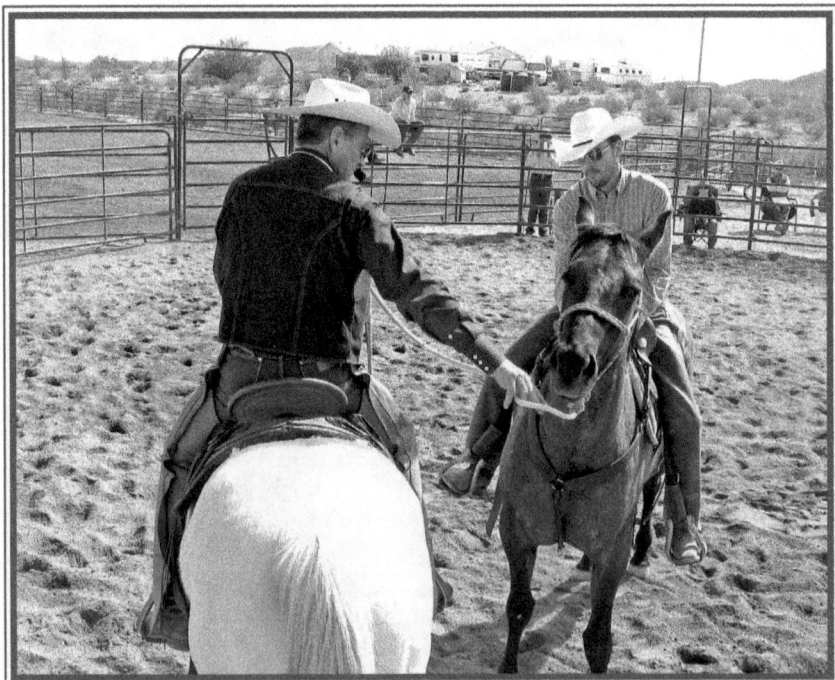

Ty gets ponied on Smoke for her first ride as Harry offers for her to step forward.

Ty led Smoke about 15 feet away in the direction Harry had indicated, and he prepared to put his boot in the stirrup.

"Well, you can do one [side] at a time if you want," Harry joked about his previous statement. "See we're just exposing her without me there supporting her, that maybe she could deal with him stepping up there. And if he gets up in each side and everything's smooth and looks good, we're going to eat lunch."

Ty, with the lead rope now in hand, stepped up in the saddle at a distance from Miss Muffit. It was fine until he went to get down on the side opposite from the one he'd mounted on.

"Naahhh," Harry snorted as Ty went to dismount. "Don't ever get off the side your rope's not on!"

Ty settled back in the saddle realizing that indeed the lead rope was on the side of the mare's neck opposite the one that he'd gone to dismount from. It is a safety thing—if you go to dismount (from any horse, but especially from a colt during the early rides who may be particularly unpredictable) and the horse spooks, if you grab the lead rope and it is coming across her neck and shoulders then you can cause the horse to bend and flee right over top of you. If you have the lead rope in hand on the same side as you're dismounting on and something goes wrong, then the horse will bend and flee away from you and you will have a better chance of hanging onto the rope as well.

Ty, realizing the error, tossed the halter rope across her head to the other side. This prompted Harry to show us the art of maneuvering a lead from one side of a horse's head to the other from the saddle.

"In changing that rope," the clinician began, "people always want to do this. [Harry demonstrated on Miss Muffit with one of the split reins attached to the snaffle bit.] They want to flip it over there [flip it over the horses head]. Well then, if you don't quite get it, you're whacking your horse. But if you get a piece between your two hands here, and you just think about tossing that piece out over the ears it'll end up on the other side. If I toss this over their ears, it'll end up on the other side and it's not coming in here. It just drops down over their head and lands on the other side. So you don't worry about getting it across to the other side, and then you're not whacking them upside the head. I don't see anybody else do it that way so it must not be too important, but I think it's helpful. People are always trying to get it to the other side, but it can't help but go to the other side where you're hanging on to it. It just can't help but go over there. Just toss that over their ears."

Ty worked at that for a few moments, complimented Harry on yet another brilliantly helpful and simplistic tip, and then dismounted, this time with the lead rope on the same side as he slid down.

"Now turn her around just about three steps and get right back on this side," Harry said. "Almost like you are in a hurry. There you go. Now just change your rope and bail off the other side and we'll go eat lunch."

Ty did so. Smoke did great.

"She was so good yesterday with that saddle," Harry pointed out. "She's done so good here today—a little exposure there—tomorrow this will go even better...well, Monday."

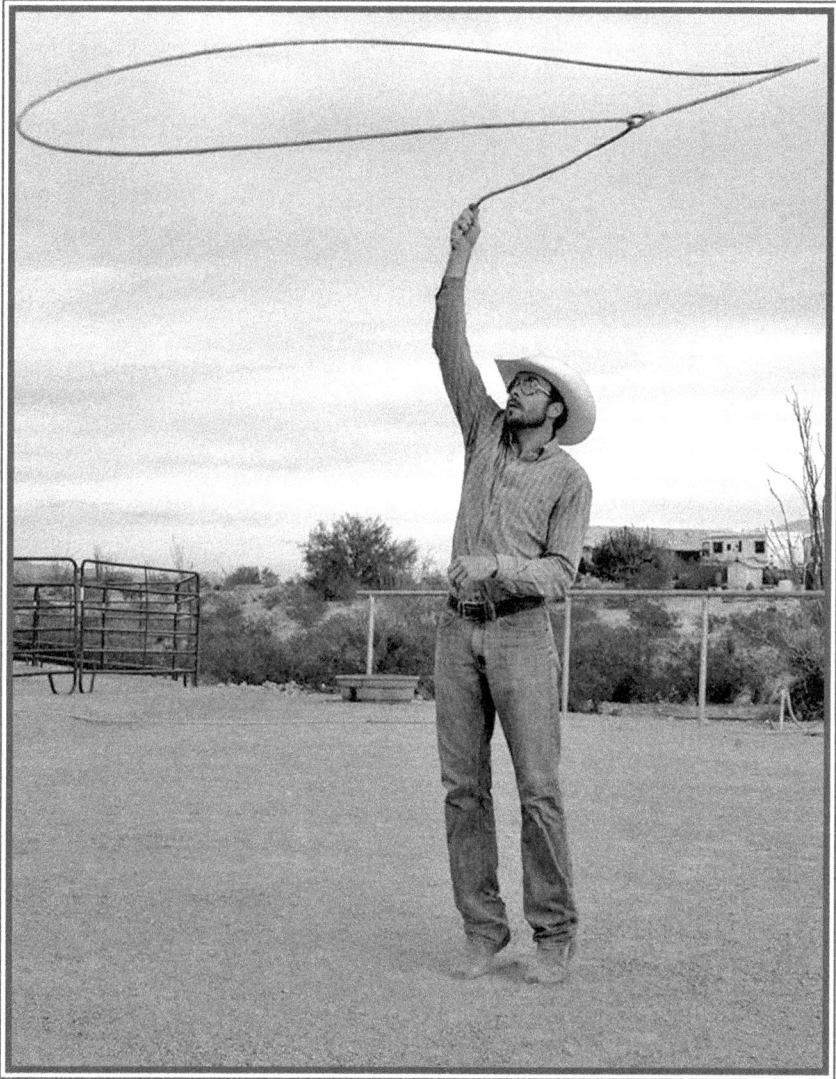

Ty has picked up some of Harry's trick roping skills over the years and there were several breaks during the clinic where he had fun teaching some of the auditors a few of these amazing talents. (Photo: Nancy Lawson)

Chapter Twenty-Three

Lunch Discussion, Day Five
Friday, 14 February 2014

"If you can see when a horse gets ready, he's trying to get himself arranged to allow you to touch him, then that's what you're waiting on."
Harry Whitney

Lunch discussions tended to be lively during the colt starting clinic. After a morning of horse work, we would pile into the bunkhouse and feast on the great and varied spreads prepared by cook, Lynn Wechsler, and her helper for this large clinic, Judy Marsh. The food revitalized us after full mornings of concentration and outside activity (often amounting to a great deal of sitting and observing) had begun to dull our senses.

As we finished up eating, the room clattered with chatter and laughter which only ebbed when Harry asked if anyone had questions. With this group, there never seemed to be a shortage of great questions, and there certainly was plenty to process from the huge range of horse work we were witnessing as the colts progressed.

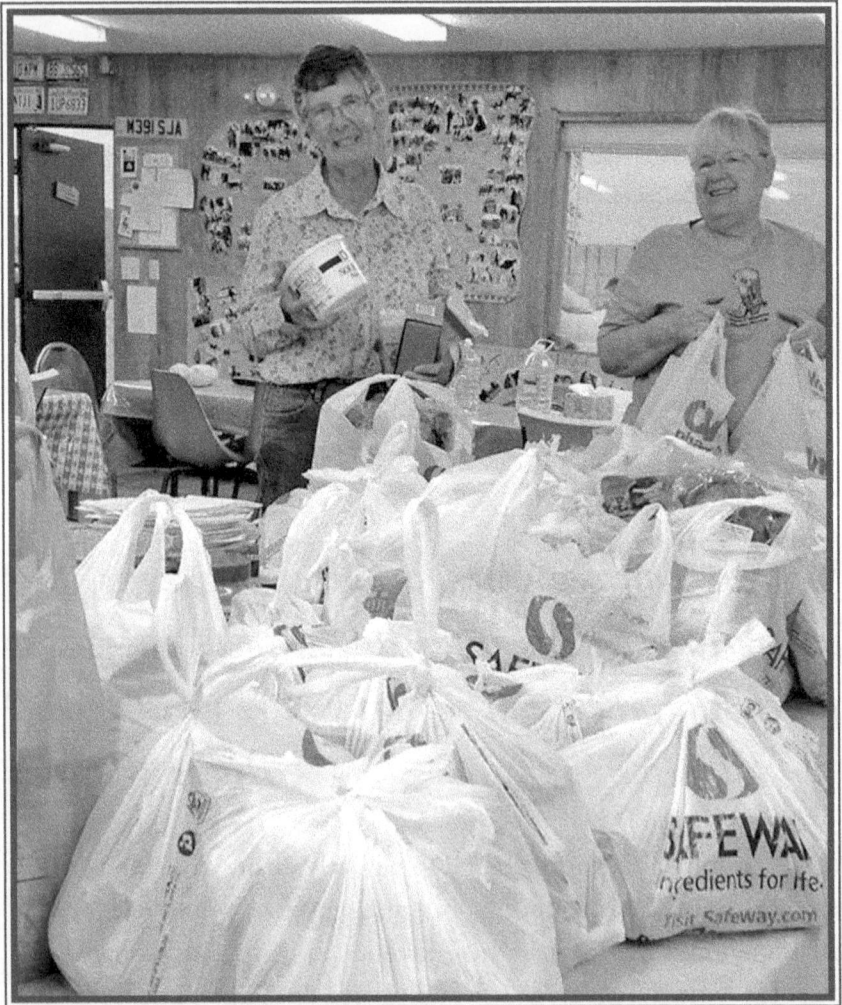

Cook, Lynn Wechsler, and her helper for the clinic, Judy Marsh, in the kitchen begining preparations for a week of colt starting clinic. (Photo: Nancy Lawson)

"You've talked about when you approach a horse, that your going to them is like the worry about the mountain lion jumping on them," Kathy began, "and once you're touching them, they can know that they're not going to die. And so, you can get something working with a horse standing still like the sound of the lariat, clackity, clackity, clackity, all over their body. And you can get them moving and get that working, but you step out on the line and you start coming back in and it seems like you're starting all over sometimes. Like with Smoke."

"It's that advance, coming in to them, that's the worry," Harry replied. "Once you get there, then they're okay. They have to experience that interim a lot of times before they realize that *that* isn't going to get them—that you're just coming in to touch them."

"So you might have to hang in there quite awhile doing that?" Kathy added.

"Oh my," Harry agreed.

"So on the same subject," Anna said, "the way you ran in yesterday with Sky...you were rushing but how would you adjust yourself to fit, to help her? If you eased off too much she would have just stopped and you wouldn't have helped her get through it—could you talk about that please?"

"If you can see when a horse gets ready," Harry said, "he's trying to get himself arranged to allow you to touch him, then that's what you're waiting on. In the meantime, you keep a little activity going. I think it's helpful, or important, to get the horses to make that change within themselves. We often do it for them. We get so anxious to touch them, or we see them go to stop, so we take that instead of waiting for them to make the change while they're moving, and letting them make the change at least towards feeling better about it."

"But on some of them, the first time you did it, would you just go over and touch them?" Anna asked.

"You might," Harry replied. "A horse that's had extremely

little handling you might need to prove to them that you could touch them without it being damaging. I told Ty to touch that horse the other day [Houston] because that was coming at his eye and he was sure that was going to be totally unsafe. So just touch him in amongst it, but that doesn't mean you quit. Touch him and at least let him feel the contact, and it didn't poke him in the eye, and build his confidence a little that it *could* come out good."

"And when you do it there's a smoothness in you," Anna said.

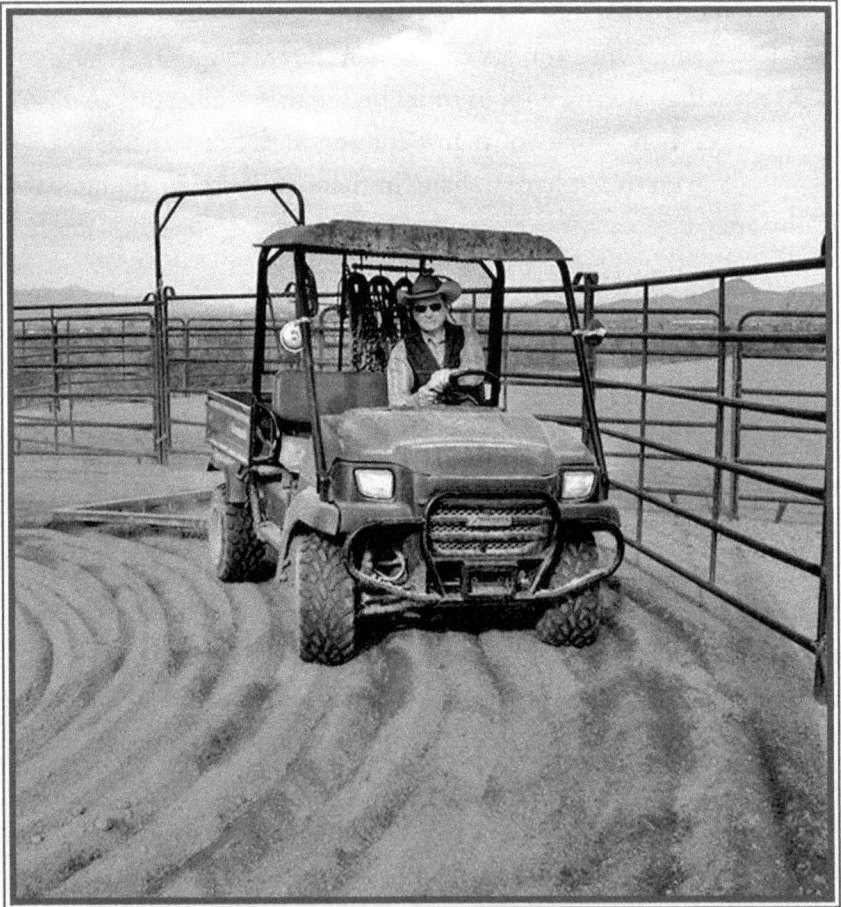

Harry drags the round pen one morning preparing for the day's clinic. (Photo: Nancy Lawson)

Harry ground driving one of the colts during a session earlier in the week. (Photo: Nancy Lawson)

"It's fluid. There's a rhythm in it, don't you think? That they can predict?"

"Yes, I know there is," Harry agreed. "It's not that I'm trying. It's not that I put an extra emphasis on thinking about that. But it's something that I guess, if you're trying to be smooth, that kind of comes with it. You learn over time that it's helpful for the horse."

The talk turned to confidence in horses and how that can transfer from the human. Ground driving, in particular, was a point of interest since a person on foot must project a feel from well behind the horse.

"If a horse has confidence in another horse and they come up to something that's a little questionable, who goes first?" Harry asked the lunch crowd.

"The confident one," came the answer from several folks.

"And the other horse draws from that, watches the other one

physically in front of them live through it and they come behind," Harry stated. "So when we're leading them it's the same thing. We're a physical being in front of them, something to follow. But then, when you watch a couple horses like that and the more worried one doesn't follow the lead of that one, you just don't see the confident one circle around, come in behind, and try to drive the other one across there.

"Nor do you see him jump on the back of the other horse. So in the real world there is no real direction that comes from that—other than a move-away type thing. But to get the confidence to be able to handle it, they always follow. So we can lead them through all kinds of things, but to send them ahead of us, that's a foreign concept, kind of. And so, that's where you start working back beside them more. Pretty soon you're sending them out further [in front of you]. Pretty soon you're clear back at their hip.

"You come to something worrisome, you can get off and lead them through—nothing wrong with that. But if you do that with everything worrisome you come to, pretty soon they'll just stop and wait for you to get off. If you have to lead them through, lead them through if they'll follow you. Hopefully they don't run over top of you or step on you, but lead them through. Then come right back, lead them through, but then try to send them a little out there ahead of you. And one day you'll come to something worrisome and you'll step off and send them on. Pretty soon, you send them right between your legs and reins. It's no different sending them out there—sending that thought right on out there. But if we never work it back here, then it is a really foreign concept when we're up there.

"So the ground driving can be very similar to that, see. You don't have to ground drive them [with two proper long reins], all you need is a long enough lead that you can get back here somewhere and send them on out ahead.

"The other thing about ground driving, which we plan to do [with some of the colts], is it gives a lot of people way more confidence to take a horse out. Especially out of the pen. Because most folks when they've got their own two feet on the ground, they figure they're going to live through it easier. And so they get confident and that helps the horse. I just do very minimal of it because I'm lazy—that's too much walking. He can pack me—why should I be walking? But, there's nothing wrong with it."

The talk paused for a few moments as we soaked up what Harry had just said. Then we were off on another topic.

"So when you're starting a horse to work another horse off of, and that horse hasn't worked another horse very much," Ginna began, "is it probably better to start with an old broke horse that you're

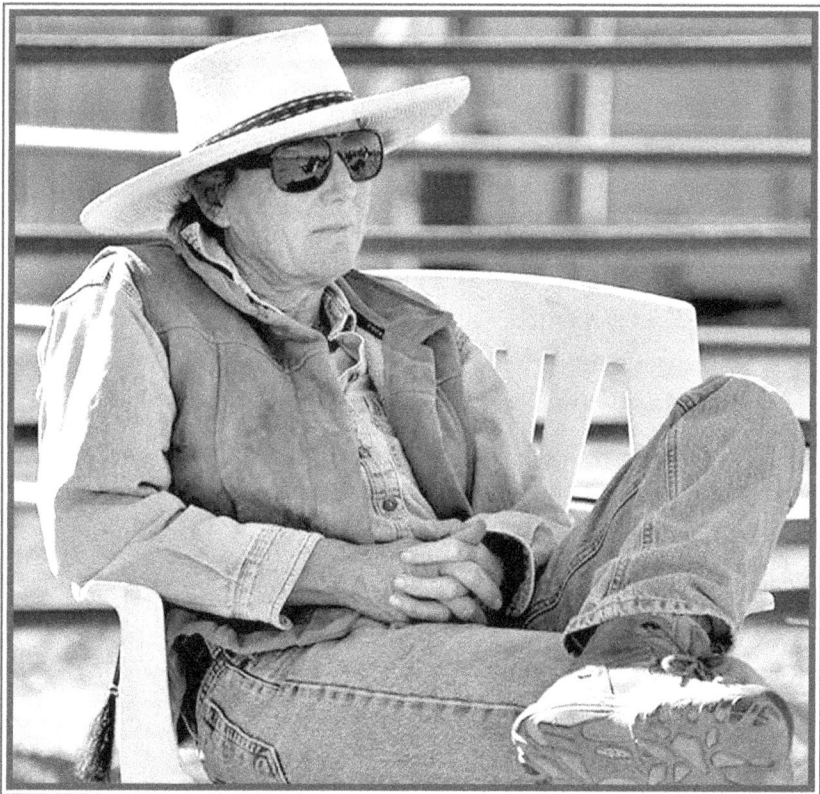

Auditor, Ginna Ciszek, watches the action in the arena one afternoon. (Photo: Nancy Lawson)

working and take care of your riding horse more—get them started like with the flag? Anything in there that you would do to prepare a horse to work another horse before you worked the other horse?"

"Well," Harry answered, "it kind of goes back to what we were talking about this morning—before you work a cow you need this, this, and this. But, how good does it have to be? Yet, in amongst working with Smoke there, I had to forget about Smoke and take care of the horse under me [Miss Muffit] and then go back. Well, those things come up. But if I'm going to have a horse that's reliable under me then that's almost got to be my priority for awhile. There are moments where you'll let that slide to get this, but then you immediately take care of that. So, judgment call, judgment call, judgment call of which is a priority."

"I find myself getting more involved with the horse I'm working and not taking care of the horse underneath me and troubling them," Ginna said.

"It was cute today how Smoke—you would stop working on Smoke and you would work on Muffit, and Smoke would go to the farthest part of the pen, turn around, and just watch you work on that," someone commented.

More observations and question ensued, but just for a few minutes. With only two horses worked so far, we instinctively wound down the discussion so Harry, Anna, and Ty could get outside and get back to working colts; otherwise, they would be working in the dark that evening. I reflected on how hard it was to believe we were heading outside for the final afternoon of the first week—so much had happened it was getting hard to keep track of it all, and yet how could a whole week be nearly gone already?

Chapter Twenty-Four

Day Five, Afternoon,
A Trip to the Playground
Friday, 14 February 2014

"As good as things have been, and as gentle as this little guy is, he still has learned to brace and protect himself."

Harry Whitney

Harry has a rather elaborate permanent "playground" set up in the washes beyond the far end of his arena. It spreads out among the mesquite bushes near the enormous twin saguaro cacti that stand and tower in the backdrop of so many photos taken during clinics at his place. It is not unusual for a group of riders to head to the playground for several hours of work with Harry's adult supervision, especially towards the end of a clinic where some of the changes they have made in the round pen and arena can be tested and enjoyed in more difficult, worldly settings.

The playground boasts a great variety of challenges for people and their horses. There is a mailbox that can be opened and closed from horseback, a railroad tie edged square on the ground that looks like a big sandbox but holds a bunch of crushed plastic bottles for horses to walk through, large logs to step over or walk around, a horse teeter totter, a wooden bridge, large equipment tires packed with dirt for horses to stand on, a bunch of plastic 55 gallon drums stood on

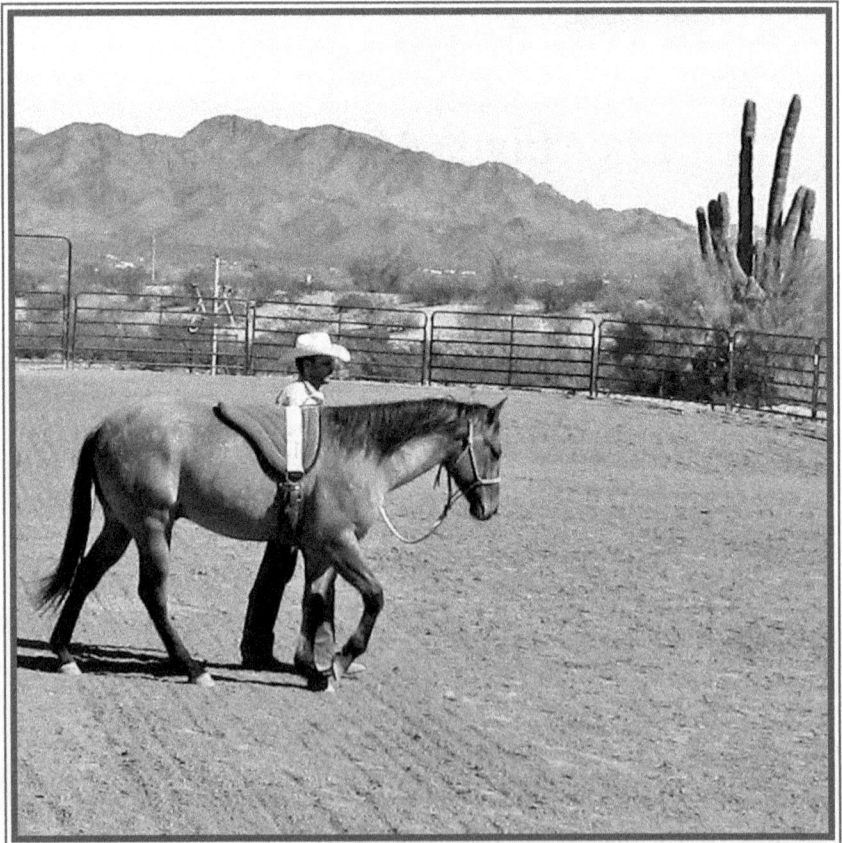

Ty and Houston in the arena with the huge twin saguaros in the background before heading to the playground on day five.

end to navigate through, and so forth.

After the lunch discussion on this final day of the first week, the afternoon horse work began with Ty and Houston in the arena. Before long, they would head out the gate at the far end of the arena to the playground. Anna would fetch Chic and follow, and the rest of us would migrate that way as well to watch. But first, Ty and Houston continued working together in the arena with us gathered around. He began with some basic ground work with the gelding on line—circling, stepping laterally, and backing. The recently dragged sand made a soft crunch, crunch, crunch as the horse stepped.

Houston was clearly not interested in what Ty was offering—not ill behaved but unengaged. Harry made mention that with a horse like this it is sometimes helpful to go into a smaller area and spend some time working at liberty to get the horse to "look you up." Houston remained a horse that had not yet been worked in the round pen as a point to show that any number of approaches can be successful when starting a colt regardless of what you have available to you. Ty continued working to get a better response from Houston with the simple things he asked in the arena on line.

"What you're really working on when you're working on the responsiveness is what he's thinking," Harry explained. "If he lets go of these other thoughts, he can be responsive. Until then, he's not very responsive. Now, they might be reactive, but I'm talking about good responsiveness. So, this is where people talk about getting to the mind through the feet. You're doing some directing, you're getting some movement, you're directing the movement, and yet it wouldn't come through if you weren't getting to the horse's mind at some level. But, often they get conformity—obedience—but they don't really get the willingness to come in there because that's all they're thinking about. They miss that he's doing it mechanically and begrudgingly."

Ty continued to work with Houston. In among the various movements Ty asked the gelding to perform were plenty of stops.

Harry, who never seems to miss even the minutest detail when it comes to horses, had been quietly watching for a few minutes and then spoke again.

"Now every time that you've done that," Harry said referring to how Ty stopped Houston, "that head's away from you. His head turns away from you when you stop. Tip his thought to you. After his feet stop, take a moment and just tip his head to you. That tells me he's still thinking away, still thinking about a plan of escape. And, he doesn't back straight anyway, see? But if you allow him to continue doing that it'll never get much straighter."

"So this horse is a year younger than the others," I asked, setting up my question.

"Yes," Harry confirmed.

"I know physically there are characteristics that change what you're going to do when training young horses as relates to their physical maturity," I continued, "but mentally, are horses very similar regardless of their ages? Or is that something you have to allow for? Do you approach a horse like Houston, being a two-year-old, any differently than some of the others being three-year-olds?"

"No," Harry replied. "Now physically, yes, but as far as thinking about what they can deal with mentally, no. It's amazing. On a foal still on its mother, or a weanling, you might not push it quite as long as you would an older horse on the mental side. And yet, you can present these same things, it's just the time frame there might be a little different. But, it's amazing how you can treat them just like grown horses, but unlike humans, horses are born horses. Humans are born just kinda helpless, so you've got to handle that totally different, see.

"You wouldn't treat a puppy that doesn't have his eyes open yet like you would a year old dog, but a horse is pretty much born a horse. He's ready to hit the ground running with his mother— fleeing when he needs to flee, saving himself. There's a big difference in there. So these things can come in there real early with a horse.

And yet, there is a maturity that comes later and so you don't push it too hard and too long, but it's amazing what they can do and deal with."

Ty continued the ground work as Harry spoke, focusing plenty on getting Houston to back.

"Years ago a guy brought a mare with a foal on its side to a clinic," Harry began. "He wanted help with the mare, and the foal had been halter broke. There was a lady there who had been to quite a few clinics and done all kinds of horse stuff in her life and she volunteered to hold the foal while he was riding the mare. Oh, that foal got busy when Mother left! It was over here and it was over there and it was fussing and stewing.

"I was trying to help him and I finally took it as long as I could. I said, 'Can I see that foal?' She handed me the lead rope and I just dropped slack in it instead of trying to control him. He took off past me like he was leaving and I just swung the rope and popped him on the side and made a big noise and he spun around, shot back past me going the other way and I did it again. He spun around and looked down that rope. I petted him. He cocked a hind leg and relaxed and stood there. Later, she made an issue of that. She said, how ignorant of her that she was fumbling around there, mollycoddling this little guy. She said, 'You just treated him like a horse and it was over—Boom!' And yet on those foals you can get that so quick."

Harry had Ty go ahead and put a bareback pad on Houston before heading down to the playground. Anna went to get Chic to bring her along for a bit of outside work on line as well. The idea with tacking Houston up in the bareback pad was simply to let him begin to get accustomed to having something cinched up on him while working through some of the other things that he would be doing. Harry mentioned that putting a saddle or a surcingle on him would have served a similar purpose.

"In thinking about that backing up crooked deal," Harry

said about the challenges Ty was having backing Houston with straightness, "we'll go down to the playground and he can work backing him through some barrels and stuff where there's a place to go—a reason, a purpose—and see if he doesn't free up and start hunting how to go backwards."

Ty kept working with Houston in the arena for several minutes until he got the gelding to a particularly good spot for that session, and then he put the bareback pad on him. Houston's first tacking-up went without a hitch. Ellen pointed out that before the bareback pad went on, Houston had not had the ring rope around his barrel or even a lead rope around that cinch area—things that might be done on young horses to prepare them for a first saddling. Houston had proved he could care less about such things. Harry knew this and had not suggested they needed to be addressed.

Ty, Houston, Anna, and Chic all headed for the gate to the playground. Harry fired up the Kawasaki Mule and invited anyone who wanted a chair to pile one in the back of it to be trucked down. At that point, the huge bunch of us drifted to the playground.

Ty and Anna began working with the horses. Anna walked Chic here and there between the bushes. She allowed the mare check everything out but frequently asked Chic to let go of various thoughts and check back in with her. It looked very good.

"It's good for him to have that other horse out here," Harry said about Houston. "He's already thinking about that more than Ty. So when you hit a good spot there, Ty, you let me know."

The distractions were a challenge for Houston but not in a sense that the colt was making any big physical sidetracks—spooks or such like. Rather, it just made him dull and less responsive along the lines of what we'd seen in the arena.

"Can I see him?" Harry said to Ty who handed the lead rope over to the clinician.

Harry began to get pretty big with Houston when doing some ground work. He worked him around in a flat area without obstacles. This went on for several minutes.

"I want," Harry started, "—and I'm sure some of you already have—but I want you guys to notice how much more of the time he's prone to look like this. [Harry stopped and pointed out what the muscles were doing in certain sections of his lower neck.] He's dipped here, this is big, really hollow in here. You look at that mare; she doesn't do it as much. Now, it comes in any of them, but he's been in that position more in two years to be carrying that posture that much.

"There's a reason. See that drop down? [Again he pointed to a spot in the lower neck.] And that disappeared for a moment when he let go of that thought and he stepped around the corner. When you go to back them up and there's a lot of resistance in it, you'll see that [the poor posture mentioned above] instead of what I got right

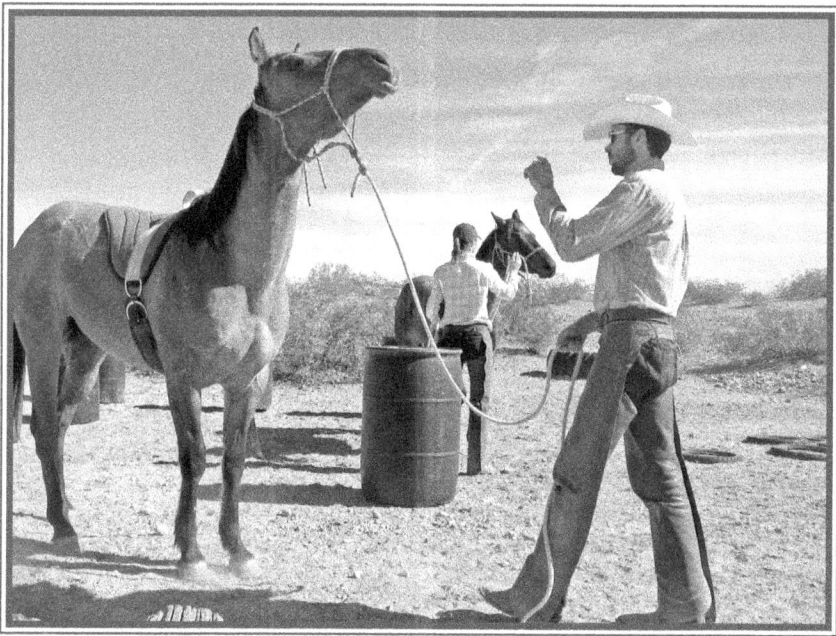

Among the barrels at the playground, Houston demonstrates his unresponsiveness and poor posture to Ty while Anna begins working with Chic in the background.

there when that head dropped and that whole posture changed. But he's been living like that a lot and so he's got the postural things that show you that there's been some tension.

"As good as things have been, and as gentle as this little guy is, he still has learned to brace and protect himself. And so you look at how quiet and gentle he seems, and yet you see that and you know that things have not been as good and as clear as they could have been or should have been. See this right here? [The head popped up and poor posture was coming in the neck again.] So I didn't let up what I was doing, but I did come in here in hopes that I could encourage a little more of this [head lowering in a relaxed posture]. Not by pulling down. I might raise up a little here and pretty soon he says, 'Well, I'll just let that go.' Like that, see. So I wanted to talk about that just a little before I backed him through the barrels here because you're going to see that probably come in there stronger when I go to play with the barrels."

Harry stopped the horse and came in close to Houston's head and faced us. He put his hands on the gelding's head.

"This is something I think about in the riding," Harry said, "and if you've been around many clinics you've heard me talk about this a bunch, that everybody seems so infatuated with them giving here [Harry indicated at the poll]. That should come in there—see him give there a little when I come in with a little pressure on his nose? But even more important to me is what happens through here. [Harry again indicated regions of the neck.] They can bring this in [the top of the neck] and shove all this down [the base of the neck and the withers] and have a tremendous brace in it. But when he let go there, this all stretched out [the entire neck]. That's more important to me than that [giving at the poll]."

Harry went back to offering that Houston do some ground work like circle him, step forward, and back up. He asked the horse to back between a couple of barrels at the edge of the barrel collection which consisted of about a dozen black and white barrels standing on end, each about a horse's width apart from the other closest barrels.

"That's pretty strong in him," Harry said, referring to the bracing. "But right there is why. He just grits his teeth and comes forward. What I want here is the same thing I wanted with Smoke at the gate the other day—is that he would *think* about it. When he thinks about getting between those barrels, he'll pick his feet up and go through there a little smoother. But he's not doing much here in the way of searching. He tried going forward until he backs up here. But you see how much effort it took [Houston got very crooked], he'll run into that bush long before he'll let go and think back."

Harry kept asking for him to go back, and the gelding suddenly softened, thought about it, and went, backwards.

"There's what I needed!" Harry exclaimed. "Whew, big lick and chew. See the effort he put into going forward long before he tried this other [backing up]. That's in this little horse pretty strong, and that is why you see this posture. That's because of how he's been handled somewhere along the line—or all the way along the line—however you want to think about it.

"Now, we're not going to get this all cleared up today," Harry remarked. "If he was really thinking back there that wouldn't have to come in there! [Harry got big on the lead rope to block the gelding's push forward.] See him just raise his head higher and start to push through that chest. I talked about that the first day, that that's so natural in a horse. [Harry backed him again.] That was better. As he backed, his head started to drop just a little. If you've been working at backing your horse for awhile and he's still throwing his head in the air pretty high to back up, then you're not getting it clear to his mind. You might have his feet going backwards but you don't have his mind thinking backwards. There see. [Harry stayed a little big with his request on the lead rope.] Back there. Back there. Thank you! Very nice.

"The thing with him that is different than with a lot of horses," Harry continued, "if we played with that horse [Harry indicated Chic, with whom Anna was working at the moment], you'd probably see a bigger difference in when she finally decided to go through there [between the barrels] because she'd worry about it. He doesn't care. It's back to his assets being his detriments—he doesn't care.

"It is amazing to me how many people you run into out there in the world that think working on this much backing up is going to take the forward out [of the horse]. It's apt to free that forward up, because what are we doing here? Nothing runs unmingled and we're freeing up those thoughts so they can let them go and be willing to go with you. And so then when we ask him forward, he's apt to be a little freer there too."

Among the work Harry was doing with Houston, he stopped and asked the horse to stop as well.

"As I stopped, he lit on his forehand and his hind quarters swung out to the left and then his head came up to get ready to push," Harry pointed out. "Just patterns of how he's used to operating."

"Nothing runs unmingled" is a remark I've heard Harry use many times before. It was brought up back in chapter 18 and I know it is part of the core of how he understands horses. Considering the gravity of the concept, it makes it easy to understand why he would spend ample time playing with a horse like Houston working on getting just a few steps backwards to shape up. Harry wasn't willing to gloss over what might be seen by some as a mundane thing.

Or one might simply discount Harry's ways here by saying, "Oh he's drilling that horse and he'll turn sour to backing." It is interesting to me that in another person's hands, this very scenario easily could become drilling and very well could sour Houston to working on backing. But we listened to Harry and observed his every move with the gelding there in the playground that afternoon. It definitely was an ongoing conversation rather than a mindless repetition of mechanical exercises.

An answer to my earlier question about what kind of training a young horse can take mentally was well displayed here. Houston didn't sour to Harry's requests or dull out because of the way Harry "spoke" to Houston. In fact, the horse got more aware and increasingly responsive. Harry got big and blocked wayward thoughts. He released for little improvements along the way. Those little beginnings towards betterness grew to be more easily observed positive changes. If the horse is improving and feeling better about things, he is hardly on the way to experiencing some kind of training burn out.

The first week group photo (which Tom managed to miss by being elsewhere on the farm). Front Row: Janice Guntner, Ginna Ciszek, Linda Davenport, Lauren Gruber, Kathy Davis Baker, Danielle Gruber, Patty Pierce, Nancy Lawson. Middle Row: Katelyn Praly, Kristin Praly, Anna Bonnage, Claudia Heath, Wes Bartlett, Frannie Burridge, Libby Lyman, Ellen Bartlett, Tim Thomas, Marcy Johnson, Connie Crawford, Bob Grave, HW, Rick Roll. Top Row: Duncan, Ty Haas, and Shirley.

Then Harry would change it up a bit, which often caused Houston to revert to his previous pattern of poor posture and smashing forwards like he was prone to do. So Harry again would address that. I found this session (and the playground certainly was useful for bringing out challenges because it was a different environment than the more hermetically sealed round pen or arena) to be a perfect example of why searching out and working on the little things is so important.

I was left with the impression that if we do not train ourselves to see the little things and seek them out with our horses, then we never can get a horse through to the best possible place. If we miss a colt not backing freely because he doesn't think along with us to go backwards, then we will never have a truly willing and straight backing in that horse. It doesn't mean we can't get it better later in the horse's life if we detect it and deal with it then, or that he won't back when asked at all. But since we were here to learn about starting colts, I was quite focused on any and all work I could do to prevent a young horse ever having a sticky spot in the first place.

And as Harry pointed out, if a horse gets more mentally tuned into any of our requests, like the backing in this example, then that improvement has the potential to help in all the other areas where we ask him to follow our lead, let go of his sidetracks, and willingly go along with us.

Chapter Twenty-Five

Day Five, Afternoon, Wrapping Up Week One Friday, 14 February 2014

"I could watch you setting up choices in everything you did—whether it was a big place [or] a small place." A closing remark made during the evening discussion wrapping up week one.

Anna and Ty continued to work with Chic and Houston at the playground. One of the more involved projects came when Anna asked Chic to step across a set of wooden planks that were close to the ground. This was a teeter-totter set up, but the ends both were propped so there was no rocking action. Instead of asking Chic to step onto the planks to walk the length of them like they were a bridge, Anna was working to get Chic to follow the feel she presented on the lead rope and willingly walk across the short width of the planks.

Chic was unsure about this obstacle. Anna was reassuring and kept presenting a feel for the mare to step a foot, and then two onto the planks, and then step back off and then step up again.

"This mare's not too troubled by that," Harry said. "But if she was a little more concerned I would tell Anna to let her go right on across instead of working on those little things like that. Getting that particular with what she's doing there, [if she was more troubled by it] you'd let her just drift on across, but that mare was dealing with that pretty decent there. See she stopped there with her back feet on [the

Ellen Bartlett and Anna Bonnage gather the colts in the pasture one morning. (Photo: Nancy Lawson)

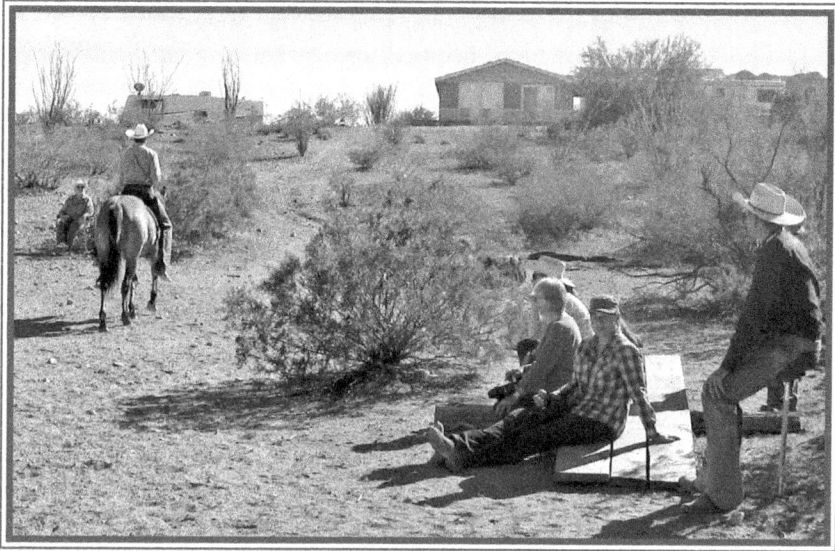

The auditors watch as Ty rides Houston around the playground.

planks]. That takes a lot with a lot of horses. But she's handling that really good, but I just want you guys to think about that. You approach something uncertain to a horse, if you can go on across, sometimes the best thing to do is get out of the way and let her cross it.

"Would you try and back her back up there?" Anna asked as she had Chic stepping across the boards now. "I wouldn't at home."

"Yes," Harry replied. "Now if she's too worried about that, don't press it. Just walk her on off. [Anna asked her to back onto the planks.] She was close, wasn't she? Now when she comes on next time, see if you can catch when the first foot steps off and put it back on. You might not, but you're striving for that."

Anna had to dial in her handling of Chic to accomplish that, but it didn't take long and she was doing great with it. As I watched her work I was thinking about how even a slight change in what we ask a horse can be a big deal for a horse and give us a new means to help her progress. And, how much more can be done in most any situation with a horse if we just think a little and exercise our imaginations.

By the end of the playground session that afternoon, Ty had stepped up on a large log, hopped up on Houston, and ridden him with the bareback pad all around the washes. Anna had Chic stepping over all kinds of things, backing between barrels, and coming along side one of the large dirt filled tires so she could place one of her legs onto the mare's back as a pre-cursor to mounting her.

As that session wound down and we migrated back to the round pen, Bailey was brought in. Ty and Harry double-teamed the mare—Ty was holding the lead rope while Harry had ahold of a lariat and had roped one of her hind feet. Harry was getting her to stop when he applied some feel on the rope, and then to go when he put bumps on it. After that, Harry got the ring rope and placed it around Bailey's barrel and proceeded to put bumps in the rope to indicate she should walk and he put a steady pull on the rope for her to stop and back up. At first, the mare would buck instead of going forward. At those times, Harry continued putting bumps on the rope until she gave up the dramatics and just went forward, at which point he released.

Anna continues Chic's progress in the playground by taking a good opportunity to let the mare feel her leg and foot on her back. (Photo: Nancy Lawson)

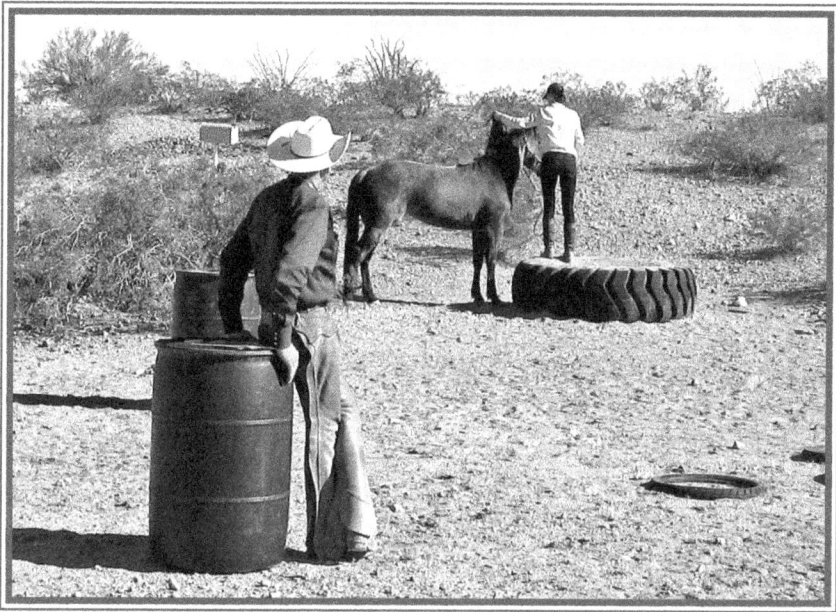

Harry monitors Anna's progress with Chic.

We had seen this type of ring rope work previously in the week. This time Harry explained that after this, "if you put the saddle on, even if she did a little kicking at first, she'd know a different option existed," that she could just go forward.

Next was something altogether new for the week. Harry got out his driving reins and a side pull. Bailey had a tendency to want to turn and face Harry when she stopped, which wound her up a little in the long lines. When this happened, Harry just maintained a little pressure on the outside line that wrapped around her hind quarters to keep her searching a way out of that predicament. Each time she would get straightened out, and he would walk her forward again.

The other point Harry made while driving the mare was that a person must be careful not to have the horse think that the long line scenario is about the horse getting away from the person. To help avoid this pitfall, Harry checked in with Bailey often by putting a feel on the reins and seeing if she responded by softening to that feel.

As Bailey's session came to an end, the afternoon was waning. The final horse of the week was Tinker. Ty worked on some ground work with her in the round pen. He got to the point of strapping a saddle pad on her, and with that the week of horse work drew to a close. Clinics at Harry's place run Monday through Friday. There is a tradition of wrapping up the week with hamburgers on the grill for supper before having the closing discussion. This week was no exception.

Another tradition when wrapping up a clinic at Harry's is for everyone to say a little something about what they will take home from the clinic. This was a huge crowd, and nearly all of us were staying for the next week, so there wasn't time to go around and hit everybody. Rather Harry asked if anybody felt they wanted to share on that topic to please speak up and do so. Below I've written down some of the comments so the eyewitnesses of this amazing week can

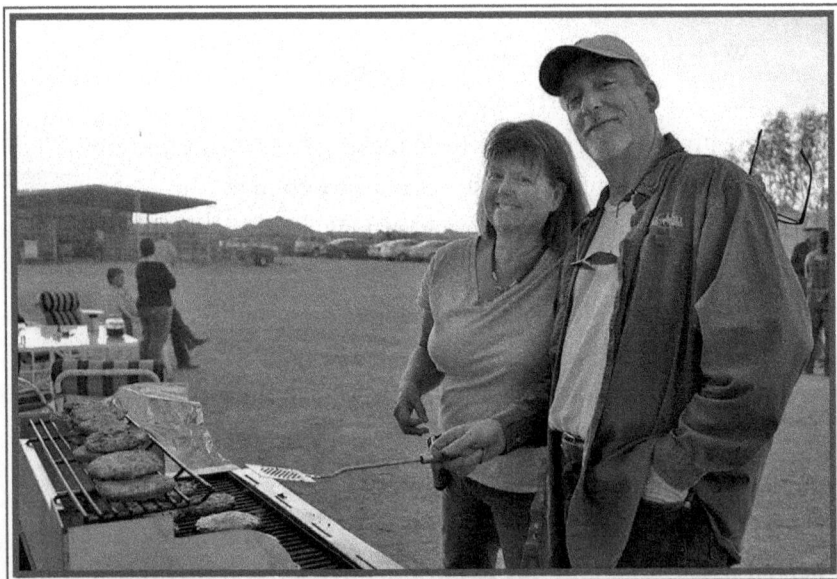

"Burger Friday" gets underway as Patty Piece and Rick Roll flip burgers for the group for the traditional hamburger night.
(Photo: Nancy Lawson)

Ty leads a colt to be turned out after a day of clinic as the sun sets behind them. (Photo: Nancy Lawson)

leave you with their lasting impressions. I'll leave them anonymous, as I think in this situation it's not so important who said what but rather what was said:

"I don't plan on starting a young horse, but even going back and checking out some of these things on older horses to see where they are, [this clinic] gives you so many ideas."

"I guess the thing that got driven home was, for once, I could watch you setting up choices in everything you did—whether it was a big place, a small place. I no longer look at just one particular thing you do and say, 'Oh well, that's what you've got to do.' Now I can see it in everything. Not that I can do it! But at least I can see it."

"Understanding and application are two separate things," Harry agreed. "Here awhile back I said our abilities will never catch up with our understanding. Every time we increase our ability because we understand it could be better, different, something...about the time that your ability catches up, you're already realizing what you could do just beyond that."

"Starting the colts—this whole colt starting clinic was a huge undertaking for you, and I get that. But, it made such a difference for me to see one right after the other, after the other, after the other. Previously, I've been here with friends of mine auditing. We've brought horses that were all different levels, but they've all worked with Harry somewhere along the line, so I've never gotten to see from the beginning—from the very bottom. He had the mind going, but I couldn't put the pieces together because I think for me, it had been just snatches, and this made a huge difference connecting more dots."

"I think seeing these horses start, it's made me realize how important, what 'important to the horse' is. Because these guys haven't really been exposed to people, and yet you see how they feel with that first coming together with a human. It gave a very good example of what a true definition of 'important' really, really is."

"I really enjoyed watching you do so many in a row. I never get to see you—I mean, here and there, and bits and pieces—but you rarely get this much of you. And I really appreciate that. Your timing, your feel, the search in all of it came out really strong this week."

"Your body might not have liked it, but we did!"
"I always am so amazed after being around so many of the clinicians, how patient you are in understanding that when we're ready to hear it then we'll understand it, but most of the time we're not at that point where we're ready to hear something. And yet you do keep repeating, and you're always so patient with taking that time for each person. It's just really appreciated."

Each evening plenty of volunteers offered a hand to lead the colts to be turned out. (Photo: Nancy Lawson)

"Watching one after the other and hearing what you're saying, to me just affirms in me how little I know. How little I see. How I yearn to see more and it just keeps me wanting that."

Towards the end of the discussion Ty and I chimed in with our impressions.

"I would say the thing that gets me when I watch Harry is it doesn't matter the situation—it's just that thought," Ty said. "I think about horses like two weeks ago that I was riding. One of them was just a total pet, a yard ornament...I look back I am just like, man, if I would have just thought of the thought! Like, oh, were going out and we've got to pass these trees, and he's scared of the trees. Well, you just have got to get the thought. You go down and you work by the trees and sure enough, there it is! You've just got to get the thought. I come in here and I think if I would have just thought like Harry thought I could have just gotten through it without fighting this horse [at home] for three days."

"One of the things that excited me so much about this, and

I knew it was going to be, and it has been fantastic in part for this reason," I began, "is that only twice before have I seen Harry work with horses that were unstarted or unhandled. I've written about one—that little three-month-old, Olive.

"There's a part of me that would rather work with an older horse that has established problems than work with a young horse because you are so responsible, and the gravity of that responsibility, and when I work with a young one, I enjoy it when I get into it, but it's always hanging there: 'Don't screw it up!'

"So a lot of working with these horses is what to do to avoid the troubles that we see all the time in clinics, that we see in our horses at home. That is such a rare opportunity to know what Harry would do to avoid the trouble in the first place so a lot of what's going on this week is not the typical problems you see. And yet, I've been able to see that there are some things inside these horses—and yeah, they've had some minimal handling—but still, it's about as minimal as it gets, and it's one after another after another, all day. And so it's really helped me distinguish what is going to be a common

Laundry dries behind the bunkhouse as attendees regrouped on the weekend between week one and week two. (Photo: Nancy Lawson)

Harry and Sandy work one of the colts during week one. (Photo: Nancy Lawson)

situation between a human and a horse when you don't have the pre-established human trouble in there. There are going to be certain bridges that have to be crossed [when starting a youngster], and this week I feel like I have a much more solid feel about that base line—what does a horse come into the world with? When a person first approaches it, what are we likely to see? I have answers to some of that now. I don't think I would have ever had that any other way, so I'm so grateful.

"Seeing one, you get a sense of it. Seeing two, you get a sense of it. But to see this this week? I really have more answers to that—I kind of know what's in there. And a lot of what we're doing maybe we've seen in clinics, but the application I think is a little different because you're really setting the youngsters up to win with what's best in them and keep that in there, bring that out, and not let that get shut down. We've been talking about, 'Okay, how do we avoid this happening?' This horse has this potential, we see it in there, okay we need to make sure this doesn't get full-blown—how can you do that?

"And I don't think there will ever be another opportunity for me to see that unless I come to another one of these [colt starting clinics] that Harry's never going to put on. And I had a sense of that coming to this, and it's one of the reasons I was so highly motivated to get here. And it's even better than I could have imagined!"

Afterword

Thus ended week one of Harry Whitney's special Colt Starting Clinic back in February of 2014. Week two—oh my, week two! Well, that's a whole other adventure. It was a week built upon the solid foundations of this first week. I can tell you that during week two the progress was amazing with colts being saddled, ridden, ridden out into the desert, and all manner of other things.

But the truly wonderful thing about both weeks was that

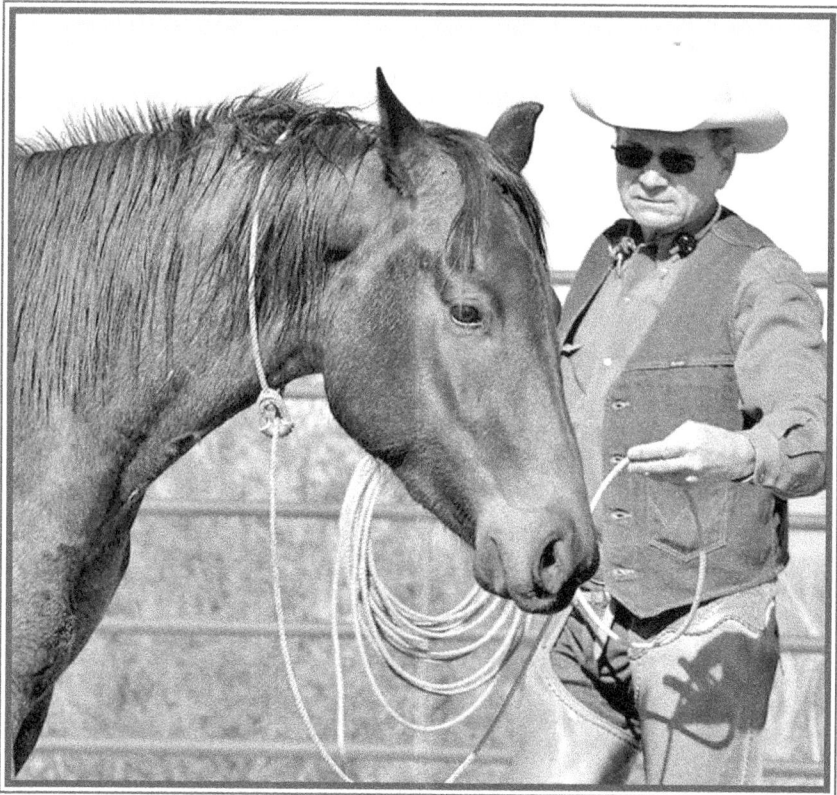

Harry presents a feel on the lariat showing us how little it takes sometimes to get a young horse to follow along with a person. (Photo: Nancy Lawson)

Harry's oversight and special kind of horsemanship made sure that every step every session—and at every other moment when the horses were being handled, too, during an official session or not—was taken with careful consideration of where each horse's thoughts were (or weren't). And that relaxation, okay-ness, and with-you-ness were *the* goals. Saddling or riding were secondary concerns and there were absolutely no cut corners to please a crowd with dramatics like getting them all saddled in a day or cracking a whip while standing on their backs by their second saddling.

I want to make a quick note about Harry's ongoing clinics for you readers, too. While Harry likely never will conduct another colt starting clinic, this special clinic has brought about a new clinic format that Harry teaches which has become very popular and is known as his "intensive clinics."

The first intensive clinic was held in Tennessee in 2014 a few months after the colt starting clinic. It occurred because the main excitement that Harry was hearing as feedback from the colt starting was that folks were excited to see him work so many horses back-to-back. So, he worked with Linda Bertani at Mendin' Fences Farm, who hosts Harry each year in Rogersville, Tennessee, to come up with an innovative format that stressed that aspect of the colt starting deal.

The new intensive clinic was six days long and had five horses with Harry riding all the horses exclusively for the first four days and then the owners getting involved for the final two days. As I write this (it is December 2015), there are now intensive clinics offered in Tennessee, Washington State, California, and in a few months Harry will put on the first one at home in Arizona as well.

I hope that bringing you readers along through the first half of this very special clinic has been inspirational and has provided many insights that we attendees enjoyed. I look forward to providing the same to the reader with volume two which will cover week two. So, the adventure continues. More soon...!

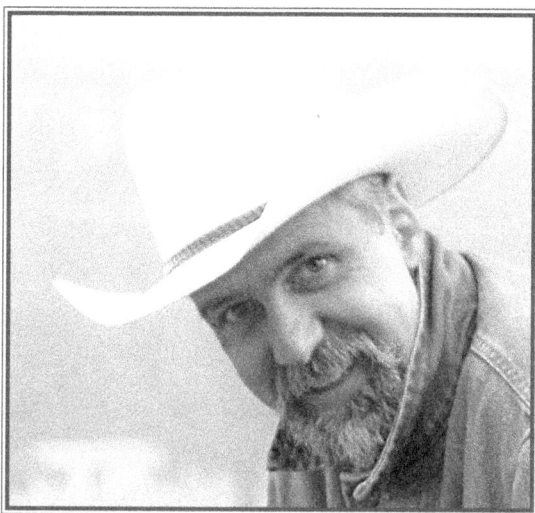

(Photo: Terry Sparks)

About the Author

Tom Moates is a leading equestrian journalist and author. This award winning writer is on the masthead of *Equus* magazine as a Contributing Writer, and his articles run in many horse magazines in the United States and abroad including: *Ranch & Reata*, *Eclectic Horseman*, *America's Horse*, and *Western Horseman*. Moates's newest book, *Six Colts, Two Weeks*, joins his other titles, *Discovering Natural Horsemanship*, *A Horse's Thought*, *Between the Reins*, *Further Along the Trail*, *Going Somewhere*, and *Passing It On*, all established titles in the library of modern horsemanship literature. A compilation of his most notable articles and essays, *Round-Up: A Gathering of Equine Writings*, was published in 2011. Moates lives on a solar powered farm with his wife Carol and a herd of horses in the Blue Ridge Mountains of Virginia. Book ordering info and Moates's latest publishing news are available at www.TomMoates.com.

www.ingramcontent.com/pod-product-compliance
Lightning Source LLC
Chambersburg PA
CBHW020605270326
41927CB00005B/192